Praise for *The Cities That Built the Bible*

"An engaging journey into the Bible and archaeology from a new perspective: instead of starting with kings, prophets, or texts, the author starts with ancient cities in which so much was born—all the while combined with a lively personal account that puts flesh and bones on the tale."

—Richard Elliott Friedman, Th.D., author of *The Bible with Sources Revealed*

"Cargill offers a riotous gazetteer, one filled with astute observations about the literal and figurative building materials that biblical authors mined—and sometimes had foisted upon them—from key cities of the ancient world. Readers will happily accompany their learned tour guide as they reconsider Near Eastern influence on the Bible and perceive its text from new perspectives."

—David Vanderhooft, Ph.D., associate professor of Hebrew Bible in the Department of Theology at Boston College

"Cargill is a lucid and expert tour guide, taking us from city to city to explain how and why the Bible is an extraordinary product of its material and urban contexts. The people, places, and peculiarities of ancient West Asia come alive in this exhilarating tour of the biblical past."

—Francesca Stavrakopoulou, D.Phil., professor of Hebrew Bible and Ancient Religion at the University of Exeter

"In a compelling narrative that sparkles with life, Cargill takes his readers on a thrilling tour through the cities that built the Bible. The expert guide leaves his readers longing for more. A wonderful way to deepen your knowledge of the biblical writings, their historical context, and the ancient world."

—Mark Goodacre, D.Phil., professor of New Testament in the Department of Religious Studies at Duke University

"With heartfelt sincerity and timely humor, Cargill possesses the historical knowledge, command of biblical languages, and archaeological expertise necessary to successfully communicate the tale of the Bible's beginnings with a passion that highlights his love for the biblical world."

—Oded Lipschits, Ph.D., professor of Jewish history and director of the Sonia and Marco Nadler Institute of Archaeology at Tel Aviv University

"Cargill explores the urban settings that influenced and shaped some of the Bible's most profound people and events. He uses archaeology, literature, and personal experience to help readers contextualize the biblical Mediterranean and gain a firm hold on the topography of the Old Testament, the New Testament, and the spread of Christianity. By tying the literature to the geography, Cargill has provided a fascinating, dynamic map for readers to navigate with."

—Sarah E. Bond, Ph.D., assistant professor in the Department of Classics at the University of Iowa

"Woven through from start to finish with insightful scholarship, humor, and the warmth of Cargill's personal experience. He will take you places you couldn't otherwise go—under the ground, into a cistern, across a border, and into closely guarded archives—to see things you'd never otherwise see, which in turn will allow you to see the Bible itself in new ways."

—James F. McGrath, Ph.D., Clarence L. Goodwin Chair in New Testament Language and Literature at Butler University

"After three decades of books that discuss how the Bible came into being, we have something new! Rather than focusing on textual or compositional history, Cargill explains, interprets, and amplifies the social settings that gave rise to the sacred books of the Hebrew Bible and the Greek New Testament. This book, written in an accessible and engaging style, is critical as a supplemental textbook for undergraduates and as background reading for all students of the Bible. Highly recommended."

—Andrew G. Vaughn, Ph.D., executive director, American Schools of Oriental Research

"The most original and entertaining approach to telling the story of the Bible that I've seen. This is both a delight to read and reliable in its scholarship. Anyone who wants to know how recent archaeological discoveries have revolutionized our understanding of the Bible should read this book."

—William Schniedewind, Ph.D., Kershaw Chair of Ancient Eastern Mediterranean Studies at UCLA and author of *How the Bible Became a Book*

The CITIES THAT BUILT the BIBLE

The CITIES THAT BUILT the BIBLE

Robert R. Cargill

HarperOne
An Imprint of HarperCollins*Publishers*

HarperOne

FIRST EDITION

Layout by Laura Lind Design

Library of Congress Cataloging-in-Publication Data is available upon request.

ISBN 978–0–06–236674–0

16 17 18 19 20 RRD(H) 10 9 8 7 6 5 4 3 2 1

For Roslyn
More every day

CONTENTS

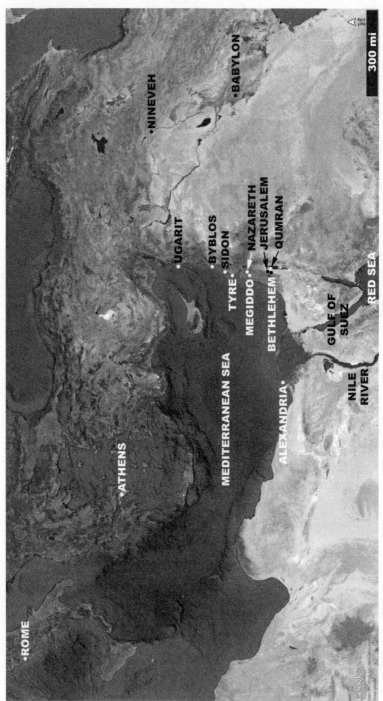

Map of the eastern Mediterranean and Ancient Near East. Image courtesy Google Earth, Data SIO, NOAA, U.S. Navy, NGA, GEBCO, Image Landsat.

ABBREVIATIONS

General

BCE	Before the Common Era (same as BC)
ca.	circa
CE	Common Era (same as AD)
cf.	compare
chap.	chapter
col.	column
DSS	Dead Sea Scrolls
Gk.	Greek
HB	Hebrew Bible
Heb.	Hebrew
lit.	literally
LXX	Septuagint
MT	Masoretic Text
NT	New Testament
OT	Old Testament
r.	ruled
v(v).	verse(s)

Bibliographic

AHI	*Ancient Hebrew Inscriptions* (Davies)
ANET	*Ancient Near Eastern Texts Relating to the Old Testament* (Pritchard)
COS	*Context of Scripture* (Hallo and Younger)
CTA	*Corpus tablettes alphabetiques* (Herdner)
EA	*Tel el-Amarna Archive* (Amarna Letters; Moran)
FGrH	*Die Fragmente der Griechischen Historiker* (Jacoby)
HAE	*Handbuch der althebräischen Epigraphik* (Renz and Röllig)

KTU   *Cuneiform Alphabetic Texts from Ugarit, Ras Ibn Hani, and Other Places* (Dietrich, Loretz, and Sanmartín)

Bible Books

OLD TESTAMENT

Gen.	Genesis
Exod.	Exodus
Lev.	Leviticus
Num.	Numbers
Deut.	Deuteronomy
Josh.	Joshua
Judg.	Judges
Ruth	Ruth
1 Sam.	1 Samuel
2 Sam.	2 Samuel
1 Kings	1 Kings
2 Kings	2 Kings
1 Chron.	1 Chronicles
2 Chron.	2 Chronicles
Ezra	Ezra
Neh.	Nehemiah
Esth.	Esther
Job	Job
Ps(s).	Psalms
Prov.	Proverbs
Eccl.	Ecclesiastes (Qohelet)
Song	Song of Songs
Isa.	Isaiah
Jer.	Jeremiah
Lam.	Lamentations

Ezek.	Ezekiel
Dan.	Daniel
Hos.	Hosea
Joel	Joel
Amos	Amos
Obad.	Obadiah
Jon.	Jonah
Mic.	Micah
Nah.	Nahum
Hab.	Habakkuk
Zeph.	Zephaniah
Hag.	Haggai
Zech.	Zechariah
Mal.	Malachi

APOCRYPHA

Tob.	Tobit
Jth.	Judith
Add. Esth.	Additions to Esther
Wisd.	Wisdom of Solomon
Sir.	Sirach (Wisdom of Sirach, Ecclesiasticus)
Bar.	Baruch
Let. Jer.	Letter of Jeremiah
Pr. Azar.	Prayer of Azariah and the Song of the Three Jews
Sus.	Susanna
Bel.	Bel and the Dragon
1 Macc.	1 Maccabees
2 Macc.	2 Maccabees
1 Esd.	1 Esdras
2 Esd.	2 Esdras

Pr. Man.	Prayer of Manasseh
3 Macc.	3 Maccabees
4 Macc.	4 Maccabees

NEW TESTAMENT

Matt.	Matthew
Mark	Mark
Luke	Luke
John	John
Acts	Acts of the Apostles
Rom.	Romans
1 Cor.	1 Corinthians
2 Cor.	2 Corinthians
Gal.	Galatians
Eph.	Ephesians
Phil.	Philippians
Col.	Colossians
1 Thess.	1 Thessalonians
2 Thess.	2 Thessalonians
1 Tim.	1 Timothy
2 Tim.	2 Timothy
Titus	Titus
Philem.	Philemon
Heb.	Hebrews
James	James
1 Pet.	1 Peter
2 Pet.	2 Peter
1 John	1 John
2 John	2 John
3 John	3 John
Jude	Jude
Rev.	Revelation

Introduction

You have Nicole Kidman to thank for this book. In the fall of 2004, I had the good fortune to be hired by Ms. Kidman (yes, the Academy Award–winning actress) to teach her a private version of the Introduction to the Old Testament course I was teaching at Pepperdine University.[1] I kid you not. (For those of you rolling your eyes at my name-dropping, I'm telling you this to demonstrate this book's topic is of interest to everyone—even celebrities.) Not only did she prove to be wicked smart—she still remembered her Latin—but she was kind, clever, and funny, and she has one of the most caring hearts of anyone I've ever met.

One day we met on a Culver Studios set where Ms. Kidman was filming the movie *Bewitched*. During breaks in between shooting, she and I would go to her trailer and do our course lessons. One day while reading the book of Genesis, Nicole asked a simple question: "Where did the Bible come from?"

I didn't have an answer, at least not a simple one. And she's not alone in wondering. It's a question we've probably all pondered at some point. The Bible is the bestselling book in the United States; chances are, most people reading this will have at least one copy at home or on their computer, iPad, or smartphone. Whether we consider ourselves religious or not, we hear the Bible quoted everywhere from pop culture to politics. It's part of the fabric of our nation. But the elusive question remains: Where did it come from?

I've spent over a decade formulating an answer to that question, and that answer is found throughout the pages of this book. Also, now you know the answer to your book club's first trivia question: What was the author doing with Nicole Kidman in her trailer? The answer is one that fulfills the dreams of men around the world: reading the Bible. And Ms. Kidman, thank you. It was truly an honor to work with you. I hope this book serves as an adequate answer to your question.

WHERE DID THE BIBLE COME FROM?

So, to answer the question about where the Bible came from, we should start with the fact that the Bible did not one day just magically appear. It did not float down from heaven as a complete document. It was not revealed verbatim to a single person whose utterances were then recorded, a claim that Islamic tradition makes about the Qur'an. Rather, the Bible's contents were repeatedly argued over, voted on, and seldom decided upon with unanimity. In fact, the early church councils rarely took up the issue of the canon of the Bible and, instead, left the decision to certain prominent individuals tasked with reforming liturgical practices or creating copies or translations of the official Bible for various political and religious leaders. And when the church councils did issue decisions on the canon of Scripture, those decisions were often not consistent from one council to the next, so that many of those decisions aren't reflected in the Bible we have today.

Furthermore, the creeds of the early church, like those stemming from the most famous of early church synods, the First Council of Nicea, were actually declared *before* the contents of the biblical canon were established. This means that the church was making decrees *prior* to a decision about what officially belonged in the Bible. What this tells us is that the popular notion, especially among religious conservatives, that the Bible is a "blueprint" for the church and that all decisions should be rooted in "Scripture" is backward, as this was not the practice of the early church. Rather, the church fathers decided what the church was to believe based on *some* of the writings of the Bible with *other* doctrines based on what they thought *should* or *ought* to be true.

The remainder of the Bible was then filled out by books that supported these doctrinal decisions.

This book examines how the Bible we know today, both the Hebrew Bible and the Christian New Testament (including the Apocrypha), came to be. But rather than examining the councils and individuals who decided what would make up the Bible, I want to take a new approach. We will examine important *cities* that contributed to the formation of the Bible, including its composition, redaction, and canonization. We will explore the cities that built the Bible by telling of their backgrounds, histories, and archaeology, and then we will examine the significance of these cities for the written text of the Bible.

As an archaeologist and professor of biblical studies at the University of Iowa, I study and teach about the relationship between the archaeology of the ancient Near East and the text of the Bible. This book uncovers some topics that will be surprising to many people. For example, the books of the Bible weren't the only Jewish and Christian books written in antiquity. There were numerous other books written about Moses, Jacob, and Jesus in antiquity, and there are far more books that were left out of the Bible than were let in. Furthermore, the process by which the books of the Bible were chosen was a messy, often political process. Of the books that *were* allowed into the Bible, there were multiple versions in circulation at the same time as well as various translations, and the modern English Bibles we read today pull from *all* of these versions.

This book will also explore some of the more difficult biblical verses, how they got there and how the early Christians and Jews interpreted them. We'll see what the Bible says about the birth of Jesus, and how his place of birth and virginal conception caused problems for the early church. We'll see exactly how tall Goliath really was. At the end of this book, you should be well versed in the archaeological evidence for the literature of the Bible, what international events shaped the Bible's stories, and who was ultimately responsible for the final form of the biblical canon. Perhaps most important, you will possess a knowledge of the stories *behind* the stories of the Bible, and this behind-the-scenes look at the making of the Bible will change the way you read the Bible forever.

EXPERIENCING THE BIBLE PHYSICALLY

The Bible cannot simply be read; it must be experienced. Put another way, you cannot read and understand the Bible without understanding the geography—the land, the cities, the rivers and lakes, the oceans, the mountains, and the weather—in which the biblical stories are set. You simply cannot understand the Bible without a knowledge of its physical context.

In this book, I will take you with me as I travel through the Holy Land, acting as your guide through many important sites and sharing little-known information, crucial background, and even some interesting trivia. I encourage you to visit the cities described in this book (although in the interests of safety, you should refrain from visiting some of them for the time being), and it is my hope that you can take this book with you to the various cities described here and use it to understand better how each city's geographical context and archaeological history interconnect with the formation of the Bible and the specific passages dealing with each specific city. For those of you who won't have a chance to make the trip any time soon, I've included photos of the locations, so that you can get a feel for what it looks like from the comfort of your chair or study.

DISCOVERING THE LINK
BETWEEN CITIES AND THE BIBLICAL TEXT

An important part of this book is looking at how the cities that built the Bible ultimately influenced the actual text we find in our Bibles today. The idea of how the Bible actually became a book has been the topic of many recent volumes. My UCLA doctoral adviser, Bill Schniedewind, wrote a book entitled *How the Bible Became a Book,* in which he articulates how the Hebrew Bible, or Christian Old Testament, went from being a set of oral teachings to a written volume commanding authority. Other books, like Neil Lightfoot's *How We Got the Bible,* examine the physical manuscripts that were used to establish the standard texts we have of the Bible. The late Bruce Metzger's classic work, *The Text of the New Testament: Its Transmission, Corruption, and Restoration,* which was recently updated and expanded by Bart D. Ehrman, looks at how the text of the New Testament was altered both accidentally and intentionally over the first few centuries. Still other volumes, like *The Canon Debate,* edited by Lee M. McDonald and James A. Sanders, have examined the process of canonization, that is, the process by which it was determined which books would become part of the authoritative Bible, and thereby considered to be part of the "Word of God," and which books would be cast out as merely "instructional" or condemned outright as "heretical."

Books such as these have become increasingly important as people look more seriously at both the process by which the practice of writing evolved and how it came to have authority in society. In the earliest societies, the highest authority came not from written documents but from kings who verbally spoke commands and laws, but who themselves were not necessarily subject to them. The king was often above his own laws, prompting the famous Mel Brooks line, "It's good to be the king." But within many ancient Near Eastern societies, we see laws transition from words that may have been spoken by kings, prophets, and priests, or that may have been normative cultural practices, to words that were written down and often attributed to a deity or deities. Over time, the writing down of these laws as words steadily transfers legal authority from the one speaking the words to the written document recording those words. As subsequent generations gradually learn to revere the authority of the written word, and these written words outlast the particular kings or deities who originally were believed to have spoken them, the written word itself comes to be increasingly authoritative, until soon a "nation of laws" is established that is founded upon a legal code that becomes more authoritative than any single ruler. This very process describes the origin of the Bible, which today is understood by the faithful to be the "Word of God," and which many believe to be more authoritative than any ruler or government.

Of course, whenever texts are copied, there is always a chance for scribal errors, interpretations, and explanations as well as deliberate alterations over time. We can identify discrepancies within the texts by setting them side by side and examining the historical development of the textual changes from copy to copy. This is one form of what scholars call textual criticism, and I'll demonstrate plenty of examples of textual criticism in this book. This will allow us to go beyond the mere history of these cities and instead explore the influence the cities had upon the written text of the Bible, which many people today look to as a source of great authority in their lives.

A NOTE ABOUT THEOLOGICAL
CLAIMS AND DIVINE INSPIRATION

The purpose of this book is not to make theological or doctrinal claims. I have no denominational preference, nor do I favor one religious or nonreligious tradition over another. It's my hope that this book will appeal to both theists and nontheists alike, devout Christians and atheists, conservative Jews and secular humanists.

I present facts and data, explain what this information means, demonstrate how the archaeological and geographical data affect the biblical texts, and then leave what to do with that information up to you. Some people will use it to become more literate about the history and background of the Bible. Some will use this book to plan their trip to the Holy Land's archaeological sites and museums. Others might use it in a Bible study at church or synagogue. Still others will use it to point out some problems with the texts sacred to Judaism and Christianity. However you use it is up to you; my job is not to tell you what to believe, but rather to give you the information necessary to make and hold an informed belief.

A quick word about divine inspiration. Most people of faith, both Jews and Christians, believe that there was *some* divine aspect to the composition of the Bible. Although very few people believe that the Bible is the verbatim word of God and that every letter is perfect, inerrant, and infallible (and we'll discuss this belief later in the book), the majority of people of faith today believe that there was some level of divine "inspiration" to the creation of what today is known as the "Word of God." This book will touch a bit on this subject toward the end, *after* we read the stories that resulted in the text of the Bible. But the process of canonization, that is, the process of determining which books came to comprise the Bible and which books did not, is similar to what is said about the making of laws and sausage: most people like the end result, but few want to see how they are actually made. In the same way, the canonization of the Bible is actually a very messy process, which we'll examine in the second half of this volume. For now, understand that I am not as interested in how the divine realm "inspired" (directly or indirectly) the composition of the Bible. Rather, this book examines the *human* part of this process, as people of faith understand that the Bible is *both* a divine and a human phenomenon.

HOW TO READ THIS BOOK

Let me offer a few notes on formatting and abbreviations and then explain how I've structured the book. First, I use the scientific and professional dating standard of BCE (before the common era) and CE (common era) to represent the dates that many know as BC (before Christ) and AD (*anno Domini,* "In the year of the Lord"). I do this for two reasons. The first is that BCE/CE is the standard modern way to represent dates in history, as it removes dating from a purely Christian calendar. By using the same dates, but attributing them to BCE and CE, we don't have to redate everything, but we remove the explicitly Christian reference point of the dating system. The second reason is related to the first. Many people do not realize that the "before Christ" and "Year of the Lord" dates are flat-out wrong. Jesus was not born in "AD 1," and it's quite simple to prove. We know from multiple literary and archaeological sources that Herod the Great died in 4 BCE according to our existing calendars. If we use a BC designation, it means Herod the Great died four years "before Christ," and this is a problem if Jesus was supposed to have been born *during* the reign of Herod. However, if we simply use BCE, then we can keep the exact same dates and spare the embarrassment of using a miscalculated date for Jesus's birth.[2]

Some might also observe that the majority of this book deals with the composition of the Hebrew Bible or Old Testament. This is to be expected since approximately 75 percent of the Christian Bible is, in fact, the Old Testament.[3] When Jesus quotes "the Scriptures," he's not quoting the Gospels, which weren't written until at least a half century after his death; rather, he is quoting the *Hebrew* Scriptures, which was the Bible of the earliest Christian church. When Jesus is heralded as the promised messiah of Israel, that is not a Roman invention, but a thoroughly *Jewish* notion.

As you see above, I use the term "Hebrew Bible" (abbreviated HB) to refer to the Old Testament (OT). It wasn't until a number of centuries after Jesus that later Christians canonized the writings of early Christians and distinguished them from the accepted Jewish writings by calling them the "Old Testament" and their own Christian Scriptures the "New Testament" (NT). All quotations of biblical verses are from the New Revised Standard Version (NRSV) unless otherwise noted, and all emphasis in Bible quotations and other quoted material is mine.

The Masoretic Text (MT) of the Hebrew Bible is the standard, received text of the Hebrew Bible that was edited from the sixth to the eleventh centuries CE by a group of Jewish scribal scholars referred to as the Masoretes, who not only preserved and copied the Hebrew Scriptures by hand, but also added the well-known vowel vocalization system used today to pronounce the Hebrew text in a standardized way. The Masoretic Text differs from other versions of the Hebrew texts, such as the Samaritan Pentateuch (SP), the texts of the Hebrew Scriptures found among the Dead Sea Scrolls (DSS), the Greek Septuagint (LXX, or "Seventy," after the legend of the seventy-two scribes who supposedly translated the Hebrew Scriptures into Greek), and the various Aramaic Targums (Tg), which preserve the Aramaic translations of the Bible along with additional interpretations by the Aramaic-speaking Jews of the first few centuries CE.

I'll provide a literally transcribed English equivalent for many Hebrew personal names (e.g., Ḥizqiyahu), followed by their common anglicized form (Ḥezekiah). You will often notice small half circles raised above the letters, as in the names Baʿal, Canaʿan, and Yisraʾel (anglicized as Israel). These represent the Hebrew letters ʾaleph and ʿayin and are brief pauses in the names, rendering the pronunciations *bah-al* and *cana-an*. The dots under some of the letters are not problems with the printing press, but rather represent more intensively vocalized letters. I do all of this in an effort to show you how the names are actually pronounced in Hebrew and to entice you to learn Hebrew.

This book proceeds in a largely chronological order. Chapter 1 begins in Phoenicia (modern Lebanon and coastal Syria) with an examination of the cities of Byblos, Tyre, and Ṣidon. In addition to giving us the word for Bible, these cities contributed both the physical materials needed for writing and the very alphabets used to write the Bible. These cities also contributed the early Phoenician deities that would become so prominent in the narrative of the Bible.

Chapter 2 examines the city of Ugarit, the Mediterranean coastal city that not only provided evidence of the transition from Semitic languages written in pictorial and syllabic cuneiform alphabets to those written in later consonantal alphabets (like Aramaic and Hebrew), but also, like Phoenicia, provided a pantheon, or assembly of deities, that came to be worshipped throughout Cana'an with familiar names line Ba'al, 'Asherah, and 'El, many of which also show up in the Bible.

Chapter 3 looks at the city of Nineveh, the capital of the ancient Neo-Assyrian Empire, which dominated Cana'an and ultimately conquered Samaria and ancient Israel. Chapter 4 examines Babylon, the capital of the ancient Neo-Babylonian Empire, which destroyed Jerusalem and the Temple to YHWH (God's personal name found throughout the Hebrew Bible) and ended the line of Davidic rulers in Jerusalem.

Chapter 5 explores the city of Megiddo, which played an important role in the politics of ancient Israel and contributed one of the most famous biblical concepts known today from the New Testament book of Revelation, namely, Armageddon.

Chapter 6 looks at Athens, which gave rise to Western civilization largely through its Platonic philosophical academy. This chapter surveys some of the philosophies that are mentioned in or had tremendous influence upon the Bible. This chapter also looks at the process of hellenization, brought to the Holy Land by Alexander the Great and his successors, which thoroughly influenced and ultimately altered Jewish theological beliefs and shaped many early forms of Christianity.

Chapter 7 examines the city of Alexandria, on the Mediterranean coast of Egypt, home to the famed Library of Alexandria, which provided the legendary motivation for the translation of the Hebrew Scriptures into Greek, yielding the Septuagint. This chapter also provides a survey of the books that comprise the Apocrypha, which were included in the Septuagint, but were ultimately left out of the Hebrew Scriptures.

Chapter 8 looks at Jerusalem, the capital of the ancient United Kingdom of Israel, the later Kingdom of Judah, and home of the Jewish Temple and the modern Western Wall. This chapter examines Jerusalem's significance for the ideology and theology of

the Hebrew Bible as well as its importance in the life and death
of Jesus.

Chapter 9 moves to the tiny settlement of Qumran and its significance to the Dead Sea Scrolls, which contain the earliest copies of
the Hebrew Bible known to us by over a thousand years and which
have altered the content of nearly every Bible published since 1950.
Chapter 10 looks at the cities of Bethlehem and Nazareth, which
are inexorably linked with the birth, life, and ministry of Jesus.

Chapter 11 examines the city of Rome, the Roman Empire, and
its role in late Second Temple Judaism, the life and death of Jesus,
and the birth of the early church. We discuss Paul's Letter to the
Romans as the best treatise of Paul's gospel of Jesus and the book
that more than any other shaped Western civilization. We also
examine Rome's role in the canonization of the Bible. Finally, the
Conclusion summarizes what we've learned and shows what we
can do with this information.

Last, I reiterate my promise to you. I'll never tell you what to
think or what to believe; that is up to you. What I *will* do is present you with the archaeological, historical, and literary evidence
that we have along with the consensus opinions of the world's best
biblical scholars, archaeologists, historians, and linguists regarding that evidence.

Now, I hope you'll do me a favor by not just reading the information presented in this book, but *challenging* it. If you're reading
the eBook, make use of the copious links to websites and defini-
tions that I've included with each important term. Use the Google
Earth virtual tour included at the Cities That Built the Bible website to travel virtually to these locations and view the evidence for
yourself. If you have the means and the opportunity to do so, book
tickets to travel to these physical places and see them for yourself.
I strongly encourage you to challenge *everything*—and not just
what you read in this book—but every claim made by a pastor,
preacher, minister, scholar, rabbi, author, cable TV documentary
host, or ancient-alien enthusiast to see whether what is being
claimed is simply what you *want* to believe or reject or whether

there is historical, archaeological, and literary evidence to support the claim and whether it is logical. Do this and you're already on your way toward thinking like a critical scholar.

And one last thing. I tell a lot of jokes and incorporate humor into every aspect of my life, both professionally and personally. I hope you'll have as much fun reading this book as I had writing it.

So grab a comfy spot on the couch or on a sandy beach, grab your beverage of choice, and join me as we walk through *The Cities That Built the Bible*.

CHAPTER 1

Phoenician Cities

If we're going to write a book about writing *the* book, the Bible, we have to start at the beginning. How did societies develop the skill of writing? And if we're going to examine writing, we must begin with Phoenicia, the birthplace of Western writing, which gave us the alphabet that allowed written documents like the Bible to be written at all. In fact, the early capital of Phoenicia holds claim to being the first city responsible for building the "Bible," since it is where the Bible derives its name: Byblos. By taking a look at Byblos and the later cities of Tyre and Ṣidon, we will see how, at its most elemental level, Phoenicia is the perfect starting point for exploring how these ancient cities built the Bible.

An Illegal Drive to Lebanon

The pinnacle of Phoenician culture was located in what is now Lebanon, and travel to Lebanon can be a bit dicey, especially if you've ever traveled to Israel. This is because the two countries are still technically at war, and given the hostilities between the two countries, travelers attempting to enter Lebanon with Israeli stamps in their passports will usually be denied entry. The remnants of the war between the two countries are still visible today; entire fields full of land mines are fenced off and bright yellow signs written in English, Hebrew, and Arabic still warn, "DANGER MINES!" One area, Shib'ā Farms, is still a point of contention today, as Israel controls the land, but the Lebanese say it belongs to them.

A sign near Banias (ancient Caesarea Philippi) in the Golan Heights near the Israeli border with Lebanon.

In 2000, I was digging at Banias (ancient Caesarea Philippi) with a team from Pepperdine University. The dig director was Vassilios Tzaferis, who served as the Israel Antiquities Authority's Director of Excavations and Surveys from 1991 to 2001. Vassilios and I became fast friends, and he was a mentor to me during my early years as an archaeologist. A Greek Orthodox monk who left the priesthood to marry his beautiful wife, Efti, Vassilios went on to earn his doctorate and become an archaeologist. He discovered the first evidence of a crucified man in Jerusalem—a Jewish man named Yehoḥanan ben Ḥagqol, whose ankle bone was discovered with a nail driven through it inside an ossuary (or burial bone box) bearing his name.[1]

One afternoon following an exhausting day digging at Banias, Vassilios called to me, "Bob! Let's go for a drive."

I didn't ask any questions. I got in the car, and Vassilios started driving. But instead of turning south back to Kibbutz Snir (cf. Deut. 3:9), where the team had been staying, he continued on toward the west. I knew something was up when we crossed an unmarked, flattened barbed-wire fence that had been driven over repeatedly.

"So, where are we going?"

Vassilios responded in his deep, booming Greek voice, "Over there."

I looked down the winding dirt farm road on which we were driving and in the distance saw a pile of tires burning in the middle of the road. Residents of a small local village appeared to be protesting something.

I asked Vassilios nervously, "Where are we?"

"It depends on who you ask. Some call it Lebanon," he replied calmly, without looking up or altering the path of our slowly progressing vehicle.

I stoically suppressed my suddenly increasing anxiety and pointed out to Vassilios in my coolest voice possible, "Um . . . the road is on fire, and those people appear to be protesting. And did you say 'Lebanon'?!"

Vassilios again replied peacefully, "They're just kids."

As our vehicle pulled to a stop in front of the tire fire, Vassilios rolled down the window and in perfect Arabic began speaking to one of the teenagers who approached the vehicle. They had a whole conversation. I sat nervously waiting for them to begin pelting our vehicle with the rocks they each had in their hands, but it never happened. Our fearless, peacemaking Greek leader finished the conversation, rolled up the window, turned the truck around, and began driving back to Israel.

"They want their farm back," Vassilios said, scanning the land around us. "They're just farm kids, they're angry, this is all they've got, and burning tires on their own property doesn't hurt anyone."

Vassilios continued, "It's complicated up here, Roberto. Don't be afraid. They want the same thing you want: to be happy, have a job, get married, raise a family, and be left alone."

I always liked it when Vassilios called me Roberto. I knew he was being sincere. And it was there, in a truck that had illegally crossed into Lebanon with a colleague I admired, that I began researching and learning about the conflict between Israel and its neighbors from *all* sides, including that of the children who just want what all kids want: to play and not be in constant fear. This experience influenced how I read and study the Bible, especially as I look at cities, such as those in Phoenicia, that so deeply impacted the creation of the book that still causes a stir in my heart today.

THE HISTORY OF PHOENICIA

Before the Romans, Greeks, and Persians dominated the Mediterranean, the Phoenicians ruled the sea from 1200 to 800 BCE and made a fortune as traders throughout the area. Phoenicia is actually a Greek name from the word *Phoiníke* (Φοινίκη). The Phoenicians were experts in the extraction of red-purple dye from murex shells, giving us the word *Phoinix* (Φοῖνιξ), meaning "deep purple, crimson." Phoenicia came to be known as the "land of purple" because of its monopoly over the production and export of its most famous product, purple-dyed cloth. The vast wealth derived from this and many other commodities and crafts traded throughout the eastern Mediterranean resulted in a collection of independent Semitic city-states in northern Cana'an that came to be known as Phoenicia, one of the most economically prosperous cultures of the late second to early first millennium BCE.

These Cana'anite Phoenician states formed colonies on several Mediterranean islands, including Cyprus, Crete, Sicily, Malta, Sardinia, and Ibiza; along coastal Europe from southern Turkey to Spain; and along the entire coast of northern Africa. Their best-known colony is Carthage (modern Tunis, Tunisia, located between modern Libya and Algeria), which later became their capital. Carthaginian Phoenicians came to be known as the Punics and were rivals of Rome until their destruction as a result of the Punic Wars, fought between Rome and Carthage from 264 to 146 BCE.

Long before the biblical kingdom of Israel existed (ca. 1000 BCE), ancient Phoenicia ruled the eastern Mediterranean and northern Cana'an. In addition to the archaeological and nonbiblical literary evidence attesting to the wealth of Phoenicia,[2] the

Bible acknowledges the success of its cities. Joshua 19:29 describes Tyre as a "fortified city," which we would expect of a major port town. Acts 21:3 records that the apostle Paul's ship docked at Tyre, as this was one of the major coastal ports in Syria as late as the Roman period.

And it is this success—particularly the success of its three major port towns, Byblos, Tyre, and Ṣidon—that made Phoenicia a target for neighboring nations seeking to take advantage of its economic success and therefore its political power, as we see with the Neo-Assyrian conquest of Phoenicia in 883 BCE. It was also Phoenicia's success that made it a subject of condemnation by Israelite prophets admonishing foreign nations for their greed while the poor in Israel suffered.

Isaiah 23 is a poem recounting the fall of Tyre and Ṣidon at the hands of the Babylonians in the seventh century BCE. In it, Yesha'yahu (Isaiah) bemoans the demise of the once proud and wealthy coastal city-states, "whose merchants were princes, whose traders were the honored of the earth" (23:8). The prophet states that Phoenicia will remain in this ruined state "for seventy years, the lifetime of one king" (23:15).

So although the destruction of these three Phoenician cities at the hands of the Babylonians provided a point of reference that later Israelite prophets (including Jesus, as we'll see later) used to scare Israelites and later Jews into behaving properly, these cities were actually far more than just historical reference points; in fact, they quite literally provided the materials for three of the most essential items for the building of the Bible: the alphabet, paper, and the Jerusalem Temple itself! Let's start by looking at the early capital of Phoenicia, Byblos.

BYBLOS

Byblos served as the early capital of Phoenicia from 1200 until around 1000 BCE, when the capital was moved to Tyre. You may not recognize Byblos as a city in the Bible because it was known by a few different names. During the Bronze Age, it was known as the Cana'anite city Gubal. The Amarna Letters, which were correspondence between the Egyptian pharaohs in Amarna and various Cana'anite city-states, refer to it as Gubla. The Phoenicians referred to the city as Gebal, and the Bible preserves this Iron Age (1200–586 BCE) name, referring to Byblos as Geval (גבל).[3]

However, you may recognize the city by its later Greek name, Byblos (Βύβλος), as the city lent its name to its most famous export: the book. In fact, although the earliest "paper" came from the stalks of the papyrus plants largely found in Egypt, papyrus earned its early Greek name, *byblos* or *byblinos,* from the fact that it was exported to the Aegean through the Phoenician city of Byblos. The name for paper eventually evolved into *biblion* (βιβλίον), the Greek word for "book, scroll," the plural of which, *biblia* (βιβλία), "many books," gave us the word "Bible." Thus in the purest sense, the first city responsible for building the "Bible" is the very city whence the Bible derives its name: Byblos.

THE PHOENICIAN ALPHABET

But Phoenicia didn't just give us the word for the Bible. The Phoenicians are credited with the very invention that allowed the Bible to be written down in the first place—the Phoenician alphabet.

As the Phoenicians engaged in trade over the centuries, their influence throughout the Mediterranean increased.[4] But these seafaring traders needed a system to streamline their invoices, orders, receipts, and logistical organization as they brokered goods between Asia, Europe, and northern Africa. Although the Phoenicians gathered and exported a myriad of products, arguably their most lasting gift to the world is something far more ubiquitous: a simple, consonantal alphabet.[5]

The Phoenician alphabet is actually responsible for *both* the Greek and Hebrew alphabets. The Phoenicians are credited with transitioning from earlier systems of writing like cuneiform (those chicken-scratch impressions made by a wedge-shaped stylus tip on a clay tablet to form pictures that represent either words or syllables) to a much easier system. Cuneiform required the memorization of hundreds, if not thousands, of symbolic pictograms to represent the nouns, verbs, and other parts of language required to communicate complete thoughts in rudimentary "sentences." The Phoenician system was a much easier consonantal system made up of only a few graphemes (letters). These "letters" did not stand for *things*, but for the *sounds* that made up words.

The development of a consonantal alphabet meant that scribes had to memorize only a few symbols—twenty-two to be exact—and place them together to form the *sounds* that make up a word, instead of drawing the entire object they were trying to communicate. Having to remember only twenty-two shapes (instead of thousands of pictograms) made writing much easier and the composition of letters much faster, which in turn allowed writing to become easier to learn and therefore more common during this period. Thus, the Phoenician alphabet is the first necessary component to "building" the Bible, and the Phoenician cities of Byblos, Tyre, and Ṣidon represent the glorious culture of the Phoenicians from which Western alphabets derive.

THE SPREAD OF THE PHOENICIAN ALPHABET THROUGH THE MEDITERRANEAN

It is thought that the Phoenicians spread their new writing system to their ports and colonies throughout the Mediterranean. The Greek historian Herodotus claims that the Phoenicians brought their alphabet to the Greeks.[6] Indeed, the chart on the next page demonstrates the similarities between the Greek and Phoenician alphabets. Of course, the Greeks went on to write tomes of classical literature and philosophy that serve as the foundation for Western thought, subsequent Western literature, and essentially most of Western culture.

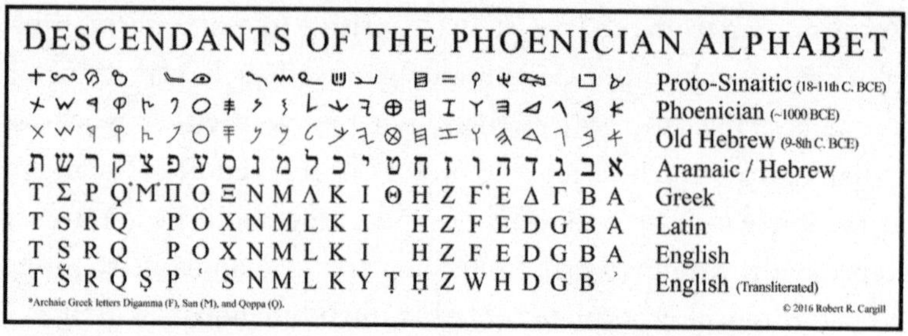

DESCENDANTS OF THE PHOENICIAN ALPHABET

				Script
✝ �ᶜᵇ ᖇ ⬮	ᐭ ᐤ	ᔑ ᗰ ᖰ ᗐ ᗑ ᗒ	ᗸ = ᖰ ᖺ ᗏ	☐ ᖴ	Proto-Sinaitic (18–11th C. BCE)
✗ W ꟼ Ϙ ᖶ ⌐ Ο ⧧ ᔿ ξ ᒪ ᭼ ᖰ ⊕ ᖺ I Υ ᗐ ◁ ᐳ ᔕ K	Phoenician (~1000 BCE)
X W ꟼ Ϙ ᖰ ᒎ Ο ⧧ ᒎ ᒪ ᖰ ⊗ ᖺ ᒡ Υ ᗷ ᗰ ᐳ ᔕ ✝	Old Hebrew (9–8th C. BCE)
ת ש ר ק צ פ ע ס נ מ ל כ י ט ח ז ו ה ד ג ב א	Aramaic / Hebrew
T Σ P Q̓ M̓ Π O Ξ N M Λ K I Θ H Z F̓ E Δ Γ B A	Greek
T S R Q P O X N M L K I H Z F E D G B A	Latin
T S R Q P O X N M L K I H Z F E D G B A	English
T Š R Q Ṣ P ʿ S N M L K Y Ṭ Ḥ Z W H D G B ʾ	English (Transliterated)

Archaic Greek letters Digamma (F), San (M̓), and Qoppa (Q̓).   © 2016 Robert R. Cargill

The chart above demonstrates how the Phoenician alphabet provided the foundational shapes of the letters that would become the Greek, Hebrew, Aramaic, Latin, and ultimately English alphabets.

Other groups adopted the Phoenician alphabet, for example, the Arameans, a group of Semitic peoples who resided in what is now Syria. The Arameans used the Phoenician alphabet for their Aramaic language, which came to be the dominant language throughout the Near Eastern empires until the coming of the Greeks and the hellenization (and subsequent romanization) of the Levant. In fact, so superior in ease of use and learnability were the Phoenician alphabet and the Aramaic language that, following the Persian Achaemenid conquest of Mesopotamia in the sixth century BCE, King Darius I jettisoned his own people's traditional Akkadian cuneiform language and adopted (Old) Aramaic as the official language of the empire.[7] Because it was easy to learn and use, the Persians felt it was the best language for governing their vast empire made up of many different peoples speaking various native languages.

Because the Phoenician alphabet was the dominant one used by Cana'anite peoples, it is no surprise that the Hebrews also adopted it and used it to write the earliest known epigraphic Hebrew inscriptions, like the Gezer Calendar, discovered in the city of Gezer, about twenty miles west of Jerusalem.[8] This tenth-century BCE tablet acted like an ancient *Farmers' Almanac,* instructing farmers when to plant and harvest their crops. Scholars refer to Hebrew written in Phoenician script during this early period as Old Hebrew (see chart above).[9] Later, while they were in Babylon, exiles from Judah adopted the local Aramaic language as their native tongue. Evidence for this comes from the fact that some books of the Bible written after the return from exile, namely, 'Ezra' (Ezra) and Dani'el (Daniel), contain large portions of text written in what has come to be known as biblical Aramaic.[10]

After the exiles returned to Jerusalem, they continued speaking and writing the Aramaic language down through the time of Jesus. This is why Jesus is always quoted in the Gospels as having spoken Aramaic—it was his native tongue! They also adopted the Aramaic square script to write *both* Aramaic and Hebrew, which is why the Hebrew that we have in the Bible (and today) uses the Phoenician alphabet and the Aramaic square script.

Thus, since the Phoenicians, who popularized the consonantal alphabet, saw their alphabet become adopted by the Hebrews, Arameans, and Greeks, and since their three languages were used to compose the books of the Old and New Testaments of the Bible, we can confidently claim that the Phoenicians are ultimately responsible for the literary raw materials—paper and alphabet—used to write the Bible. But the Phoenicians didn't just give us the devices used in the writing of the Bible; they also inspired some of the text of the Bible. And believe it or not, Phoenicia also gave us the holiest place in Judaism, the house of God itself, the Jerusalem Temple. So let's turn to Tyre and Ṣidon, two cities that greatly influenced the contents of the Bible in different ways.

TYRE AND ṢIDON

Two other ancient Phoenician port cities, Tyre and Ṣidon (both in modern Lebanon), ultimately surpassed the early Phoenician capital of Byblos in size and importance. The island city of Tyre grew in prominence throughout the Late Bronze Age (1550–1200 BCE) and supplanted Byblos as the Phoenician capital around 1000 BCE. In 333 BCE the capital was moved to Carthage (in modern

Tunisia), where it remained until the destruction of Carthage at the hands of the Romans in 149 BCE during the Third Punic War.

Tyre is mentioned often in the Bible, where it is known as Ṣor (צור), pronounced "Tsor" or "Tsur." The Greeks later called it *Turos* (Τύρος), whence we get the modern anglicized name Tyre.

TYRE'S CONTRIBUTION TO THE CREATION OF THE TEMPLE IN JERUSALEM

Although Tyre was not an Israelite town, this regional trade center *did* provide ancient Israel with its most prominent structure. Few people realize that the palace of King David as well as the Temple of King Shlomoh (Solomon), both in Jerusalem, were made possible through materials and craftsmen from Tyre. Tyre was responsible for the *physical* building of David's palace and the Temple in Jerusalem. Second Samuel 5:11 states: "King Hiram of Tyre sent messengers to David, along with cedar trees, and carpenters and masons who built David a house." Later on, 1 Kings states that Ḥiram also provided the materials—specifically the famed cedars of Lebanon (take a look at the Lebanese flag today to see just how proud the Lebanese are of their cedars!)—to build the Jerusalem Temple: "Now King Hiram of Tyre sent his servants to Solomon, when he heard that they had anointed him king in place of his father; for Hiram had always been a friend to David" (5:1).

Note that the verse also says, "Hiram had always been a friend to David." This implies that there had been a strategic alliance between Israel and Phoenicia. Solomon confirms this alliance by sending a message to King Ḥiram asking him (quite flatteringly) for Lebanese cedars to use in building his Temple:

> *Therefore command that cedars from the Lebanon be cut for me. My servants will join your servants, and I will give you whatever wages you set for your servants; for you know that there is no one among us who knows how to cut timber like the Sidonians. (1 Kings 5:6)*

King Hiram consented, responded with his counterdemands, and then proposed a clever way to transport the lumber to Jerusalem. Rather than carry it overland, which would incur tremendous expense in labor and animals as well as an increased delivery time to navigate the mountains between the Lebanese coast and Jerusalem, Hiram decided he would ship the lumber down the coast. Instead of taking valuable trade ships out of service for use in transporting the lumber to Jerusalem, 1 Kings says that King Hiram bound the lumber itself into rafts and floated them down the Mediterranean coast, which allowed his shipping vessels to continue on their business of international trade:

> *"My servants shall bring it down to the sea from the Lebanon; I will make it into rafts to go by sea to the place you indicate. I will have them broken up there for you to take away."* (5:9)

In exchange for the lumber requested by Solomon for use in his Temple, King Hiram asked Solomon to pay him an annual allowance.

> *"And you shall meet my needs by providing food for my household."* So Hiram supplied Solomon's every need for timber of cedar and cypress. Solomon in turn gave Hiram twenty thousand cors of wheat as food for his household, and twenty cors of fine oil. Solomon gave this to Hiram year by year. (1 Kings 5:9–11)

The language used in 1 Kings 5 appears to imply some sort of trade deal, if not a formal treaty between Tyre and Israel. Near Eastern scholar Edward Lipiński states: "Israel and Tyre were complementary countries from the economic point of view, Israel appearing as a continental, agricultural land, while Tyre was oriented towards seafaring and maritime trade."[11] Israel, which produced wheat, millet, honey, oil, and balm, among other commodities (cf. Ezek. 27:17), traded regularly with Tyre, which likely exported much of the goods it received from inland states; in exchange, Israel imported many handcrafted objects that were produced locally in Phoenicia. Thus, it makes sense that Solomon would ask King Ḥiram of Tyre for the materials for the Temple, as Lebanon was known worldwide for its timbers and Solomon wanted only the best for YHWH's Temple.

We also know that laborers from both Tyre and Israel are said to have worked together on the Temple according to the Bible. According to 1 Kings 5:18, "Solomon's builders and Hiram's builders and the Giblites did the stonecutting and prepared the timber and the stone to build the house." Thus, we have additional biblical claims that the two kings worked together to procure the materials and build the Jerusalem Temple.

Given this textual evidence, we can conclude that Tyre contributed significantly to the construction of the Jerusalem Temple. Furthermore, the Bible explicitly states that much of Solomon's wealth was the result of joint trade expeditions with Phoenicia. First Kings 9:26–29 tells of one joint venture in which Solomon provided trade access to the Gulf of ʿAqaba, the Red Sea, and the Indian Ocean for King Ḥiram. Such a trade agreement would have cut the distance of ocean voyages from Europe to South Asia by over forty-three hundred miles, making commercial trade with India viable for Phoenicia. Thus, although the biblical tales of Solomon's wealth may indeed be exaggerated, the fact that Solomon engaged in trade with Phoenicia may stand at the root of the legends of his wealth, as those trading with Phoenicia would have certainly profited greatly by doing so.[12]

Now, scholars and many readers may take pause and rightly ask, "How do we know that this is historical and not just a made-up story?" This is a fair question. The best scholarly response is that the later compilers and editors of the Bible (i.e., the scribes who collected these stories and arranged them in the Bible) would likely not have highlighted positive interactions with foreign nations (who worship foreign gods) if they had not actually happened. Express commands from God like those found in Exodus 23:32 and Deuteronomy 7:2 prohibit the Israelites from making treaties with foreign peoples. The fact that David and Solomon both are said to have had positive interactions with Phoenicia is a problem for the Bible. Thus, it is unlikely that such a violation of YHWH's commands would be invented and introduced into the text by later composers or editors of the Bible. Rather, although the tales of Solomon's wealth and the vastness of his "kingdom" are almost certainly embellished, it is likely that the use of Phoenician cedars to build the Jerusalem Temple and the tales of joint trade ventures and agreements with Phoenicia are rooted in some historical reality.

THE FALL OF TYRE AND ṢIDON

But as is the case with every nation that has ever existed, Phoenicia's heyday eventually gave way to foreign conquest. Tyre and Ṣidon were attacked and conquered a number of times by various enemies including Egypt; the Assyrian king Shalmaneser V; the Babylonian king Nebuchadnezzar II, who forced them to pay him annual tribute; the Persian Achaemenids, who ruled Tyre and Ṣidon from 539 to 332 BCE;[13] Alexander the Great, who overthrew Ṣidon and orchestrated the Siege of Tyre before razing the city to the ground when taking it from the Persians; and Antigonus I Monophthalmus, who again besieged the city in 315 BCE.[14]

And it is these destructions of Tyre and Ṣidon that were burned into the cultural memory of Israelites, Judahites, and later Jews by a number of Hebrew prophets. Because of the history of power and economic excess and the subsequent destruction of these cities, the Hebrew prophets looked to Tyre and Ṣidon as examples of what God does to those who do not care for the poor or heed his word.

The prophet Yeḥezqi'el (Ezekiel) condemned the king of Tyre not only for his vast wealth, but because he "compared his mind to the mind of a god":

> *Therefore thus says the Lord GOD: Because you compare your mind with the mind of a god, therefore, I will bring strangers against you, the most terrible of the nations; they shall draw their swords against the beauty of your wisdom and defile your splendor.*

*They shall thrust you down to the Pit, and you shall die a violent
death in the heart of the seas. (28:6–8)*

In fact, Ezekiel 27–28 is a lengthy prophecy against Phoenicia, a
portion of which is particularly condemnatory of Ṣidon:

*Thus says the Lord God: I am against you, O Sidon, and I will
gain glory in your midst. They shall know that I am the Lord
when I execute judgments in it, and manifest my holiness in it;
for I will send pestilence into it, and bloodshed into its streets; and
the dead shall fall in its midst, by the sword that is against it on
every side. And they shall know that I am the Lord. (28:22–23)*

The prophet Isaiah offers an entire prophecy against Tyre. Isaiah
23 describes the destruction of Tyre, and vv. 13–14 specifically
highlight the deeds of the Babylonians (here called the Chaldeans):

*Look at the land of the Chaldeans! This is the people; it was not
Assyria. They destined Tyre for wild animals. They erected their
siege towers, they tore down her palaces, they made her a ruin.
Wail, O ships of Tarshish, for your fortress is destroyed.*

Thus, a prophetic tradition developed that cursed Tyre (and Ṣidon
by proxy) for amassing wealth and not heeding the words of God.

TYRE AND ṢIDON IN THE NEW TESTAMENT

It is this destruction of the main city-states of Phoenicia that Jesus
would remind his opponents of in a harsh sermon against cities
near the northern shore of the Sea of Galilee. In Luke 10:13–15 (cf.
Matt. 11:20–24), Jesus invokes Tyre and Ṣidon as a point of comparison while chastising the Jewish cities of Chorazin, Bethṣaida,
and Kfar Naḥum (Capernaum):

*Woe to you, Chorazin! Woe to you, Bethsaida! For if the deeds of
power done in you had been done in Tyre and Sidon, they would
have repented long ago, sitting in sackcloth and ashes. But at the*

judgment it will be more tolerable for Tyre and Sidon than for
you. And you, Capernaum, will you be exalted to heaven? No,
you will be brought down to Hades.

Jesus tells Chorazin, Bethsaida, and Capernaum, cities in which Jesus
has performed his "deeds of power" (cf. Matt. 11:20), that the well-
known non-Jewish cities of Tyre and Ṣidon will have an easier time
at the final judgment than they will.

And yet, interestingly, we also have an account of Jesus retreat-
ing to Tyre and Ṣidon in Matthew: "Jesus left that place and went
away to the district of Tyre and Sidon" (15:21). Mark adds that
he went there and "entered a house and did not want anyone to
know he was there. Yet he could not escape notice" (7:24). And
while he was in Tyre, Jesus is said to have performed one of his
more controversial miracles.

Mark 7:24–30 (cf. Matt. 15:21–28) tells the story of the Syrophoenician woman. (Syrophoenicians are Phoenicians from Syria.)
This miracle is controversial because Jesus not only initially refuses to perform the miracle, but also calls the woman a dog (Gk.
κυνάριον), which was as insulting then as it is now:

Now the woman was a Gentile, of Syrophoenician origin. She
begged him to cast the demon out of her daughter. He said to
her, "Let the children be fed first, for it is not fair to take the
children's food and throw it to the dogs." But she answered him,
"Sir, even the dogs under the table eat the children's crumbs."
Then he said to her, "For saying that, you may go—the demon
has left your daughter." So she went home, found the child lying
on the bed, and the demon gone.

I once told my college class a version of this story: "On my way
to class today, a homeless person asked me, 'Teacher, can you answer some questions about the Bible for me?' I responded, 'I'm on
my way to teach my students. I need to teach them first, because
it's not fair to take the children's food and throw it to the dogs.'"

My students were appalled (and rightly so). I could hear one of the students whisper under her breath, "What a jerk!" They stared at me, wondering how I could be so rude to a homeless man who was simply asking for my help.

Then I said to my class, "I didn't *really* say that to a homeless man. But could you imagine if someone had recorded my saying that and then posted it on YouTube? At the very least I'd get called into the dean's office, and I'd certainly be labeled on some website as the worst person in the world."

And yet *that's* what Jesus said to the Syrophoenician woman! Of course, he ultimately healed the woman's daughter, but the text makes clear that it was because of the woman's clever comeback—"even the dogs under the table eat the children's crumbs"—that he healed her. Note that she didn't give Jesus an "Oh no you didn't" response along with a finger wag, but instead spun Jesus's "dog comment" and threw it back in his face, matching him cliché for cliché. And here's the fun part: Jesus was so impressed with her *cleverness*—"*For saying that,* you may go"— that he healed the woman's daughter.

Of course, some people argue that the healing by Jesus makes up for his harsh words or that the addition in Matthew 15:24 of Jesus's statement that he "was sent only to the lost sheep of Israel" makes his healing of this Gentile woman some sort of extracurricular bonus healing, compensating for his initial denial of the woman's request and his rude behavior toward her. Whatever its interpretation, it is worth noting that, although Jesus may have initially ministered to his fellow Jews, he ultimately ministered to *all* people, regardless of race, gender, and nationality, and he first did so *not* in Jerusalem or the Galilee, as one would expect, but on a trip to Tyre.

———

The ancient Phoenician cities of Tyre, Ṣidon, and Byblos contributed to both the Old and New Testaments. Phoenicia gave us paper, the alphabet, and the word "Bible" itself. These cities assisted with the building of the Jerusalem Temple and are credited with helping Solomon become rich, not to mention the fact that their prosperity became the target of condemnation for Hebrew prophets. The destruction of these cities became a lingering memory in the minds of Jews at the time of Jesus, who performed a unique miracle there, expanded his ministry to include Gentiles, and chastised cities surrounding the Sea of Galilee by saying that they would suffer more than Tyre and Ṣidon. Indeed, the ancient cities of Tyre, Ṣidon, and Byblos are cities that directly helped build the Bible.

CHAPTER 2

Ugarit

In 1928, an Alawite peasant named Maḥmoud Mella az-Zir was plowing his field in the Mediterranean port town of Minet el-Beida, about seven miles north of the modern city of Latakia, Syria. While he was plowing, az-Zir accidentally unearthed an ancient tomb. Archaeologists from the Service des Antiquités en Syrie et au Liban investigated the tomb and the pottery it contained. Noticing that pottery was thirteenth-century BCE Mycenaean and Cypriot pottery similar to vessels found in tombs in Crete, and given that the presence of imported vessels in a burial is typically a sign of a wealth, French archaeologists René Dussaud and Claude Frédéric-Armand Schaeffer and their team began to focus on the nearby tell of Ras Shamra, about a half mile inland.

Their curiosity paid off. The French team uncovered an entire city full of residences as well as several monumental buildings, including a palace and two temples. They had discovered the ancient city of Ugarit. Within the buildings, archaeologists discovered multiple caches of various cuneiform texts that not only tell us about the economic wealth and political standing of the city in the Late Bronze Age, but, more important for our purposes, also shed more light on the origins of Israelite religion than perhaps any other discovery in history.

These Ugaritic texts detail the lives of many deities that were worshipped not only at Ugarit, but also throughout Cana'an to the south, including in Israel. Likewise, the Ugaritic language provides a linguistic bridge from Mesopotamia to Cana'an. Thus, the texts discovered at Ugarit are significant because they inform our understanding of the origin of many of the Bible's stories and provide a backstory for many of the deities mentioned in the Bible. So the next stop in our journey is Ugarit, where we'll take a look at how this city changed what we know about the Bible.

THE ARCHAEOLOGY OF UGARIT

Using the texts discovered at Ras Shamra, archaeologists in 1935 were able to identify the site as ancient Ugarit, a kingdom first mentioned around 2300 BCE in the Ebla Tablets, in the eighteenth-century BCE Mari Archives from Mesopotamia, and in the fourteenth-century BCE Amarna Letters from Egypt. The texts were discovered in multiple locations near various monumental buildings discovered on the site. Archaeologists interpreted one building to be either a library or the house of the city's high priest. The remains of two temples honoring two deities—the Temple of Ba'al Hadad and the Temple of Dagon—were also discovered in the northeast quarter of the walled city. These buildings formed the central areas of worship on the city's acropolis.

TEMPLE OF BA'AL HADAD

The temples of Ugarit are on the acropolis of the city to the east of the royal palace. The palace's ninety rooms are guarded by the iconic postern gate that provides entrance to the city from the west. As you make your way through the city up the tell, you come to the Temple of Ba'al Hadad, an impressive structure whose 52-by-72-foot building and walled enclosure covered 9150 square feet on the acropolis. It was identified by the presence of a large stele (an inscribed monumental stone) of Ba'al, the "Ba'al with Thunderbolt" (which is actually an image of Ba'al with a mace), and a stele of a local "scribe and attendant of the royal domain" named Mami, which contained an Egyptian hieroglyphic dedication to "Ba'al of Ṣafon."[1]

The main structure of the Temple of Ba'al Hadad complex was a rectangular building divided into a larger and a smaller room, with an altar to the south in front of it. Archaeologist Marguerite Yon claims that the temple was about 65 feet tall. Because the acropolis itself rises another 65 feet above the plain below, the Temple of Ba'al Hadad would have ascended 130 feet above the surrounding area, making it easily visible to sailors at sea.[2] In fact, the presence of seventeen stone anchors found within the temple precinct demonstrates just how thankful sailors must have been to Ba'al for protecting them while they battled the stormy seas.

TEMPLE OF DAGON

Another nearby temple, the Temple of Dagon, was also located on the acropolis of Ugarit to the east of the Temple of Ba'al Hadad. Archaeologists attribute the temple to Dagon because two steles (*KTU* 6.13 and 6.14) were discovered within the temple enclosure, one of which possessed a dedicatory inscription to Dagon written in Ugaritic.[3] Dagon was originally a Mesopotamian fertility deity (likely specific to grain) who was worshipped at Ugarit. The earliest references to Dagon are from the Mari Archives (2500 BCE), where he held the titles "King of the Land" and "Lord of all the Great Gods,"[4] and at Ebla (2300 BCE).[5] King Sargon of Akkad credits Dagon with his victories in western Mesopotamia, and the Philistines are said to have adopted Dagon as their national deity (cf. Judg. 16:23). Dagon also features prominently in 1 Samuel 5:1–5, when the Philistines capture the ark of the covenant and place it in the temple next to the statue of Dagon. In the story, the statue of Dagon falls on its face before the ark during the night, shattering and losing its head and hands. The text is designed to show that YHWH (represented by the ark) is greater than Dagon (represented by the idol).

LIBRARY OR HOUSE OF THE HIGH PRIEST

The House of the High Priest (which some have called the Library of the High Priest) stood between the two temples. Although this building possesses all of the expected features of any other fine house in Ugarit, what was buried *inside* changed the way we understand Ugarit *and* the Bible. The excavation of the building yielded seventy-four weapons and bronze tools including "a hoe and four adzes with dedicatory inscriptions on them that were used in 1930 to decipher Ugaritic."[6] But most important for our purposes were tablets upon which were written mythological poems containing texts from several important Ugaritic literary masterpieces, including the Ba'al Cycle, the Legend of Kirta (Keret), and the Epic of 'Aqhat (or Dan'el), which provided the key to understanding Ugaritic literature.[7]

These three buildings crown an impressive city full of remains that speak to the importance of Ugarit in the Late Bronze Age. But for our journey it wasn't the monumental structures that helped build the Bible, but rather the texts that were discovered inside them; what those written texts *say* has been of interest to scholars for decades. Once scholars began deciphering the Ugaritic tablets, they discovered something dramatic: the content of the narrative texts (e.g., the names of the deities, the tales of certain men, the poems, and the wisdom texts) and of the religious texts (e.g., how the ancient Ugaritic peoples worshipped and *did* religion) were remarkably similar to and possibly influenced many of the stories found in the Hebrew Bible. Some readers are surprised to learn that many of the stories found in the Bible were often inspired by *earlier* stories about characters and gods from *other* cultures. We'll discuss this more later on, but first let's meet the gods who were prominent both at Ugarit and in the Bible.

THE UGARITIC PANTHEON

People at Ugarit worshipped deities known from the Phoenician pantheon. This is to be expected, given Ugarit's proximity to Phoenicia. But significantly, the texts discovered at Ugarit revealed much about the background of many of the deities mentioned in the Bible, including why encounters with various gods so frequently take place on top of holy mountains. The answer may lie in the holy mountain of Ugarit, which perhaps not coincidentally is also mentioned in the Bible.

Jebel 'Aqra' (Mt. Aqra), lying to the north of Ugarit, is known in the Bible as Mt. Ṣafon (Zaphon).[8] Mt. Aqra, or Mt. Ṣafon, is to Ugarit and northern Cana'an what Mt. Olympus is to the Greeks: the tallest mountain in the region and home to the assembly of the gods.[9]

Among the various deities mentioned in the Ugaritic texts as dwelling atop Mt. Ṣafon were some that came to play an important role in the development of religion in ancient Israel. Because these deities were worshipped at Ugarit hundreds of years before the so-called United Kingdom of Israel existed, scholars believe that much of what became Israelite religion was an incorporation of, or a reaction to, the popular Ugaritic deities that were worshipped throughout Cana'an. Below, we'll meet the most important Ugarit deities and learn how they may have influenced the Israelite religion.

'EL

'El was the father of the gods at Ugarit. However, he was viewed as more of an initial creator who now plays a less active role in the daily lives of the Ugaritic people, but whose consent was still required in major decisions. 'El was like the chairman of the board (as opposed to the CEO) of a company or the Deity Emeritus of the pantheon, who was respected for contributions made long ago.

'El is mentioned in the Bible several times, but it is difficult to distinguish in some cases whether the actual deity is being named or whether 'El is being used as an epithet for the Hebrew God, YHWH, or a shortened form of the Hebrew word 'Elohim ("God"). For instance, the 'El in the name Beth-'El (Heb., "house of 'El" or "house of God") in Genesis 28:19 (cf. 31:13), where Jacob consecrates the place he wrestled with God, most certainly refers to YHWH. However, Judges 9:46 mentions the temple of 'El Berit (Heb., "'El of the covenant") at Shechem, who is a decidedly *different* deity from YHWH.[10] Likewise, Psalm 82:1 says, "God has taken his place in the council of 'El," and many versions of the Bible translate "council of 'El" as "divine council" to avoid mentioning the deity 'El. Thus, 'El's presence in the Bible is sometimes a synonym for the Hebrew God (YHWH) and sometimes the foreign deity with roots at Ugarit.

'ASHERAH

'Asherah is 'El's consort, or wife if you will, in the same way she is the wife of Anu, the sky god ('El's equivalent), in Sumerian mythology. At Ugarit, she is called 'Athirat. (The *sh* sound in Hebrew is pronounced and spelled as a *th* sound at Ugarit.[11]) She came to be associated with the sea at Ugarit; twelve different references to her in the Ba'al Cycle alone are to the deity as "Lady 'Athirat of the Sea."[12] 'Asherah is mentioned in the Bible several times, often in association with Ba'al.[13] According to 2 Kings 21:7, at one point during the reign of King Manasseh of Judah an idol of 'Asherah even stood in the Temple in Jerusalem!

BA'AL HADAD

Ba'al is the champion of the Ugaritic pantheon. Pronounced like *ball* (and not like a hay *bale*), the name Ba'al literally means "lord" or "master" in Ugaritic in the same way that it does in Hebrew. In fact, the word *ba'al* is still the modern Hebrew word for "husband." (My wife despises this fact when I mention it.) Most important, Ba'al is the storm god, who brings rain and therefore fertility to the land—an important role in arid agrarian areas. Ba'al's voice is the thunder, in the same way that YHWH's voice is thunder (Heb. *qol,* קול) in Exodus 19:19.[14]

Like 'Asherah, Ba'al was a popular deity. Not only were the Israelite prophets constantly warning against worship of Ba'al, but 1 Kings 16:30–33 says:

Ahab son of Omri did evil in the sight of the LORD *more than all who were before him. And as if it had been a light thing for him to walk in the sins of Jeroboam son of Nebat, he took as his wife Jezebel daughter of King Ethbaal of the Sidonians, and* went and served Baal, and worshipped him. *He* erected an altar for Baal in the house of Baal, *which he built in Samaria. Ahab also made a sacred pole (Heb. 'Asherah). Ahab did more to provoke the anger of the* LORD, *the God of Israel, than had all the kings of Israel who were before him.*

Clearly, ancient Israel, especially the kingdom of Israel in the north, which was much more closely affiliated with Phoenicia to its north, worshipped Ba'al openly.

The aforementioned Ba'al stele, which provided the identification for the Temple of Ba'al Hadad on Ugarit's acropolis, is a white sandstone bas-relief stele, 4 feet 8 inches high, depicting a horned Ba'al in a typical power pose with his left foot forward and right arm raised holding a mace or club (often misinterpreted as a thunderbolt); it was discovered about 60 feet from the temple. This Ba'al

Bronze statue of a storm god poised to strike, from Ḥaṣor, dating from the fifteenth to thirteenth centuries BCE. *The image closely resembles other depictions of the storm god Ba'al discovered at Ugarit and elsewhere. Image courtesy Israel Museum.*

stele, now on display at the Louvre in Paris, reflects the literary descriptions of Ba'al as both a warrior deity and a fertility deity.[15]

Ba'al's popularity throughout Cana'an and within ancient Israel is evident not only from the number of Ba'al statues that have been uncovered throughout the land, but also from the number of texts in the Bible essentially saying, "Stop worshipping Ba'al!"[16] There is also a specific mention of a place called Ba'al Safon ("Ba'al of Mt. Safon") in Exodus 14:2, 9 and Numbers 33:7 and of another place called Bamot-Ba'al ("the high place of Ba'al") in Numbers 22:41, along with dozens of other place-names and personal names with the name Ba'al in them.

'ANAT

'Anat is Ba'al's sister, who loved and defended Ba'al vigilantly and viciously. Scholars debate whether 'Anat is also Ba'al's consort or

wife as the Ugaritic texts pair the two together in a number of stories. Like Ba'al, she too promoted fertility by serving as goddess of both love and war in ancient Ugarit. A statue of 'Anat in a pose similar to Ba'al's was uncovered at Ugarit by Dussaud, Schaeffer, and their team.

However, unlike 'Asherah, 'Anat is rarely mentioned in the Bible. The name does appear, however, in place-names and personal names, including the fortified city of Beth-'Anat (Josh. 19:38; Judg. 1:33), 'Anatoth (a priestly city and the hometown of the prophet Jeremiah, mentioned in Josh. 21:13, 18), and the name of Shamgar son of 'Anat (Judg. 3:31; 5:6), who, true to his namesake, reputedly slew six hundred Philistines with an ox goad.[17]

Bronze figurine of a striking goddess, probably 'Anat or 'Astarte, discovered at Tel Dan in northern Israel dating to the fifteenth to thirteenth centuries BCE. Image courtesy Israel Museum.

It is likewise noteworthy that the name 'Anat also appears as part of the name of the deity 'Anat-Yahu (or 'Anat-YHWH) in a fifth-century BCE Aramaic papyrus from Elephantine (modern Aswan), Egypt.[18] There was a large Jewish community in Elephantine in the sixth and fifth centuries BCE that included a priesthood facilitating worship in a temple to Yahu (YHWH) there, which had been built by Jews who had fled various foreign campaigns into Israel and Judah. One Elephantine Papyrus (B52) preserves an oath that was drafted and signed as part of a court case involving the half ownership of a donkey (believe it or not), demonstrating that suing people over the smallest things is not a modern invention. The oath affirms that the defendant is telling the truth and swears "in/by the place of prostration, and by 'Anat-Yahu."[19] The reference provides evidence that worship of 'Anat reached as far south as Upper Egypt and that the Jewish deity YHWH was associated with her.[20]

YAM

Yam is the god of the Mediterranean Sea and of rivers, streams, and lakes at Ugarit. Yam is also referred to as "Judge *Nahar*," or "Judge River," as his cooperation is necessary for securing the proper amount of river water for crops and avoiding drought and flooding. Like the ocean itself, Yam is chaotic, unwieldy, and unconquerable. As in the story of creation in Genesis 1, the watery abyss must be restrained and put in its place to allow for dry land and human existence by a more powerful deity. It should come as no surprise that Yam's immortal enemy is Ba'al, as Yam controls the ocean and its abysmal depths, while Ba'al is lord over the dry land, bringing life to the very creatures—humankind—that Yam's oceans regularly seek to destroy.

Yam appears in the Bible in a clever way; the Hebrew word for "sea" is *yam*! Thus, in Israelite religion, Yam the deity has become a depersonified natural entity—the sea—possessing all of the same characteristics, the unruliness and fear-inducing power over humankind, but *without* being considered a god. Many scholars have suggested that the battles between the "depths" (Heb. *tehom,* תהום) and YHWH are parallels to stories of battles between Yam and Ba'al. Think about it. God battles the watery abyss during creation in Genesis 1, holds back the floodwaters during the flood in Genesis 6–9, parts and then collapses the waters of the Reed Sea[21] in Exodus 15, and parts the Jordan River to allow the Hebrews to cross over into the promised land in Joshua 3:16. Repeatedly YHWH is said to conquer the waters in much the same way that Ba'al conquers Yam at Ugarit.

Mot

Mot is the god of death at Ugarit. Like Yam, Mot also takes on Ba'al and ultimately concedes defeat. In much the same manner as Yam, Mot is depersonified in Hebrew, and the name Mot (מות) becomes the word for "death." Although Mot does not appear as a deity in the Bible, Habakkuk 2:5 preserves the line, "They open their throats wide as Sheol; like Death (*mot*) they never have enough," which, as we'll see, is remarkably similar to the story of Mot and Ba'al in the Ba'al Cycle. Similarly, Job 18:13 preserves the expression, "the firstborn of Death (*mot*) consumes their limbs," offering again a very personified view of death and perhaps providing evidence that, just like all of the above gods from Ugarit, Mot too was well known in ancient Israel.

Now that we've been introduced to the most important gods in the Ugaritic pantheon, let's look at the texts from Ugarit that mention these deities and whether these gods and stories may have influenced the creation of the Hebrew Bible.

UGARITIC TEXTS

Many classic Mesopotamian texts were discovered within the six archives of tablets found at Ugarit, including copies of stories similar to those found in the Bible, for example, the Gilgamesh Epic[22] and the Atraḫasis Flood Epic.[23] Other tablets unique to Ugarit were also discovered. These texts are written in a language called Ugaritic, which employs an alphabetic cuneiform script that at first resembles typical Mesopotamian syllabic cuneiform, but is actually a version of the Phoenician consonantal alphabet written in cuneiform wedges.[24]

One humorous text from Ugarit is *KTU* 1.114, commonly called "'El's Divine Feast." In this story, the god 'El hosts a banquet for the other deities. 'Asherah and 'Anat and Ba'al are all there. The moon, Yariḫ, even sneaks in posing as a dog under the table looking for scraps. Eventually 'El drinks too much wine, gets sloppy drunk, falls down, wets himself, and ends up rolling around in his own poo. But here's the funny part: the back side of the tablet reads like a recipe for a hangover cure. The fact that 'El presents this Ugaritic "hair o' the dog that bit you" recipe essentially makes it the ultimate product endorsement: "Hi, I'm 'El, and when I'm sloppy drunk, I use the hairs of a dog, the top of a *pqq*-plant and its stem, and mix it with virgin olive oil to cure my hangover!" (And yes, that's the *actual remedy* from the last few lines of *KTU* 1.114.)[25]

However, three important texts discovered at Ugarit have heavily informed our understanding of the origins of many biblical stories and provide backgrounds for many of the deities mentioned in the Bible. These three are the Ba'al Cycle, the Legend of Kirta (Keret), and the Epic of 'Aqhat, which we'll explore at length below.

THE BA'AL CYCLE

Arguably the most important text from Ugarit is the Ba'al Cycle, dating to somewhere between 1500 and 1200 BCE. The six tablets containing the story at Ugarit are part of a much larger myth that scholars estimate to contain 2,350 lines and 1,500 poetic verses. The story is essentially comprised of two major conflicts: one between

Ba'al Hadad and the sea god, Yam, and a second between Ba'al Hadad and the god of death, Mot, separated by two poems about Ba'al, 'Anat, and Ba'al's palace. The Ba'al Cycle introduces us to the father of the gods, 'El, the goddesses 'Asherah and 'Anat, and other deities that form the supporting cast in an epic drama demonstrating how the god Ba'al became the most powerful god of all.

The first conflict begins with the god of the sea and rivers, Yam, who with the backing of the chief god of the Ugaritic pantheon, 'El, sought to be the most powerful god of all—something we might expect from a city on the eastern Mediterranean shore with an economy and culture built on maritime trade. However, Ba'al feels he is the greatest god of all. In preparation for the battle, the divine craftsman, Kothar wa-Ḥasis, constructs two maces for Ba'al, which he names Yagrushu ("drive out") and 'Ayyamurru ("expel"). Ba'al uses the maces to defeat Yam and scatters him over the earth (explaining why oceans and rivers cover so much of the earth). This battle parallels remarkably the account of creation described in Psalm 74:12–17, which is perhaps the oldest preserved Hebrew creation story—even older than the accounts in Genesis chapters 1 and 2.[26]

Ba'al Hadad defeats Yam, becomes the most powerful god of all, and seeks to build his own royal palace. So Ba'al enlists 'Anat to pressure 'El to agree to build Ba'al a palace. 'Anat goes so far as to threaten to bust 'El upside the head and make his "gray hair flow [with blood], the gray hairs of [his] beard with gore."[27] When this fails, Ba'al bribes 'El's consort, 'Asherah, with gifts in an effort to get her to support his bid for a palace. 'El then concedes to 'Asherah's request, and the divine craftsman, Kothar wa-Ḥasis, builds Ba'al a palace (after a contractor squabble about a window),[28] which Ba'al inaugurates by hosting a royal banquet for all the gods at which he humbly proclaims himself king of them all.

The second conflict of the cycle begins when Mot does not take kindly to Ba'al Hadad's self-appointment as king of the gods. So Mot, the god of death, invites Ba'al to another feast at which he challenges Ba'al to battle. Acknowledging defeat, Ba'al makes preparations to descend into the underworld along with the clouds, wind, and the rain (explaining the drought that follows Ba'al's death) by having sex "seventy-seven—even eighty-eight times" with 'Anat, who had transformed herself into a heifer and who eventually bears him a bull-calf, whom he loves and clothes in a manner reminiscent of Israel's actions toward the birth of Joseph in Gen. 37:3, explaining how the bull became the symbol of Ba'al.

After finding and burying her beloved Ba'al, 'Anat seeks to avenge him; she ruthlessly attacks Mot with a sword, kills him, burns him, pulverizes his body into powder, and scatters his remains to the birds. With Mot dead, Ba'al Hadad reemerges and returns to Mt. Ṣafon, where many of the gods live. However, Mot is resurrected from the dead and fights Ba'al Hadad in a rematch. This time, however, Mot realizes that, because 'El is siding with Ba'al, the battle is futile; Mot submits to Ba'al and declares him king of the gods. Thus, the Ba'al Cycle tells the story of how Ba'al became the most powerful of all the gods, which may explain his continued presence throughout the Hebrew Bible.[29]

THE LEGEND OF KIRTA (KERET)

The Legend of Kirta (commonly called "Keret") is a Ugaritic epic poem written on three rectangular tablets dating somewhere between 1500 and 1200 BCE. The tablets can presently be found in the National Museum of Aleppo in Syria.

The poem recounts the story of King Kirta of Ḫubur, who despite being a king and a favorite son of the god 'El, saw his wife, all his brothers, and all his children die in a series of tragedies ranging from death during childbirth to disease and warfare. He petitions 'El for an heir, and 'El instructs him to attack a nearby kingdom and demand that the king give him a daughter as a wife to produce an heir. Kirta does as 'El suggests, and King Pubala of the nearby kingdom of Udum gives Kirta a daughter, Hariya, who bears him two sons and six daughters.

However, after Kirta witnesses the birth of his new children, he breaks his promise to the goddess 'Asherah that he would bring gifts of gold and silver, should his plan to procure a wife be successful. 'Asherah retaliates by striking Kirta with a disease once again, which 'El ultimately cures. But as Kirta reassumes his throne, his son, Yassub, challenges his integrity. Kirta responds by asking the god of the underworld to crush his son's skull. Unfortunately for us (and fortunately for Yassub), the tablet breaks off at this point in the story, and we never learn the end of the tale.

Some clever readers may note some similarities between the Legend of Kirta and the biblical book of 'Iyov (Job) and are right to do so, as scholars have debated these similarities as well. Both Job and Kirta are called "good" or "righteous" individuals, both were said to be of high rank (Job 1:3 says Job was "the greatest of all the people of the east," while Kirta was a king), both suffer horrible calamities including the deaths of their families to disease and the sword, both are stricken with illness, both are accused of neglecting the poor by individuals close to them (Job by 'Eliphaz in 22:6–9, and Kirta by his son, Yassub),[30] both petition their respective gods for help, and both ultimately experience the birth of new children.[31]

Thus, the Legend of Kirta may have been the inspiration, if not the template, for the book of Job, as Job is ultimately a contest between heavenly beings—God and "the satan"[32]—who debate the fate of a noble man who lost his family, was accused of improprieties by those close to him, and had his fortunes restored. It is yet another way that Ugarit may have helped to build the Bible.[33]

EPIC OF 'AQHAT

The Epic of 'Aqhat is also sometimes referred to as the Epic of Dan'el or Dan'il, after the father described in the story. Dan'el means "'El is Judge", a name similar to the Hebrew name Dani'el (דניאל). He is said to be a "man of Rapa'u," which University of Chicago professor Dennis Pardee suggests is a reference to the

Repha'im, who are well known from the Bible.[34] 'Aqhat the Youth
is the name of Dan'el's son, for whom he prayed and offered sacrifices to the gods when he had no heir. The god Ba'al Hadad pleads
with 'El on Dan'el's behalf, reasoning that he deserves a son (and,
kids, pay attention) "who takes him by the hand when he's drunk,
carries him when he's drunk, carries him when he's sated with
wine"[35]—a line of reasoning with which Isaiah 51:17–18 is certainly familiar, as it echoes the fact that one of the expected duties
of a son is to carry his father home when he's drunk:

> *Rouse yourself, rouse yourself! Stand up, O Jerusalem, you who
> have drunk at the hand of the LORD the cup of his wrath, who
> have drunk to the dregs the bowl of staggering.* There is no one
> to guide her among all the children she has borne; there is no
> one to take her by the hand among all the children she has
> brought up.

Ultimately 'El grants Dan'el's request, and 'Aqhat is born. As
a gesture of thanks, Dan'el instructs his wife, Danatay, to pre-
pare a meal for the divine craftsman, Kothar wa-Ḥasis, who in
turn gives 'Aqhat a beautiful bow he had originally been making
for the goddess 'Anat. 'Anat still wants her bow and offers silver
and even eternal life to 'Aqhat in exchange for the bow. 'Aqhat
taunts 'Anat in response saying, "My bow is [a weapon for] war-
riors. Shall now women hunt with it?"[36] 'Anat is furious and plots
with Yaṭpan the Drunken Soldier (yes, that's his name) to kill
'Aqhat, which Yaṭpan the Drunken Soldier does.[37] Unfortunately
for 'Anat, the bow appears to have been broken and lost during
the attack (the text is broken at this point).

Dan'el is overcome with grief, and because of the violent death
of his son 'Aqhat, a massive drought and death consume the land.
The storm god Ba'al ("he who rides upon the clouds") stops sending rain. Dan'el utters a spell in an attempt to end the drought,
but to no avail. He then hatches a plan to find 'Aqhat's remains
and give him a proper burial (to perhaps end the drought).[38] After

finding 'Aqhat's remains and burying them properly, Dan'el returns home, curses the various elements of the environment for their complicity in 'Aqhat's murder, and mourns his son's death for seven years. Meanwhile, 'Aqhat's sister, Puġatu, plots to avenge her brother's death, but the texts breaks off and we never learn whether she succeeded.[39]

What is noteworthy about the story is Dan'el's constant devotion to the gods. He appeals to them for assistance even when he believes they have treated him unfairly. Readers of the biblical book of Job, of course, recognize this same characteristic in Job. Furthermore, it is Dan'el's desire to give his son a proper burial—an important obligation in antiquity—that motivates him throughout the story. We see righteous individuals seeking proper burials for the dead—and well-deserved chastisements for failing to do so—in a number of literary characters: Dan'el (for 'Aqhat), Odysseus (for Elpenor),[40] Abraham (for Sarah),[41] and Joseph of Arimathea (for Jesus).[42]

The character of Dan'el may also be mentioned (or at least referenced) in the Bible. The prophet Ezekiel mentions a character named Dan'el (דנאל; 14:14, 20; 28:3) who is *different* from the character Dani'el (Daniel) featured in the canonical book of Daniel (despite the fact that medieval Masoretes tried to "correct" the three instances of Dan'el in Ezekiel to read as if they said Dani'el). But scholars realize that Ezekiel likely meant the character Dan'el mentioned in the texts from Ugarit, as he places the figure chronologically in between the patriarchs Noaḥ and Job, who lived long before the Babylonians exiled the people of Judah in the sixth century BCE, precluding the biblical character of Dani'el from consideration by Ezekiel.[43] So the name Dan'el actually fits the lists in Ezekiel 14:14 and 20, as he was understood to be a pre-Israelite foreigner who exhibited righteousness and apparently wisdom.[44]

All of this means that the prophecy of Ezekiel may preserve references to the legendary figure of Dan'el from Ugarit, which would be direct evidence of Ugarit's influence on the Bible.[45]

UGARITIC INFLUENCE ON THE BIBLE:
MONOTHEISM VS. POLYTHEISM

Although you may had never heard of Ugarit prior to reading this chapter, you can now understand the significance of the site for the Bible. The texts discovered at Ugarit help paint the backdrop for many of the stories contained in the Bible, which were adopted and altered and retold over time until they were stories that told of a distinctly Hebrew deity.

We've seen how the stories from Ugarit may have inspired or outright shaped some of the stories we have in the Bible. However, we should close with how the Bible dealt with these stories, given the fact that, after all, Israelite religion and later Judaism are supposed to be monotheistic. So we must ask: How were the polytheistic Ugaritic legends and deities incorporated into a monotheistic religion?

The short answer is that various attributes, names of deities, and deities themselves from Ugarit (and elsewhere) were harmonized and incorporated into the Hebrew God, YHWH. Now I admit, when I first say this to my students, many of them balk at this conclusion (especially those from conservative religious traditions, both Christian and Jewish). But if we look at the evidence that has been discovered over the past hundred years, it becomes clear that the portrait of God and the traditions about him in the Bible are the result of prior foreign influences on early Israel.

The fact that 'El and 'Asherah are a couple at Ugarit contributes to the claim that 'El eventually morphed into the Hebrew deity YHWH. Archaeological evidence in the form of the discovery of two late ninth- to early eighth-century BCE *pithoi* (jars) in the 1970s at Kuntillet 'Ajrud in the Sinai desert just south of Israel support this claim. Two inscriptions from the jars and a third from a pillar of a burial cave at Khirbet el-Qom read:

> *Utterance of 'Ashyaw the king: "Say to Yehallel and to Yaw'asah and to [...]: 'I bless by* Yahweh of Samaria and his 'Asherah.' " [46]

The burial inscription from the Judean hills site of Khirbet el-Qom, ten and a half miles west of Hebron in the modern West Bank. Discovered in 1967, this inscription dates to the mid-eighth century BCE and offers a blessing invoking the deities YHWH and 'Asherah together. Image courtesy Israel Museum.

———

Utterance of 'Amaryaw: "Say to my lord: 'Is it well with you? I bless you by Yahweh of Teman and his 'Asherah. *May he bless you and keep you and may he be with my lord.' "*[47]

———

'Uriyahu the rich:[48] *(This is) his inscription. Blessed was 'Uriyahu to* Yahweh, *and from his enemies,* by his 'Asherah, *he saved him. (Written) by 'Oniyahu.*[49]

The fact that 'Asherah is said to be the consort of 'El in thirteenth-century BCE Ugarit and later the consort of YHWH in eighth-century BCE Israel suggests that the deity known as 'El in Phoenicia and Ugarit was incorporated into the deity YHWH, who became the God of the Hebrews and later the Israelites, Judeans, and Jews, Christians, and Muslims.

Now what about the fact that Judaism is a monotheistic religion? Although we often refer to Judaism as "monotheistic," this term is somewhat misleading if understood as meaning belief in the *existence* of only one God. This is not the case with ancient Israel. Ancient Israel believed in *multiple* gods, and if we are to believe the Bible, apparently God did too! On any number of occasions the Bible warns Israel not to worship "other gods." It's one of the earliest commands. Exodus 20:3 says, "You shall have no *other gods* before me," and 34:14 adds, "Because YHWH, whose name is Jealous, is a jealous God." YHWH didn't want any of his followers worshipping any *other* gods, only him.

It wasn't that ancient Israel didn't *believe* in the existence of other gods—or else they wouldn't have made a golden calf at the foot of Mt. Sinai and claimed it was a god (Exod. 32:4). Rather, they were *allowed to worship* only one god: YHWH. Scholars call the worship of one deity while acknowledging the existence of others "monolatry" to distinguish it from "monotheism." (It should be noted that much later in Judaism, Jewish monotheism shifted to the *belief* in the existence of only one God [see 1 Cor. 8:4], but early in Israel's history, there was a general acceptance of the existence of multiple gods.)

A maṣṣeboth, *or set of standing stones (stelae), discovered in a temple at Tel Ḥaṣor, Israel dating from the fifteenth to thirteenth centuries* BCE. *Each stone in the shrine represents a deity venerated by the community. Note the horizontal offering stone lying in front of the standing stones. Image courtesy Israel Museum.*

THE CITIES THAT BUILT THE BIBLE

Evidence of multiple gods appears elsewhere in the archaeological record in the form of *maṣṣeboth*. The Bible describes many *maṣṣeboth* (Heb. מצבות), or a series of tall standing stones representing multiple deities worshipped in an area. The most famous in Israel are the monolithic standing stones at Tel Gezer and at Tel Dan and one from Tel Ḥaṣor presently on display at the Israel Museum in Jerusalem. Because there are *multiple* stones, they testify to the fact that *multiple* deities were worshipped in these cities.

So how did ancient Israel go from the worship of multiple gods, to the command to worship only one God above all the other gods, to the belief in the existence of only one God? This question is addressed by examining the answer to another question: Why are there so many different names for God in the Hebrew Bible? And I don't just mean his personal divine name, YHWH, first revealed to Moses at the burning bush in Exodus 3 (although it is used long before that in Gen. 2). And I'm not speaking of derivatives of YHWH like Yah (יה) or YHWH Ṣaba'oth (יהוה צבאות, commonly translated as "Lord of Hosts," but meaning "Lord of the Army"), or the etymology for YHWH given in Exodus 3:14, *ehyeh-asher-ehyeh* (אהיה אשר אהיה), often translated "I Am Who I Am," or more accurately, "I Will (Cause to) Be What I Will (Cause to) Be."[50] I mean truly *different* names like 'El and its plural, 'Elohim, and other derivatives like 'Elyon and 'El Shaddai.

New York University professor Mark Smith's *The Early History of God* lays out how the many deities that were worshipped in ancient Cana'an and Phoenicia came to be either rejected as "foreign gods" or synthesized into the Hebrew god YHWH. This is true not only for divine characteristics attributed to these deities, like power over the sea and water (Yam) or destructive storms and fertility in both crops and people (Ba'al), but for the divine names as well. Simply put, the reason that there are so many different names for YHWH in the Bible is that many of the names of *other* gods were simply attributed to YHWH, so that when a text honors 'El, as in Genesis 35:7[51] or Psalm 82:1,[52] readers simply understand 'El as another name for YHWH. Or when Abram tithes to the priest-king Melki-Ṣedeq (Melchizedek) in Genesis 14:18–20, who blessed Abram by his deity, 'El 'Elyon, later biblical traditions interpret 'El 'Elyon as simply "God Most High," as is regularly done by the Septuagint (the Greek translation of the Hebrew Bible), which translates 'El 'Elyon with the Greek word ὕψιστος (*hupsistos*), or "most high."[53] So although one way to fight polytheism is to send prophets to rail against the Israelites and criticize them for worshipping 'El and Ba'al and 'Asherah, a slightly more subtle way is simply to redefine the names of these foreign deities as alternative epithets for YHWH.

———

We've traveled through the archaeological treasure trove of Ugarit, where we read stories with some remarkable "parallels" to what we read in the Bible, which scholars believe may have been the origin, or at least the *inspiration,* for many of the Bible's stories. These texts also provide many of the names that would become the names of the Hebrew God as well as the backstories for other Cana'anite deities that Israel was not supposed to worship. Thus, it is clear that Ugarit played a tremendous part in helping to build the Bible. Indeed, the title of R. W. L. Moberly's book can be appropriated to describe Ugarit: Ugarit is essentially *The Old Testament of the Old Testament*!

Next, we travel east to Mesopotamia and forward in time to encounter the two empires that influenced and ultimately destroyed ancient Israel and whose exploits (along with the Israelite and Judahite responses to them) contributed greatly to the text of the Bible.

CHAPTER 3

Nineveh

The city of Nineveh is well known for different reasons. Many people are familiar with the writings of the Hebrew prophet Naḥum, who chastises the old Assyrian capital city. Nineveh is also verbally assailed by the prophet Ṣefanyah (Zephaniah; 2:13–15) and serves as the setting for the apocryphal book of Tobit. Most know Nineveh from its appearance in the story of Jonah, in which Jonah childishly despises God because he refused to destroy Nineveh as Jonah wanted. Unfortunately, far too many people are now familiar with Nineveh because of its present-day occupiers, Da'esh (commonly called ISIS, or Islamic State of Iraq and Syria), Islamic militants who are in the process of physically destroying the irreplaceable architectural and cultural remnants of one of the greatest civilizations of its time, ancient Assyria.[1]

Nimrud (ancient Kalhu) was the ancient Assyrian capital while Israel and Judah existed as separate kingdoms. But Nineveh came to represent the foreign domination and ultimate destruction of Israel, the Northern Kingdom. The devastation of Israel at the hands of the Assyrians gave the later editors of the Bible the theological ammunition they needed to argue that God was displeased with Israel for rebelling against the United Kingdom of Israel, ruled by Sha'ul (Saul), David, and Solomon and for repeatedly embracing the "sins of Yarov'am (Jeroboam), son of Nebat," the Northern Kingdom's first king. Because it served as the subject of critique for multiple Hebrew prophets, influenced the politics of ancient Israel, and ultimately represented the destruction of Israel, Nineveh was a city that greatly influenced the creation of the Bible.

THE HISTORY OF THE NEO-ASSYRIAN EMPIRE

When scholars speak of "ancient Assyria," they distinguish between three Assyrian periods: an earlier one, a middle one, and a later one, the so-called Neo-Assyrian Empire. The first is referred to as the Old Assyrian Kingdom, traditionally said to be founded by King Puzur-ashur I, whose dynasty ruled in northern Mesopotamia from 2025 to 1809 BCE. The Old Assyrian Empire was displaced by the Amorites and then by the brief Old Babylonian dynasty, which gave us King Hammurabi, famous for his law code, which we'll discuss in the next chapter. The Old Assyrian Kingdom was reestablished by King Adasi (r. 1726–1701 BCE) and lasted until 1451 BCE, when it fell into decline. The Middle Assyrian Kingdom essentially ended with the mysterious Late Bronze Age collapse, which saw the rapid decline of nearly every Mediterranean and Near Eastern empire.[2]

The reign of the Assyrian king Adad-nirari II (r. 911–892 BCE) marks the beginning of what scholars call the Neo-Assyrian Empire, the third Assyrian period. The Neo-Assyrian Empire is the "Assyria" mentioned in the Bible, as it is contemporaneous with ancient Israel and Judah and directly affected their politics, economics, and religion. The Neo-Assyrian Empire exhibits the qualities of a true empire in that it ruled over a number of otherwise independent kingdoms and peoples, and it regularly campaigned against neighboring kingdoms in order to annex them, expand the Assyrian civilization, and increase revenue in the form of tributes to Assyria. When the Assyrian army showed up, the terms of the deal were pretty simple: you (small kingdom X) send Assyria money and goods annually, and we won't kill you.

Many noteworthy Neo-Assyrian kings influenced the political policies of ancient Israel, including Shalmaneser III (r. 858–824 BCE); Tiglath-pileser III (r. 745–727 BCE), who was known as "King Pul" in 2 Kings 15:19; and Shalmaneser V (r. 727–722 BCE).

King Sargon II (r. 722–705 BCE) built a new capital at Dar-Sharrukin (the "Fortress of Sargon") in present-day Khorsabad, about nine miles northeast of Nineveh. Following Sargon II's death in battle, the capital was moved to Nineveh.

Nineveh rose in importance as it became an increasingly critical crossroads on the lucrative trading route from the Indian Ocean along the Fertile Crescent, both north to Europe and south through the Levant and into northern Africa. Located on the eastern bank of the Tigris River (cf. Gen. 2:14), just across the river from the modern city of Mosul, Iraq, Nineveh was settled as early as 6000 BCE. By about 3000 BCE, Nineveh had become an important center for worship of the Akkadian goddess Ishtar, goddess of fertility, sex, love, and war, who was known in the Bible as her Aramean counterpart, 'Astarte, whom King Solomon worshipped.[3]

We can only imagine what ancient Nineveh must have looked like in its heyday. The closest parallel I can imagine is walking through the capitals of other famous empires like London or Paris or Rome. If you've ever had the good fortune to wander through these cities and their respective museums, you begin to ask yourself, "What are all these foreign objects doing here?"

Empires bring back the spoils of imperial victories to their capitals for the same reason that emperors built up their capitals: this is the language of *empire*! Assyria was the first true empire in the world, and its next king, Sennacherib (r. 705–681 BCE), wasn't just the king of Assyria; he was king of the world! And Nineveh came to represent the world-dominating empire of Assyria.

King Sennacherib transformed this riverbank Assyrian town into the center of the Neo-Assyrian Empire by embellishing and expanding it. He fortified the city by building massive walls with multiple ornamental gates and by constructing an elaborate system of canals, including some of the world's earliest aqueducts, which expanded the city's water supply, facilitating city growth and the ability to withstand the effects of a siege. Sennacherib made Nineveh into one of the most impressive cities of its time in the world.[4]

Archaeological work has uncovered two buildings that represent the ways Nineveh became the cultural and political center of Assyria: the Palace of Sennacherib and the Library of Ashurbanipal. The discovery of Sennacherib's palace in 1849 and Ashurbanipal's library in 1851 is credited to the English archaeologist (and later politician) Sir Austen Henry Layard and his assistant, Hormuzd Rassam. The buildings yielded thousands of clay tablets and fragments of seventh-century BCE texts, including what are considered the earliest great works of literature: the famous biblical flood parallel, the Epic of Gilgamesh; the Babylonian creation myth the Enûma Elish; and the myth of the first man, Adapa. The library today consists of fragments of about thirty thousand tablets, most of which are housed in the British Museum in London. However, the tablets from the two buildings were mixed up on their way to London, rendering it impossible to know for sure which tablets came from which building.[5]

But perhaps most pertinent to our discussion, Sennacherib devoted an entire room in his southwest palace to large, alabaster artistic commemorations of the Siege of Lachish, which resulted in the destruction of the Judahite city, the exile of its inhabitants, and the torture and execution of its nobility (they were beheaded and flayed alive; heads were hanged on trees and stacked into piles, etc.). The panels from Sennacherib's palace in Nineveh are important because they provide detailed information about the Assyrians' siege warfare, including the instruments and techniques they used to conquer their enemies' cities. The Lachish Relief Panels depicting the Assyrian victory at the Siege of Lachish are now in the British Museum,[6] and a partial replica of the reliefs is on display at the Israel Museum.[7]

The rapid expansion of Nineveh under King Sennacherib, especially the public displays of his various conquests, reflects the rise of Assyria as an imperial superpower and explains the repeated allusions to Nineveh in the Bible. Nineveh was the Assyrian capital when Sennacherib besieged Jerusalem, and therefore it was Nineveh that became the symbol of Assyrian domination.

Nineveh's status as the symbol of foreign domination also explains why Judith 1:1 mistakenly claims, "Nebuchadnezzar . . . ruled over the Assyrians *in the great city of Nineveh*." Despite the fact that Nebuchadnezzar II ruled from *Babylon* after his father overthrew the Assyrians and destroyed Nineveh in 612 BCE, Nineveh remained the symbol of foreign oppression for many Jews of the Second Temple period (530 BCE–70 CE).[8]

As the main player in the ancient Near East from the late tenth to the late seventh century BCE, Assyria dominated Cana'an and single-handedly altered the history of the Northern Kingdom, Israel, when it sacked its capital, Samaria, in 722 BCE, essentially ending the kingdom. As a result, much of the Bible is written in response to havoc wreaked by the encroaching Assyrian Empire. Furthermore, the Assyrian menace caused the single event in the late eighth century BCE that changed Jerusalem, the capital of the small backwater kingdom of Judah, into the inviolable city that became the dwelling place of almighty God and the center of the Western world.

When Assyria destroyed ancient Israel, it ironically catapulted Jerusalem into the position of sole remaining stronghold for the ancestors of the Jewish people. For this reason, Nineveh is partly responsible for the composition and the preservation of the Bible's anti–Northern Kingdom, anti-Samaritan theology—a theological perspective that not only dominates the Old Testament, from edited stories of David's usurpation of Israel's throne from Saul and his descendants down through the writings of the late Second Temple period, but also shaped the beliefs of several Jewish sectarian offshoots, including the Qumran sectarians and the early Christians.

ASSYRIA AND ISRAEL

Following the death of King Solomon, recorded in 1 Kings 11:43, his inept son, Reḥav'am (Reḥoboam), succeeded him on the throne. It was during King Reḥoboam's rule that the ten tribes seceded and formed Israel. They did so because Reḥoboam wanted to demonstrate that he was every bit as tough (and endowed) as his father and continue his father's harsh rule over his own people.

I put the word "endowed" above in parentheses, because this is one of the funnier (albeit unwise) passages in the Bible. Note that, due to its frat-boy level of sexual boasting, even the Hebrew text resorts to using sexual euphemisms in recounting this episode. In 1 Kings 12:10, King Reḥoboam gets some bad advice from his contemporaries:

> *The young men who had grown up with him said to him, "Thus you should say to this people who spoke to you, 'Your father made our yoke heavy, but you must lighten it for us'; thus you should say to them, 'My little finger is thicker than my father's loins* (matnei).'"

In this text, it is clear that the Hebrew word *matnei* (מתני), which is the plural (technically dual) possessive form of the noun *matnayim* (מתנים), commonly translated as "lions" or "thighs," is a euphemism for Solomon's penis. The point of the passage is that Reḥoboam is attempting to convince his subjects that he's tougher than his infamously virile father, Solomon (he of three hundred wives and seven hundred concubines). Thus, Reḥoboam is essentially resorting to the sophomoric locker-room claim that his little finger is bigger than his father's penis.[9] Needless to say, this boastful claim did not go over very well with the people of Israel.

Reḥoboam's refusal to lighten the tax and public-service burden on the people of Israel caused the ten tribes of the north to rebel and form into a separate kingdom, which kept the name "Israel." This new nation set up a local labor leader, Yarov'am (Jeroboam), son of Nebat, of the tribe of 'Ephraim, just north of Judah, as the first king of the Northern Kingdom. According to the Bible, Reḥoboam was left as king of only two tribes: the tiny tribe of Benjamin, and Judah, his kingdom's namesake.

It is here where we must address the theological disposition of the Bible as it relates to the socioeconomic and political reality of ancient Israel and Judah. Simply put, Israel had all the people, all the money, all the land, and all the power, while Judah had little more than Jerusalem and the hill country to the south of Israel. This is what the archaeological and extrabiblical literary records tell us, so, as the kids say, Israel was "where it's at." When Assyria became the main player in Cana'an in the ninth century BCE, Israel became a strategic vassal state that could assist in Assyria's battles with Egypt to the south and Phoenicia to the northwest.

Although the Bible makes reference to alliances between the Northern Kingdom and its Assyrian overlords, the archaeological record makes Israel and Judah's vassalage (i.e., the state of being a subject under the control of another, dominant country) to Assyria crystal clear. For example, artifacts such as the Black Obelisk of Shalmaneser III, which depicts King Jehu' of Israel (whom we recognize from 2 Kings 9–10) bowing to the Assyrian king Shalmaneser III (r. 858–824 BCE)[10] in defeat, represent Israel's submission as a vassal state to Assyria.[11] The Mesha Stele too provides archaeological evidence of Assyria's influence in Israel's politics. Dating to about 830 BCE, the 3-feet-8-inches-high basalt inscription contains thirty-four lines of text describing the Moabite king Mesha's rebellion against Israel by refusing to pay taxes. This is significant because it demonstrates that Israel was perceived as a significant political player in Cana'an at the time.

The Assyrian king Sargon II ultimately conquered Samaria in 722 BCE, ending the Northern Kingdom, placing it under direct Assyrian control, and forcibly deporting many of its inhabitants to Assyria. The Nimrud Prisms, so called because they were discovered during excavations at Nimrud, tell of Sargon II's actions in Samaria:

> [The inhabitants of Sa]merina (Samaria), who agreed [and plotted] with a king [hostile to] me, not to do service and not to bring tribute [to Aššur] and who did battle, I fought against them with the power of the great gods, my lords. I counted as

spoil 27,280 people, together with their chariots, and gods, in which they trusted. I formed a unit with 200 of [their] chariots for my royal force. I settled the rest of them in the midst of Assyria. I repopulated Samerina (Samaria) more than before. I brought into it people from countries conquered by my hands. I appointed my eunuch as governor over them. And I counted them as Assyrians.[12]

Using an archaeological lens that brings history and human experience into focus, we can clearly see how the Bible was written by people who were reflecting upon the political events of the day. The authors of the Bible had worldviews that were conditioned by war, power, and political struggles not only between the twelve tribes and foreign nations, but between Israel and Judah as well. We see this when the Bible regularly condemns Israel and favors Judah. This is due to one important event rooted in Nineveh; when the Assyrians conquered Samaria and the Northern Kingdom in 722 BCE and yet spared the Southern Kingdom, the Judahite editors of the Bible felt justified in their condemnation of Israel, because they interpreted their survival as divine favor. So although the reality was that, of the two, Israel was the true power in the region and Judah played second fiddle, the Bible as it is written and edited for the most part favors Judah.

ASSYRIA AND JUDAH

After the fall of Samaria and the Northern Kingdom, Jerusalem feared it would be next. To prevent just that, King Ḥizqiyah (Ḥezekiah) of Judah, according to 2 Kings 18:13–16, did exactly what King 'Asa' of Judah had done: he looted the Temple and paid off King Sennacherib of Assyria with three hundred talents of silver ("all the silver that was found in the house of the LORD and in the treasuries of the king's house") and thirty talents of gold ("stripped . . . from the doors of the temple of the LORD").

Unfortunately, bribing the Assyrian king only worked for a while. Whether it was because Judah could no longer afford the heavy tribute payments, or because Hezekiah saw his kingdom expand to such an extent that he felt he might actually have a chance against Assyria, Hezekiah rebelled against Assyria. The Bible credits him with instituting a series of religious reforms (2 Kings 18:1–5) that refocused the worship of the people only upon YHWH and only in Jerusalem.

Of course when Assyria learned that Judah was in rebellion, it saw fit to campaign once again into Cana'an and this time to teach the king of Judah a lesson. It was this contest between King Hezekiah of Judah and the Assyrian army that began the snowballing legend of Jerusalem as the inviolable city of God.

Second Kings 18–20 and its nearly word-for-word parallel in Isaiah 36–39 tell of Jerusalem's miraculous survival of the Assyrian siege, which includes the famed encounter between Hezekiah's ministers (Yo'ah, Shebna', and 'Elyaqim) and the Rab Shaqeh, the Assyrian vizier and royal messenger of the Assyrian king Sennacherib. The scene always reminds me of the classic "French taunting scene" from *Monty Python and the Holy Grail*, where King Arthur and his knights of the Round Table attempt to convince a French castle minister to open the gates and let them in, only in reverse.[13] In the same way that that scene generated a classic final insult, so too does the Assyrian Rab Shaqeh loft an insult at Hezekiah's ministers (which the eleventh-century CE Masoretic redactors of the Hebrew Bible attempted to paper over).

Hezekiah's ministers make an almost comical request of the Rab Shaqeh: "Please speak to your servants in the Aramaic language, for we understand it; do not speak to us in the language of Judah [i.e., Hebrew] within the hearing of the people who are on the wall" (2 Kings 18:26), as they were becoming frightened. The Rab Shaqeh taunts back the following insult: "Has my master sent me to speak these words to your master and to you, and not to the people sitting on the wall, who are doomed with you to eat their

own dung and to drink their own urine?" (18:27).[14] Hezekiah's
ministers essentially scream at the Assyrian negotiators, "Please
don't speak in Hebrew, because you're scaring our people. Speak
in Aramaic so only we can understand you," forgetting that the
whole purpose of the Assyrians' siege negotiation is to scare the
living dung and urine out of the people inside the city.

The remainder of 2 Kings 18–20 records the siege of Jerusalem
and the miraculous deliverance of Jerusalem from the hands of
the Assyrian army. It was an episode so important that the Bible's
editors didn't mind recording it twice—in 2 Kings and Isaiah
36–39. But the story of this failed siege isn't just detailed twice in
the Bible; it also appears in the Assyrian chronicles, which corroborates both this siege and Jerusalem's survival.

SENNACHERIB'S PRISMS

Sennacherib's royal annals preserve his deeds in cuneiform on multiple hexagonal prisms. Toward the end of the records, the prisms
record a campaign of Sennacherib into Cana'an and address King
Hezekiah specifically:

> *As to Hezekiah, the Jew, he did not submit to my yoke. . . .*
> Himself I made a prisoner in Jerusalem, his royal residence,
> like a bird in a cage. . . . *I reduced his country, but I still in-
> creased the tribute and the* katrû-*presents (due) to me (as his)
> overlord which I imposed (later) upon him beyond the former
> tribute, to be delivered annually. Hezekiah himself . . . did send
> me, later, to Nineveh, my lordly city, together with 30 talents of
> gold, 800 talents of silver, precious stones, antimony, large cuts
> of red stone, couches (inlaid) with ivory,* nîmedu-*chairs (in-
> laid) with ivory, elephant-hides, ebony-wood, boxwood (and)
> all kinds of valuable treasures, his (own) daughters, concubines,
> male and female musicians. In order to deliver the tribute and to
> do obeisance as a slave he sent his (personal) messenger.*[15]

Note that Sennacherib's summary is vastly different from the account in 2 Kings 19 and Isaiah 37, which state that Hezekiah's prayer to YHWH resulted in God's striking down 185,000 Assyrian troops besieging Jerusalem (2 Kings 19:35; Isa. 37:36). The account preserved on the Sennacherib Prisms much more resembles the accounts of payment of tribute to an overlord for the purposes of making him go away peacefully like those we regularly find in the Bible.[16] Sennacherib states that he besieged Jerusalem and only departed without destroying the city after Hezekiah paid him off precisely as 2 Kings 18:13–16 says he did.

Thus, the Sennacherib Prisms confirm two claims made in the Bible: Assyria did, in fact, besiege Jerusalem, and *Jerusalem survived*! Sennacherib never says he "laid waste" to Jerusalem and never says he killed Hezekiah. Rather, Sennacherib says he made Hezekiah a prisoner in Jerusalem, "like a bird in a cage." That is language of a siege, not of destruction.

Sennacherib's hexagonal prism, from Nineveh, Assyria, dates to 691 BCE and contains cuneiform writing that mentions Hezekiah, King of Judah, and the Assyrian Siege of Jerusalem. Image courtesy Israel Museum.

So not only were four chapters in Isaiah (36–39) and three parallel chapters in 2 Kings (18–20) dedicated to the Assyrian siege of Jerusalem, but it was Jerusalem's survival against the seemingly invincible Assyrian menace that propelled it into its lofty status as an impregnable city under the constant protection of God—the kind of protection that Jeremiah later mocked as overconfident when he warned the residents of Jerusalem, "Do not trust in these deceptive words: 'This is the temple of the LORD, the temple of the LORD, the temple of the LORD'" (7:4).

Jerusalem's survival against the superior Assyrian army (however it came about) was credited to YHWH and held up as evidence of Judah's righteousness, its people's "chosenness," and Jerusalem's inviolability, especially in the face of the Assyrian conquest of Samaria and the defeat of the "rebellious" Northern Kingdom, Israel. Jerusalem's escape from the Assyrian siege helped produce other legends about Jerusalem, which in turn inspired the biblical texts praising Jerusalem as God's sole dwelling place. Many of these texts are found among the biblical prophets who address Nineveh and Jerusalem's response to it, and it is these prophetic texts to which we turn next.

NINEVEH AND THE PROPHETS:
JONAH, ZEPHANIAH, AND NAHUM

JONAH

The Assyrians were so feared and hated that they warranted condemnations by multiple prophets, including Zephaniah and Nahum (the entire book). Nineveh is also known from the story of Jonah and the Great Fish that takes up the first two of four chapters of the book of Jonah.[17] Many scholars treat Jonah differently from the other prophetic books of the Hebrew Bible, and not simply because it is the only prophetic book that is *about* a prophet instead of a record of the words of a prophet. In fact, only *one line* of prophecy is recorded in Jonah, and that is in 3:4, where the text says: "And he cried out, 'Forty days more, and Nineveh shall be overthrown!'"

That's it. One line. As far as we know, that is the sum of God's "message that I tell you" mentioned in 3:2. Remember that in 1:2 Jonah was instructed, "Go at once to Nineveh, that great city, and cry out against it; for their wickedness has come up before me." It is interesting that Jonah is never recorded as having preached a message of *repentance,* only that God has noticed their wickedness and is about to destroy the city.

And yet, after Jonah is punished by God for his disobedience by suffering through a storm and having to spend three days and three nights in the belly of a great fish, Jonah finally does God's bidding and preaches to the Ninevites. And of course, the Ninevites do *exactly* what Jonah was afraid they'd do: they repented, which is precisely why Jonah didn't want to go and prophesy against Nineveh in the first place.

Most scholars view the story of Jonah as a critique—some even say a satire—aimed at the Jews, and specifically the Jewish concept of "chosenness." In this canonical book, Jonah represents an overconfident Jew (depicted as an Israelite in this case) who feels that God has made *only* Israel his "chosen people" and *must* destroy Israel's oppressive enemies, like the Assyrians of Nineveh.

God thinks otherwise. God makes abundantly clear in the book of Jonah that *God* is God, and he'll save whomever he wants. So hateful was Jonah when God spared Nineveh (3:10) that 4:1 says, "This was very displeasing to Jonah, and he became angry." God then goes on to have a little fun with Jonah, creating a bush (possibly a castor oil plant) to provide shade for him, and then sending a worm to eat the bush, which made Jonah even angrier. When Jonah became so faint from the sun that he asked to die, God replied:

> "Is it right for you to be angry about the bush?" And he said, "Yes, angry enough to die." Then the LORD said, "You are concerned about the bush, for which you did not labor and which you did not grow; it came into being in a night and perished in a night. And should I not be concerned about Nineveh, that great city, in which there are more than a hundred and twenty thousand persons who do not know their right hand from their left, and also many animals?" (4:9–11)

Thus, many think the story of Jonah is about obedience and a great fish, but it is actually about God's sovereignty and his right to save whomever he wants to save. In this case, God chose to save Nineveh—an event that Jesus would praise centuries later. Jesus praised Nineveh for its immediate repentance upon hearing the words of the prophet Jonah. In fact, Jesus is so frustrated with "the evil and adulterous generation" around him that he states: "The people of Nineveh will rise up at the judgment with this generation and condemn it, because they repented at the proclamation of Jonah" (Matt. 12:41; cf. Luke 11:32). The implication is that the Ninevites were wise enough to respond to Jonah, yet the people of Jesus's generation do not recognize him as sent from God.

Thus, as he did in the parable of the good Samaritan, Jesus once again holds up a traditional archnemesis of the Jews to highlight just how evil he believes those who do not accept him really are. In the same way that a Samaritan—a remnant of the kingdom of Israel destroyed by Nineveh—was the hero of Jesus's parable about what a true neighbor looks like, Jesus also highlights those who *destroyed* Israel and Samaria to argue that even *they* knew to recognize God and repent.

But not every reference to Nineveh was in praise of its repentance. In fact, the Bible mostly views Nineveh as the epitome of savagery and wickedness and an instrument that God uses to punish his own people. And no prophets condemn Nineveh any more harshly than Zephaniah and Naḥum.

ZEPHANIAH

The prophet Ṣefanyah (Zephaniah), who is claimed to have prophesied during the days of King Yo'shiyahu (Josiah) of Judah (r. 641–610 BCE), also discusses the city of Nineveh as a symbol of power. The purpose of Zephaniah's prophecy was to convince his readers to stop worshipping deities other than YHWH, namely, Ba'al, Milcom (Molek), and the "heavenly host" (cf. Zeph. 1:4–5), which is understood to be either other Cana'anite deities or YHWH's heavenly army.[18] As a deterrent, Zephaniah warns the Judahites that what happened to the Northern Kingdom of Israel will also happen to them if they do not repent. But Zephaniah also prophesies the downfall of Nineveh:

*And he will stretch out his hand against the north, and destroy
Assyria; and he will make Nineveh a desolation, a dry waste
like the desert. Herds shall lie down in it, every wild animal; the
desert owl and the screech owl shall lodge on its capitals; the owl
shall hoot at the window, the raven croak on the threshold; for its
cedar work will be laid bare. Is this the exultant city that lived
secure, that said to itself, 'I am, and there is no one else'? What a
desolation it has become, a lair for wild animals! Everyone who
passes by it hisses and shakes the fist. (2:13–15)*

Although Zephaniah has some harsh words for Nineveh—no
one wants an owl hooting in the window of their now-deserted
home—the words of the prophet Nahum are considered some of
the most damning in the Bible.

NAHUM

One of the shorter books of the Bible is the text of the prophet
Nahum, whose name in Hebrew derives from the word "to
comfort." Nahum is a mere forty-seven total verses, yet it provides one of the most condemnatory indictments of Nineveh in
the Bible.

The opening verse declares the prophecy's intent: "An or-
acle concerning Nineveh. The book of the vision of Nahum of
'Elqosh."[19] And following a majestic exordium trumpeting the
power of YHWH, Nahum lets it rip:

*It is decreed that the city be exiled, its slave women led away,
moaning like doves and beating their breasts. Nineveh is like a
pool whose waters run away. 'Halt! Halt!'—but no one turns
back. 'Plunder the silver, plunder the gold! There is no end of
treasure! An abundance of every precious thing!' Devastation,
desolation, and destruction! Hearts faint and knees tremble, all
loins quake, all faces grow pale! (2:7–10)*

Naḥum 3:1–7 gets even more graphic:

> *Ah! City of bloodshed, utterly deceitful . . . Because of the countless debaucheries of the prostitute, gracefully alluring, mistress of sorcery, who enslaves nations through her debaucheries, and peoples through her sorcery, I am against you, says the* LORD *of hosts, and will lift up your skirts over your face; and I will let nations look on your nakedness and kingdoms on your shame. I will throw filth at you and treat you with contempt, and make you a spectacle. Then all who see you will shrink from you and say, 'Nineveh is devastated; who will bemoan her?' Where shall I seek comforters for you?*

Naḥum essentially says that since Nineveh has lured nations to itself with its power like a prostitute lures men with her seduction, in the same way God will "lift up [Nineveh's] skirts over [its] face" and will "let nations look on [its] nakedness and kingdoms on [its] shame"—a clear reference to the sexual assault and domination that usually befell the women of conquered cities in antiquity. Although many modern readers may rightfully feel uncomfortable with God's using the language of rape and sexual domination as a God-ordained, God-endorsed, or God-empowered punishment for *anyone,* neither Naḥum nor the editors of the Bible had any problem with it. Such was Naḥum's hatred (on behalf of God) of Nineveh.

Naḥum prophesied about Nineveh's downfall in the same manner that Assyria conquered: brutally and savagely. In the end, the Hebrew prophets vindictively called for God to punish Nineveh and all of Assyria in the same way that they punished ancient Israel and Judah.

THE FALL OF NINEVEH
AND ITS IMPACT ON THE BIBLE

The great city of Nineveh eventually fell after the death of King Ashurbanipal in 627 BCE. Ashurbanipal's death marks the end of the Neo-Assyrian Empire and the rise of the Neo-Babylonian Empire, which will make its own contributions to the Bible, as we'll discuss in the next chapter.

Nineveh came to symbolize Assyrian dominance over the kingdoms of Israel and Judah. Nineveh was therefore representative of ancient Assyria and contributed both to the content of the Bible and its overarching theological perspective, as it allowed the Bible's Second Temple–period editors to claim that obedience to God (as in the case of Hezekiah and Jerusalem), even in the face of overwhelming odds, is always superior to rebellion against him (as in the case of Jeroboam and the Northern Kingdom), which leads to destruction. It furthermore allowed for the elevation of Jerusalem as the inviolable city of God, as it was able to survive the Assyrian onslaught when Samaria and Israel could not. Later, it was this sense of inviolability that garnered chastisement from the prophet Jeremiah (7:4) and it was Israel's sense of chosenness that was critiqued in the last half of the book of Jonah. Likewise, it was Nineveh's ability to recognize the coming judgment of the Lord and repent of its wrongdoing in the book of Jonah that Jesus highlighted while contrasting the behavior of Jews of his time who did not recognize him as the Messiah. For these reasons, Nineveh was a city that greatly influenced the Bible we have today.

CHAPTER 4

Babylon

My young son, MacLaren, once asked me where Babylonians come from. I answered him the way I answer a similar awkward question he asks: "Well, when a Daddylonian and a Mommylonian *really* love each other . . ."

Babylon played an important role in the formation of the Bible. Babylon's ziggurats influenced the story of the Tower of Babel, King Hammurabi's law code served as a template for the biblical law codes, and the Babylonian conquest and destruction of Jerusalem followed by the exile to Babylon fundamentally altered the theology of ancient Israel and provided the basis for numerous prophetic books like Isaiah, Ezekiel, Jeremiah, and the book of Lamentations. Many scholars also argue that much of the Hebrew Bible was composed (written down) or at the very least redacted (collected, arranged, corrected, altered, and generally edited) during the exile in Babylon. Thus, Babylon can be said to have been the city where what Jews today call the Hebrew Bible and what Christians call the Old Testament began to take its written shape.

AN EMOTIONAL EXCAVATION

Ancient Babylon is located in the modern city of Hillah, Iraq, which is about sixty miles south of Iraq's capital, Baghdad, on the Hillah branch of the Euphrates River. Although some of ancient Babylon's classic features have been restored, much of it lies in ruins as a result of the shifting course of the Euphrates and its tributaries, repeated ancient conquests, subsequent neglect over the centuries, the transportation of many of the city's treasures and architectural features to Western museums by nineteenth- and early twentieth-century explorers and archaeologists, and a couple of recent wars. Fortunately, an excellent virtual reconstruction of ancient Babylon is available to view for free at Babylon 3D,[1] demonstrating the importance of digital modeling to cultural heritage preservation.

Very few people travel to Iraq, and yet somehow everyone seems to have a negative impression of Babylon. I have a theory as to why this is so. It's not because of a bad interaction they once had with someone from Iraq or because of some bad hummus at a Baghdad restaurant, but rather because of the way the Bible portrays Babylon. Throughout its pages, the Bible presents a *very* negative portrayal of Babylon. Revelation 17:5 even calls the city "Babylon the great, mother of whores and of earth's abominations," and says this name was inscribed on Babylon's forehead! And since most people around the world are more familiar with the Bible than Babylon itself, the ancient city continues to have this negative reputation.

My experience with the Babylonians took place 16½ feet underground, in a cistern at Tel 'Azeqah in Israel, which was one of the last towns to fall before the Babylonians conquered Jerusalem itself (Jer. 34:7). As part of my research at Tel 'Azeqah, I was tasked with excavating a Late Bronze Age cistern that was in use through the Iron Age (from approximately 1500 to 586 BCE) on the southern slope of the tell. It took me nine weeks over two seasons to excavate the plastered water-collection facility. As at many excavation projects, the first weeks were exciting and new, and the final weeks leading to the completion were full of celebration, photos, and more than one underground toast to our success. But it was during the weeks in between—the long, dark, arduous, sweaty, dusty, frustrating, claustrophobic, and questioning-my-career-choice moments of the dig—that I encountered the Babylonians face-to-face. These weeks in the cistern gave me more time than I ever wanted

The last buckets of dirt excavated from the Area S2 water cistern 16½ feet below ground at Tel 'Azeqah, Israel. The cistern is plastered on the bottom and all sides to prevent water loss.

to reflect on the destructive things men have done to one another throughout time for God and country.

About 2 feet from the bottom of the plastered cistern there is a white chalky layer of debris about 2 feet thick. The white layer was created by annual rainwater washing the surface limestone debris into the cistern. Beneath this layer, I discovered vessel after vessel of what archaeologists call Iron IIc pottery, which is pottery that was used between 700 and 586 BCE. Each of the vessels held 1 to 2 gallons of water and, curiously, each was missing one handle. This was because when the Judahites living in 'Azeqah around 650 BCE needed water, they would tie a rope to the handle of a clay vessel and lower it into the cistern. Occasionally, the handle would break off, leaving the vessel at the bottom of the cistern and the unfortunate (and thirsty) person at the other end of the rope with nothing but a broken handle. Although this was bad for the fetcher of water (who was out a good water pitcher), it's *great* for archaeologists, as we can use this twenty-six-hundred-year-old pot to tell us about the people who lived at 'Azeqah.

We dated the pottery at the bottom of the cistern to somewhere between the seventh and sixth centuries BCE. The pottery at the bottom told us that this was the last time anyone used the cistern to draw water. This means that something happened that caused the cistern to go out of use and allowed years of limestone runoff to form the layer of white chalky debris 2 feet from the bottom of the cistern. That *something* may have been the Babylonians. I know this not just because of the pottery I found below the chalky layer, but also because of what I discovered *above* it.

During the hottest weeks of the summer, while I was digging down through the bowels of my cistern at 'Azeqah, I began to uncover bones. This is not uncommon in archaeology as the remains of animals are ubiquitous, especially down in holes that were once cisterns. But as I continued digging, I quickly realized that these weren't sheep, goat, or cow bones; these were *human* bones. I knew I wasn't in a tomb, as we had already identified the chamber as a plastered cistern. Yet there were bones in the cistern.

I am not scared of skeletons. The living are far more dangerous than the dead. Excavating human bones is part of my science and my work as an archaeologist. There is little emotion involved. Excavate. Document. That is my job. Yet these were *human* bones. And in my underground isolation, hunched over and staring into the eye socket of a skull looking back up at me, I could not help but think about the life this person lived. As I brushed the dirt from this skull's cheekbone, I wondered to myself what he did for a living. Was he happy? Was he in love? Did he ever have his heart broken? Was his father proud of him?

At that moment I felt tears welling up, which makes it difficult to work when you're on your hands and knees looking straight down. It was especially hard when I uncovered the skeleton of a small child, probably three or four years old. My mind immediately raced back to my newborn twins, Quincy and Rory Kate, and my two-year-old son, Mac. I sat frozen as I realized how absolutely devastated I'd be if anything ever happened to them.

My thoughts turned to this child's parents and how destroyed they must have been to have lost their child. I was overwhelmed.

I turned off my headlamp and just sat there, weeping silently, alone, in the dark. What horrible series of events must have transpired in order for this precious child to wind up at the bottom of an old cistern? I knew nothing about this child other than he had died and had been discarded without a proper burial. I didn't even know his name. So I made a decision. I didn't leave the cistern. I stayed right there in the dark. I wanted to experience the pain, the grief, and the sorrow. I just sat, and cried, and mourned his loss. I felt I owed it to him.

And it was there, in the dark, 16½ feet below ground in a cistern at Tel 'Azeqah, that I finally began to understand what Babylon meant to the Jews who built the Bible. As I sat on the very destruction layer created by the Babylonians and surveyed the bones of dead individuals strewn about the cistern, I came into physical contact with what Babylon brought to Judah—destruction, death, and sorrow. What had once given life to Judahites was now a Persian-period disposal site. It's no wonder why Babylon is portrayed so negatively in the Bible.

Now, if you'll pardon me for just a second, I need a moment to wipe the tears off my keyboard, get a drink, and hug my kids.

Okay. I'm a professional. Moving on.

BABYLON AND THE TOWER OF BABEL

The English name Babylon comes from the Greek (Βαβυλών), which was a transliteration of the Akkadian name Babili, which in turn was likely the name of a place or city. Over time, a popular folk etymology (i.e., a supposed origin of a word that sounds like it makes sense, but isn't actually historical) interpreted the origin of the name as *bab-ili,* meaning "gate of God."[2] In the Hebrew Bible, Babylon is rendered as an approximate transliteration, *bavel* (בבל),[3] which preserves the folk etymology and, as we'll see, offers an additional counteretymology with an entire story in the book of Genesis: the Tower of Babel.

The story of the Tower of Babel in Genesis 11:1–9 is an etiological myth, or a story that explains the origin of something like a religious tradition, natural phenomenon, or proper name.[4] In this case, the Tower of Babel explains how all of the world's different languages could have come about in such a short time after the flood.

According to the biblical narrative, the great flood wiped out every land and air creature from the face of the earth with the exception of Noah and his family, totaling eight persons, and the animals they brought onto the ark. Genesis 11:1 says that everyone on the ark spoke the same language, and therefore every descendant of Noah's three sons, Ham, Shem, and Yafet (Japheth), would have spoken the language their fathers taught them. Apparently someone in ancient history asked the obvious question, "If everyone is so closely related, how did we get so many different languages, like Moabite, Ammonite, Edomite, Phoenician, Egyptian, Aramaic, Elamite, and Akkadian, so quickly following the flood?" Languages take centuries to develop, evolve, and differentiate from one another, and since different nations spoke different languages, an explanation was needed to show how the different languages emerged.

Enter the Tower of Babel story, which is told for the very purpose of answering this question. The key to the purpose of the story is its location in the narrative. Note how the story of the Tower of Babel is strategically wedged in between the genealogies of the sons of Noah: the descendants of Shem are recounted in Genesis 10:21–32, then the story of the Tower of Babel is somewhat unexpectedly told in 11:1–9, and then 11:10 picks back up with the descendants of Shem again. The Tower of Babel story is placed where it is in the genealogies of the descendants of Noah because the editor of Genesis is attempting to preemptively address the expected question of the relatively sudden appearance of so many different languages. Its answer: the world's languages *didn't* evolve gradually over time (as is demonstrated from the linguistic and archaeological record of literary remains we have today); rather, God miraculously made them all at the same time.

Genesis 11:2–4 claims that Noaḥ's descendants wanted to build a city and a high place that could reach the heavens: "Come, let us build ourselves a city, and a tower with its top in the heavens" (11:4). Modern scholars argue that the tower mentioned in Genesis 11:4 was influenced by stories of ancient Mesopotamian *ziggurats,* or high places of worship that were usually part of ancient temple complexes. These ziggurats would have been known to the biblical authors through direct experience with them, stories told about them, or experience with their destroyed remains. A well-known ziggurat in the center of ancient Babylon, the Etemenanki, was dedicated to the god Marduk in the sixth century BCE after being rebuilt by King Nebuchadnezzar II. We also have the story of the construction of a towering religious precinct, the Esagila, mentioned in the Akkadian creation epic the Enuma Elish.[5]

What is fascinating about the next verses in Genesis is that they depict God as making a rather extraordinary claim about the builders of the tower:

> *The LORD came down to see the city and the tower, which mortals had built. And the LORD said, "Look, they are one people, and they have all one language; and this is only the beginning of what they will do;* nothing that they propose to do will now be impossible for them. *Come, let us go down, and confuse their language there, so that they will not understand one another's speech." (11:5–7)*

According to the Bible, the reason given for God's intervention in the building of the Tower of Babel was the fear that humans *could actually build* a tower that reached the heavens! The view that one could build a structure that could physically reach the divine realm is consistent with the worldview found, for instance, in the creation narratives in Genesis 1 and 2: the earth is a flat surface over which a domed firmament is stretched, separating the heavens from the earth (1:6–8). The builders wanted to construct a tower that reached beyond this barrier, and according to the Bible, God feared that they might do it!

In the story, God's solution is to confuse their languages, which would apparently keep the builders from communicating with each other (11:8) and cause them to abort the construction of the tower. Then in Genesis 11:9, we find a new etymology for Babylon, which expands on the earlier Akkadian folk etymology: "Therefore it was called Babel (בבל, *bavel*), because there the LORD confused (בלל, *balal*) the language of all the earth; and from there the LORD scattered them abroad over the face of all the earth."

Genesis 11:9 claims that the Hebrew word for the tower and the city of Babylon, Babel, results from a play on the Hebrew word *balal,* "to confuse," offering both an endorsement of the Akkadian "gate of God" folk etymology and a pejorative counteretymology that mocks the failure of the "confused" Babylonians to complete their tower to the heavens. This story offers an explanation for the presence of so many different languages so few generations after the flood: God made them from nothing. So from the very origin of the city's name, Babylon played an integral role in one of the Bible's best-known stories, the Tower of Babel.

THE FIRST BABYLONIAN
DYNASTY AND HAMMURABI'S CODE

Another early example of how Babylon influenced the Bible may be seen in its use of Hammurabi's law code. Babylon experienced two periods of dominance; biblical Babylon is actually the *second* great period in Babylon's history and is referred to by scholars as the Neo-Babylonian Empire, which ruled over Mesopotamia and the greater Near East for nearly a century from 626 until 539 BCE. But the earlier Babylonian period of domination also contributed significantly to the contents of the Bible.

The first Babylonian dynasty spanned a period from around 1830 to 1531 BCE and is best known for King Hammurapi (more commonly Hammurabi) and his famed law code, which is on dis-

The top of the Law Code of Babylonian king Hammurabi. The iconography shows Hammurabi receiving a ring and scepter (symbols of royal power) from the seated Mesopotamian sun god Shamash, whose feet rest on the mountains.

A close-up of the Akkadian cuneiform text of the Law Code of Babylonian king Hammurabi.

play at the Louvre in Paris. The Code of Hammurabi is an ancient law code that set standards of conduct and justice for most areas of human interaction, including contracts, wages, property rights, criminal behavior, divorce, inheritance, and so forth. Because Hammurabi's law code (which was created about 1750 BCE) predates the supposed historical Moses, exodus, and Mt. Sinai revelation (which cannot be dated to any earlier than 1450 BCE),[6] many conclude that Hammurabi's code influenced many of the laws in the Bible.[7] For instance, lines 196–97 of Hammurabi's code read:

> *If a man destroy the eye of another man, they shall destroy his eye. If one break a man's bone, they shall break his bone.*[8]

This is similar to the later law found in Exodus 21:23–25:

> *If any harm follows, then you shall give life for life, eye for eye, tooth for tooth, hand for hand, foot for foot, burn for burn, wound for wound, stripe for stripe.*

What's more, many of the laws in Hammurabi's law code break down very specific laws into scenarios similar to those found in the Bible's law codes. For example, lines 250–51 of Hammurabi's code state:

> *If a bull, when passing through the street, gore a man and bring about his death, this case has no penalty. If a man's bull have been wont to gore and they have made known to him his habit of goring, and he have not protected his horns or have not tied him up, and that bull gore the son of a man and bring about his death, he shall pay one-half mana of silver.*[9]

So if the bull is unaccustomed to goring, there is no penalty for the bull's owner. However, if the bull is a repeat offender, there is a penalty for the owner, presumably because he knew of the risk to others. Compare that to the law given in Exodus 21:28–29:

*When an ox gores a man or a woman to death, the ox shall be
stoned, and its flesh shall not be eaten; but the owner of the ox
shall not be liable. If the ox has been accustomed to gore in the
past, and its owner has been warned but has not restrained it, and
it kills a man or a woman, the ox shall be stoned, and its owner
also shall be put to death.*

Although the penalties are adjusted (and are much harsher)
in the Bible, the idea of different penalties for different casu-
istic laws (i.e., civil laws with varying penalties determined on
a case-by-case basis) concerning goring beasts that we find in
the Bible is parallel to that of the Code of Hammurabi, including the liability of the animal's owner for repeat offenses. If you
take a moment to read the laws in Hammurabi's code[10] and then
read the Covenant Code in Exodus 20:19–23:33, you'll quickly
understand why so many scholars believe that the laws said to
have been given to Moses by God on Mt. Sinai appear to have
been heavily influenced by earlier Babylonian law codes, specifically the Code of Hammurabi. It is a very real case of the city of
Babylon contributing to the building of the central law code of
the Bible.

THE RISE OF THE NEO-BABYLONIAN
EMPIRE AND THE FALL OF JERUSALEM

Over a millennium after the rise and fall of the first Babylonian
dynasty, the city of Babylon once again found itself under foreign
domination, this time at the hands of the Neo-Assyrian Empire
beginning in 934 BCE. Following the death of the Assyrian king
Ashurbanipal in 627 BCE, the Babylonians rebelled against Assyria
(as part of a larger coalition of Medes, Persians, Chaldeans,
Babylonians, Scythians, and Cimmerians) under the command of
the Chaldean tribal leader Nabopolassar, who served as the first
king of the newly established Neo-Babylonian Empire. But it was

Nabopolassar's son, Nebuchadnezzar II, who became the feared leader of the empire and the rebuilder of Babylon.

The Babylonian king Nebuchadnezzar II was the Assyrian-born king of the Neo-Babylonian Empire from 604 to 561 BCE and is considered one of the greatest kings of ancient Babylon. (In fact, Saddam Hussein saw himself as the reembodiment of Nebuchadnezzar II and actually rebuilt, expanded, and took up residence in the palaces of Nebuchadnezzar II; he even went so far as to depict himself in the same poses used in the earlier king's iconography in order to project his propagandist portrayal as the greatest ruler in Babylon since Nebuchadnezzar II.) Ruling from Babylon, Nebuchadnezzar II reestablished the city as a magnificent capital. He rebuilt temples and palaces, built the famed Ishtar Gate, and is said to have built one of the seven wonders of the ancient world, the Hanging Gardens of Babylon, although the actual existence of the Hanging Gardens is still debated, as there is no archaeological evidence for the gardens.[11]

With the Neo-Assyrian Empire destroyed, the former coalition of rebellious nations set out to assert their own domination over Mesopotamia, ultimately turning against one another. To this end, the Neo-Babylonians campaigned throughout the former Assyrian lands, securing support for their rule and leveling cities that refused. Following the Battle of Carchemish in 605 BCE (see Jer. 46:2), King Yehoyaqim (Jehoiakim) of Judah switched allegiance to Babylon and began paying an annual tribute to Nebuchadnezzar II.

The Fall of Jerusalem

Following an inconclusive battle between Nebuchadnezzar II and Egyptian forces in 601 BCE, some rulers of cities in Cana'an and Phoenicia, including Judah's King Jehoiakim, smelled weakness and rebelled, allying themselves once again with Egypt. In order to ensure a steady stream of income and loyalty, Babylon besieged Jerusalem in 598 BCE. King Jehoiakim died during the siege, and his son, Yehoyakin (Jehoiachin), succeeded him to the throne.[12] However, upon capturing Jerusalem, Nebuchadnezzar II deposed King Jehoiachin, who surrendered to Nebuchadnezzar II after only three months on the throne and was taken into exile along with his family, nobles, and a large number of the residents of Jerusalem. Nebuchadnezzar II replaced Jehoiachin with his uncle, the client king Ṣidqiyah(u) (Zedekiah).

Not only does 2 Kings 24:11–17 record this period of monarchic instability in Judah, but the Nebuchadnezzar Chronicle, which preserves the first decade of Nebuchadnezzar II's reign, corroborates the account:

In the seventh year [of Nebuchadnezzar II, 598/7], the month of Kislimu, the king of Akkad mustered his troops, marched to the Hatti-land, and besieged the city of Judah, and on the second day of the month of Addaru he seized the city and captured the king [Jehoiachin]. He appointed there a king of his own choice [Zedekiah], received its heavy tribute and sent to Babylon.[13]

Despite the protests of the prophet Jeremiah and the memory of what had happened to kings a decade before him, King Zedekiah also rebelled against Nebuchadnezzar II and entered into an alliance with Egyptian pharaoh Apries, whom Jeremiah calls Ḥofra' (44:30).[14] As the saying goes, Zedekiah backed the wrong horse. In order to deal with what was becoming a constant, rebellious nuisance, Nebuchadnezzar II again marched his army to Jerusalem and again besieged it (cf. 2 Kings 25:1). However, this time, Nebuchadnezzar II had had enough; instead of simply installing a new, loyal puppet king, he was intent on destroying Jerusalem.

Following a thirty-month siege, the city of Jerusalem fell to Nebuchadnezzar II's army. To make an example out of King Zedekiah for others who might consider rebelling, Nebuchadnezzar II's army captured Zedekiah, his family, and his royal guard as they attempted to flee, took them to the Babylonian king's field headquarters at Riblah, slaughtered Zedekiah's sons in front of him so that he could witness his monarchic line come to an end, and then gouged out his eyes, both as a military punishment and a personal humiliation (2 Kings 25:4–7).[15]

Nebuchadnezzar II then proceeded to level the city of God. The fall of Jerusalem is described in 2 Kings 25:8–12. The text says that Nebuchadnezzar II sent the captain of his personal guard, Nebuzar'adan, to finish the deed:

> Nebuzaradan . . . burned the house of the LORD, the king's house, and all the houses of Jerusalem; every great house he burned down. All the army of the Chaldeans who were with the captain of the guard broke down the walls around Jerusalem. Nebuzaradan the captain of the guard carried into exile the rest of the people who were left in the city and the deserters who had defected to the king of Babylon—all the rest of the population. But the captain of the guard left some of the poorest people of the land to be vinedressers and tillers of the soil.

Following the capture and mutilation of Zedekiah and the slaughter of his family, the nobility and any learned men or skilled laborers were deported to Babylon, while the poorest of the poor were left behind to work the fields for this new Babylonian province under the governorship of Gedalyahu (Gedaliah) son of 'Aḥiqam son of Shafan (2 Kings 25:22). It is *this* exile that is the final and most recognized exile of Judahites to Babylon because it accompanied the complete and utter destruction of Jerusalem and its Temple.

Jerusalem was gone. The promised eternal reign of the line of David in Jerusalem (cf. 2 Sam. 7:16) had come to an end. The unthinkable came to pass; the house of the Lord—the Jerusalem Temple—lay in ruins. *This* event in ancient Israel's history—the destruction of Jerusalem and the exile to Babylon—marks one of the lowest points in the history of Judaism and was a theologically traumatic event that would scar the collective Jewish psyche and linger in its memory for years to come.

EVIDENCE OF JUDAHITE EXILES IN BABYLON

Archaeological evidence confirms the presence of Judahite exiles in Babylon. From 1899 to 1917, the self-trained German archaeologist Robert Koldewey excavated 290 clay cuneiform tablets dated to 595–570 BCE from barrel vaults beneath a public building near the Ishtar Gate. The building possessed multiple rows of rooms that may have been the residence of the exiled Judahite king, his family, and his nobles. The tablets are presently housed in the south wing of the Pergamon Museum in Berlin. Among these tablets are what appear to be records of rations given to King Jehoiachin while in Babylon. One tablet reads:

> *10 (sila of oil) to . . . [Ia]-'-kin, king of Ia[. . .]*
> *2½ sila (oil) to [. . . so]ns of the king Ia-a-ḫu-du [i.e., Judah]*
> *4 sila to 8 men from Ia-a-ḫu-da-a-a [i.e., Judah]. . .*[16]

Another tablet reads:

> *1½ sila (oil) for three carpenters from Arvad, ½ sila each*
> *11½ sila for eight from Byblos, 1 sila each*
> *3½ sila for seven Greeks, ½ sila each*
> *½ sila to Nabû-êṭir the carpenter*
> *10 (sila) to Ia-ku-ú-ki-nu, [i.e., Jehoiachin] the son of the king of*
> *   Ia-ku-du [i.e., Judah]*
> *2½ sila for the five sons of the king of Ia-ku-du [i.e., Judah]*
> *   through Qa-na-a-ma.*[17]

The cuneiform texts appear to corroborate the text of 2 Kings 24:12–15. Furthermore, they appear to confirm the text of 2 Kings 25:27–30, specifically, that King *Ia-ku-ú-ki-nu* (Jehoiachin) of *Ia-ku-du* (Judah) gave himself up, was treated well in Babylon, and was ultimately released:

> *In the thirty-seventh year of the exile of King Jehoiachin of Judah,*
> *in the twelfth month, on the twenty-seventh day of the month,*
> *King Evil-merodach of Babylon, in the year that he began to*

reign, released King Jehoiachin of Judah from prison; he spoke kindly to him, and gave him a seat above the other seats of the kings who were with him in Babylon. So Jehoiachin put aside his prison clothes. Every day of his life he dined regularly in the king's presence. For his allowance, a regular allowance was given him by the king, a portion every day, as long as he lived.

Thus, the archaeological record appears to confirm the presence in Babylon of exiles from Judah. But the Babylonians also provided the Bible with one of its most vivid reflections on the destruction of Jerusalem—a book that was created *specifically* to mourn the loss of Jerusalem, the book of Lamentations, to which we now turn.

LAMENTATIONS

The book of Lamentations preserves a series of well-crafted poems dedicated to a single event: the destruction of Jerusalem by the Babylonians. It begins somberly, as the stunned, heartbroken poet opens his composition with the simple Hebrew word *eykah,* literally, "How?!" How did this happen? Why, God, why? This grief-stricken overture sets the tone for the remainder of the distraught author's internal struggle to find the right words to describe the depths of his depression and sorrow stemming from this disastrous event and to answer the central question: *How* the hell did we get here? How did we end up like this?

In order to understand Lamentations, it is helpful to understand the musical genre of the blues. The blues are songs about hard times. People "sing the blues" when they are sad. But people don't sing the blues because they *want* to be sad; that's what Morrissey and Radiohead are for. People sing the blues because in expressing their disappointments and sorrows in a creative, composed way, they can share those feelings with others who feel the same way, and through this shared empathy, this shared grief, they can together begin to feel better. Therefore in one sense, blues songs preserve a poetic hope within their lyrics that both performer and listener share and from which both can take comfort. The same is true for the biblical book of Lamentations.

Lamentations is part of both Jewish and Christian Bibles, but it is arranged differently in each. In the Hebrew Bible, Lamentations is found among the Ketuvim, or the "Writings," which include the Five Megillot, or scrolls (Song of Songs, Ruth, Lamentations, Qohelet [Ecclesiastes], and Esther), the poetic books (Psalms, Proverbs, and Job), and the books of Daniel, Ezra-Nehemiah (one book in the Hebrew Bible, two books in the Christian canon), and Chronicles. However, in the Christian canon Lamentations is placed after the prophecy of Jeremiah, as it is traditionally attributed to him.

In the Jewish faith, Lamentations is traditionally read during the Jewish holiday of Tish'a B'Av, or the "Ninth of Av," which commemorates the date of the destruction of both the First and Second Temples in Jerusalem.[18] Thus, Lamentations is read to collectively commemorate the sadness Judah felt when Babylon destroyed Jerusalem or, in a more accurate sense theologically, how God *allowed* Babylon to destroy Jerusalem because of Judah's sins.

What's most interesting about the book of Lamentations is that the first four of its five chapters are in the form of an acrostic, which is a clever literary construction that is artistically dependent upon the very nature of the Hebrew alphabet. There are twenty-two letters in the Hebrew alphabet, beginning with *'aleph, bet, gimel, dalet,* and so on. Chapters 1, 2, and 4 of Lamentations each have twenty-two verses—each line beginning with a successive letter of the Hebrew alphabet—and each chapter begins with the word *eykah* (איכה), "how." Chapter 3 is a triple acrostic that has sixty-six verses, with three lines for each of the twenty-two successive letters of Hebrew alphabet. The first three verses begin with words that start with the letter *'aleph,* the next three with the letter *bet,* and so on. Chapter 5 is not an acrostic, but still has twenty-two lines. Many English Bible readers do not notice the acrostic either because they do not read Hebrew, because they do not realize that the word order of Hebrew is different than in English, or because the English words used to translate their Hebrew counterparts don't always start with the equivalent letter. For instance, *eykah* (איכה) begins with an *'aleph,* but its English equivalent, "how," begins with an *h,* not an *a.*

So Lamentations is cleverly structured poetry to be sure, but it is also very theologically profound. It relays the collective Jewish community's sadness and confusion over the loss of Jerusalem from a self-blaming theological point of view: God abandoned the people *only* because of their sinfulness, not because of his ineptness. Lamentations 1:8 states, "Jerusalem sinned grievously, so she has become a mockery," placing the fault for the exile on the people, not on God. Lamentations 1:18 reads, "The Lord is in the right, for I have rebelled against his word," while in 1:22 the writer petitions God: "Deal with them [his enemies] as you have dealt with me because of all my transgressions." The Babylonian exiles blamed themselves for the destruction of Jerusalem and their deportation to Babylon; this theological use of self-blame to explain disaster also pervades many of the other books of the Bible.

We also see self-blame still commonly used by individuals today to explain disaster: "Something bad happened in my life, so God must be punishing me because of something I did wrong." This theological mind-set can easily be traced back through Jewish theology to the fall of Jerusalem.

And yet surprisingly, Lamentations is also the location of one of the best-known Bible passages offering a declaration of hope that the Lord will one day relent from his punishment of his people. In fact, many Christians may recognize Lamentations 3:22–24 from a popular praise song: "The steadfast love of the Lord never ceases, his mercies never come to an end; they are new every morning; great is your faithfulness. 'The Lord is my portion,' says my soul, 'therefore I will hope in him.'" Lamentations 3:25–33 then encourages patience from those who believe God has abandoned them.

Lamentations 5:20–22, the last three verses of the book, end with a bittersweet, openly pessimistic, and rightly confused pronouncement of hope:

> Why have you forgotten us completely?
> Why have you forsaken us these many days?
> Restore us to yourself, O LORD, that we may be restored;
>   renew our days as of old—
> unless you have utterly rejected us,
>   and are angry with us beyond measure.

The note of passive-aggressive pessimism on which the lament ends effectively conveys the level of distress that defines Lamentations as a whole. The faithful call on God to deliver them, unless, of course, God is too angry with them, in which case they understand.

Fortunately, the exiles would return to Jerusalem, and the story of the city of God would continue. It is also worth pointing out that in modern Jewish liturgy, v. 21 is reread after v. 22 to keep from ending on a negative note. Given the later Jewish successes in Jerusalem and given the optimism (albeit tempered with a dose of tentative near-comedic pessimism) with which many modern Jews operate in today's world, it is good that v. 21—"Restore us to yourself, O LORD, that we may be restored; renew our days as of old"—is repeated, as it reflects a sense of tempered hope and not of hopeless despair.[19]

PSALMS OF LAMENT

The book of Lamentations is not the only place in the Bible where we find theological reflections on the despair of losing the holy city of Jerusalem by worshippers of YHWH who wonder why he abandoned them. There are also particular psalms that are songs of lament. Communal laments, which are formal laments on behalf of a congregation of believers, include Psalms 44; 60; 74; 79; 80; 85; and 90. There are also personal laments like Psalm 22, the opening lines of which Jesus is said to have quoted from the cross:

"My God, my God, why have you forsaken me? Why are you so far from helping me, from the words of my groaning? O my God, I cry by day, but you do not answer; and by night, but find no rest."[20]

Perhaps one of the best-known lament psalms in the Bible is Psalm 137, which depicts an exiled Jerusalemite seated "by the rivers of Babylon" lamenting his fate: "By the rivers of Babylon—there we sat down and there we wept when we remembered Zion. On the willows there we hung up our harps" (v. 1). Verse 3 recalls the mocking of the Babylonian overlords, asking the exiles to sing presumably one of the hymns[21] praising Jerusalem as the inviolable city of God: "For there our captors asked us for songs, and our tormentors asked for mirth, saying, 'Sing us one of the songs of Zion!'" But the loss of Jerusalem caused their mouths to remain closed. Verse 4 asks, "How could we sing the LORD's song in a foreign land?"

The psalm then invokes a promise that the singers will never forget Jerusalem:

"If I forget you, O Jerusalem, let my right hand forget (its skill). Let my tongue cling to (the roof of) my mouth, if I do not remember you, if I do not set Jerusalem above my highest joy" (vv. 5–6; translation mine).

And speaking of *forgetting*, what many people forget is that Psalm 137 continues after this point, but many people either haven't read it or don't want to read it. This is because the conclusion of Psalm 137 is a brutal and incredibly vindictive passage, expressing a blessed happiness over bloody vengeance against the infants of Israel's enemies (which doesn't necessarily make for good praise hymns in modern churches and synagogues).

But Psalm 137:7–9 is *not* atypical for songs in the ancient Near East, which often conclude with a prayer of revenge, such as this execration against Edom (whom the Bible says mocked Judah and stood idly by as Jerusalem fell) and against Babylon, the great "devastator," who destroyed the kingdom of Judah and the previously "inviolable" capital of Jerusalem:

> *Remember, O LORD, against the Edomites*
> *the day of Jerusalem's fall,*
> *how they said, "Tear it down! Tear it down!*
> *Down to its foundations!"*
> *O daughter Babylon, you devastator!*
> *Happy shall they be who pay you back*
> *what you have done to us!*
> Happy shall they be who take your little ones
> and dash them against the rock.

As horrendous as the idea of grasping newborn babies by the ankle and swinging their soft young skulls into rocks may sound, we cannot overlook that *this* is the conclusion of Psalm 137—the vengeful prayer that the children of Babylon will be murdered by having their heads dashed against the rocks. This is the prayer of the Jerusalem exiles in Babylon—a prayer that is preserved in the songbook of ancient Israel. An immoral act against innocents such as this is abhorrent and indefensible by any modern standard, yet this is the degree to which the author of this psalm despised Babylon.

DANIEL

The book of Dani'el (Daniel) is also set during the period of the Babylonian exile, although most scholars conclude that its composition wasn't begun until the late Persian period (539–332 BCE) and its later chapters weren't composed until the late Hellenistic period (332–167 BCE). The reason for this is because chapters 2–7 of Daniel are written in Aramaic, not in Hebrew, and the first half of the book (chaps. 1–6) recounts tales of the Babylonian and later Median royal courts, while the second half of the book (chaps. 7–12) is a book of apocalyptic visions or revelations.

Scholars believe the book of Daniel was composed well into the Hellenistic period because parts of the book reflect activity that took place in the early second century BCE. Daniel 8:1–8, for instance, speaks in apocalyptic code about Alexander the Great's rise to power and conquest of the Mediterranean and Near East. Daniel 8:8 speaks of the death of Alexander and the rise of the four Diadochoi, the successors of Alexander and rulers over the remains of his segmented kingdom. Likewise, Daniel 8:9–12 speaks of the rise of "another horn, a little one, which grew exceedingly great," the Seleucid king Antiochus IV Epiphanes, who suppressed many aspects of Jewish worship and practice in Jerusalem, including circumcision and the daily sacrifices at the Temple.

Note that even Antiochus's termination of the burned offerings at the Jerusalem Temple is specifically mentioned in Daniel 8:11–12. Although some may argue that verses from Daniel 8 may be highly predictive visions of what was to come, most critical scholars see this as evidence that the latter portions of the book of Daniel were composed *after* the fact during the Hellenistic period, but literarily set in the Babylonian and early Persian periods.

The book of Daniel likely began as a collection of disparate Aramaic court tales that were later collected and expanded. Although they were written in response to later Hellenistic threats to Judaism, they were literarily set in the time of the Babylonian exile as a model to Jews suffering under Greek oppression; in the same way that Daniel and his friends remained faithful to YHWH upon threat of death by the fiery furnace (Dan. 3) and the lions' den (Dan. 6; Bel. 31–42), the book of Daniel encouraged Jews living under Greek oppression to remain faithful as well. This theme is seen in many other late Second Temple literary works that were ultimately left out of the Hebrew canon, including the Additions to Daniel (which include the Apocryphal Prayer of Azariah and the Song of the Three Jews, Susanna, and Bel and the Dragon), and manuscripts like the Aramaic Prayer of Nabonidus (4Q242), fragments of

which were discovered among the Dead Sea Scrolls.[22] The book
of Daniel was included in the Bible to give hope to Jews that one
day, *if* they remain faithful to God, he will deliver them from
foreign oppression.

JEREMIAH

Perhaps no prophet is more closely identified with Babylon than
Yirmeyahu (Jeremiah). Jeremiah was active during the reign of
King Josiah and continued his prophetic activity through the
destruction of Jerusalem and the Temple in 587 BCE. The famed
"weeping prophet" is traditionally credited with writing the
books of Jeremiah and Lamentations. However, although the
prophecies early in the book (chaps. 1–25) may be attributed
to Jeremiah the prophet, many scholars point to the narratives
about Jeremiah (e.g., chaps. 25–29, 32–44), which read much
like the text of 2 Kings, as evidence that large portions of the
book, especially the latter parts, were composed and added to
the book of Jeremiah by other authors because the materials
dealt with him.

Jeremiah 39:1–10 parallels Jeremiah 52:4–16 and 2 Kings 25:1–
12, while Jeremiah 40:7–41:18 parallels 2 Kings 25:23–26. In fact,
Jeremiah 52 is a complete parallel retelling of 2 Kings 24:18–25:30,
demonstrating that the later portions of the book are traditions
about Jeremiah that were appended to his prophecy despite appearing elsewhere in the Bible. Remember also that according to
Jeremiah 36:4 and 18, Jeremiah did not write his prophecies, but
only received oracles from YHWH and spoke them aloud. It was
Jeremiah's scribe, Baruch ben Neriah, who actually wrote down
the prophecies.

Jeremiah is unique among the prophets, because rather than
encouraging the king of Judah to rebel against its foreign oppressors and have faith in YHWH, as Isaiah had done with Hezekiah

during the Assyrian threat, Jeremiah encouraged capitulation to Babylon (Jer. 27:8; 38:17–18, 20–23). This may be due to the fact that Jeremiah did not go into Egyptian captivity with King Jeho'ahaz of Judah (2 Kings 23:30–34) or remain in Judah with King Zedekiah (2 Kings 24:17), but was taken into Babylonian captivity with King Jehoiachin. Jeremiah's capitulation to Babylon may explain why the books of Kings end with the good treatment and release of King Jehoiachin in Babylon and why Jeremiah 52 is identical to 2 Kings 24:18–25:30; he felt that capitulation would ensure survival, and his works were preserved because he was "right"— those who surrendered survived in exile, while those who didn't were destroyed along with Jerusalem.[23]

One of the problems that Jeremiah highlighted in his prophecies is that the people of Jerusalem believed their city was unconquerable (cf. Ps. 46:1–5).[24] He had even warned the Jerusalemites specifically in 7:4, 8 that Jerusalem was, in fact, *not* impregnable simply because the Temple was there: "Do not trust in these deceptive words: 'This is the temple of the Lord, the temple of the Lord, the temple of the Lord.' . . . Here you are, trusting in deceptive words to no avail." Jeremiah insisted, rather, that the Judahites had to *do* something in order to retain God's protection; they couldn't just assume that God would bless them because of the Temple. Specifically, Jeremiah pleaded with the king and residents of Jerusalem that they "act justly one with another . . . not oppress the alien, the orphan, and the widow, or shed innocent blood . . . and . . . not go after other gods" (7:5–6); and only then—because of their right actions—would God defend Jerusalem. But Jerusalem ultimately fell, and it was this destruction of Jerusalem—the city that was so thought to be inviolable due to the protection of YHWH—that forever defined Babylon in the memories of Jews.

Once again in Jeremiah we see the fall of Jerusalem, the destruction of the Temple, and the exile to Babylon explained with a heavy dose of theological self-blame: the ancient Judahites believed God allowed Babylon to destroy Jerusalem because of

Judah's sins. Thus, it wasn't God who broke his promise, but his people. Jeremiah's prophecy essentially served to explain to the people of Judah and its kings why God allowed the destruction of the Temple (cf. Jer. 1:16; 5:19). Remember, the biblical tradition states that YHWH chose Abraham and his descendants as his people, promised to bless them, and promised David through the prophet Nathan that a descendant of David would always sit on the throne (2 Sam. 7). But Jeremiah argues that because Judah acted unjustly and worshipped other gods, it would be destroyed.

As one might expect, Jeremiah's message was very unpopular among the ruling class in Jerusalem. No one likes to be told that they are treating people unfairly, especially politicians and rulers. Jeremiah 36:23 states that King Jehoiakim cut up and burned every couple of columns of Jeremiah's words as they were read to him. Even in modern times the prophetic voice bearing the message of government corruption and civil injustice is often attacked. As we see in the reaction to Martin Luther King, Jr., Mohandas Gandhi, and journalists and citizen watchdog groups that hold governments accountable for their actions, governments hate to be criticized. Jeremiah suffered greatly for criticizing those in power. The book of Jeremiah states he was attacked by his own relatives (12:6), beaten and put into the stocks (20:2), imprisoned by the king (35:17), and thrown into the cistern of Malkiah by Judah's officials (cf. 38:6).

The book of Jeremiah shows us that although we may argue about whether tragedy is a premeditated punishment from God because of our disobedience or simply a natural part of the human experience unmediated by any divine agent, we as humans ought to act justly toward one with another, refrain from oppressing the marginalized, like immigrants, orphans, and widows (Jer. 7:5–6), and defend the cause of the poor and needy. After all, isn't that *exactly* what Jeremiah 22:16 says it means to know the Lord?

The End of the Neo-Babylonians
and the End of Exile

The Neo-Babylonian Empire came to an end in 539 BCE, when the Persian king Cyrus the Great defeated the Babylonian king Nabonidus at the Battle of Opis, just north of Babylon. King Cyrus founded the Persian Achaemenid Empire and assumed the lands previously held by the Neo-Babylonians.

So great was the Bible's hatred of the Babylonians, that the prophet Isaiah actually heralds the Persian king as a *messiah* (or "anointed one") because he overcame the Babylonians:

> [*Thus says the* LORD], who says of Cyrus, "He is my shepherd, and he shall carry out all my purpose"; *and who says of Jerusalem, "It shall be rebuilt," and of the temple, "Your foundation shall be laid." Thus says the* LORD to his anointed, to Cyrus, *whose right hand I have grasped to subdue nations before him* . . . "*so that you may know that it is I, the* LORD, *the God of Israel, who call you by your name. For the sake of my servant Jacob, and Israel my chosen, I call you by your name, I surname you,* though you do not know me." (Isa. 44:28–45:4)

This text from Isaiah was likely written after the so-called Edict of Cyrus announcing the general return of all exiled peoples back to their homes. Although Jerusalem and Judah are never mentioned on the Cyrus Cylinder, which calls only for the restoration of Mesopotamian sanctuaries (and not specifically of the Jerusalem Temple), the authors of the Bible certainly interpreted the decree as pertaining to them. Ezra 1:1–4 (cf. 2 Chron. 36:22–23) states:

> *In the first year of King Cyrus of Persia, in order that the word of the* LORD *by the mouth of Jeremiah might be accomplished, the* LORD *stirred up the spirit of King Cyrus of Persia so that he sent a herald throughout all his kingdom, and also in a written edict declared:*

> *"Thus says King Cyrus of Persia: the* Lord, *the God of heaven, has given me all the kingdoms of the earth, and he has charged me to build him a house at Jerusalem in Judah. Any of those among you who are of his people—may their God be with them!—are now permitted to go up to Jerusalem in Judah, and rebuild the house of the* Lord, *the God of Israel—he is the God who is in Jerusalem; and let all survivors, in whatever place they reside, be assisted by the people of their place with silver and gold, with goods and with animals, besides freewill offerings for the house of God in Jerusalem."*

The authors (and editors) of the Bible interpreted King Cyrus's actions as the result of the hand of YHWH at work *through* King Cyrus, even though Cyrus did not "know" YHWH. They acknowledge that Cyrus did not credit YHWH for his victory, likely because they knew that in the same record that proclaimed the release of the exiled captives, Cyrus credits *Babylon's god,* Marduk, for his victory:

> *Marduk, the great lord, who nurtures his people, saw with pleasure his [Cyrus's] fine deeds and true heart, and ordered that he should go to Babylon. He had him take the road to Tintir [Babylon], and, like a friend and companion, he walked at his side.*[25]

Thus, the Bible interprets the victory of Cyrus the Great over Babylon as the work of YHWH and interprets the Edict of Cyrus as God's deliverance of his exiled peoples. Of course, referring to a foreign king as a messiah was problematic. But later Second Temple–period literature would attempt to support the notion that Cyrus the Great was, in fact, qualified to be called "messiah" by arguing that he actually converted to the worship of YHWH, as is suggested in 1 Esdras 4:42–63 and Bel and the Dragon 28 and 41. But desperate times call for desperate interpretations, and the editors of the Bible were more than willing to see the hand of God in the Persian victory over Babylon.

THE LEGACY OF BABYLON

Babylon continued to play an important role in the formation of the Bible even after it fell to Persia. Much of the Hebrew Bible was at the very least compiled and edited during the exile in Babylon, perhaps by the scribes at the court of the exiled King Jehoiachin. Some scholars even claim that portions of the Hebrew Bible may have been *composed* in Babylon perhaps by those Jews who remained in Babylon when others returned to rebuild the Temple in Jerusalem. Remember that although the Edict of Cyrus allowed Jews to return to Jerusalem to rebuild the Temple and repopulate what became the Persian province of Yehud (which would become Judea), many Jews—perhaps a majority of them—stayed behind in Babylon. This explains why areas in and around Babylon became centers of Jewish thought throughout the first six centuries CE, when the Babylonian Talmud, which preserves the teachings, interpretations, and often dissenting opinions of the most prominent early rabbis on a variety of subjects found in the Hebrew Bible, was compiled and edited.[26] Thus, Babylon, despite its place in history as the city that destroyed Jerusalem and the Temple of YHWH, remained a place of Jewish learning throughout the first centuries of the common era.

And this is how Babylon, the city that destroyed Jerusalem, contributed arguably a disproportionate amount of content to the Bible. Not only did it fundamentally alter the political plight of ancient Judah, but it also remained a symbol of destruction and evil even into the first Christian century. Revelation 17:5 adopts the symbol of Babylon, calling it the "mother of whores," and promises that one day God's people will experience vindication and victory over their oppressors, as Revelation 18:21 symbolically claims, "With such violence Babylon the great city will be thrown down, and will be found no more." And *this,* I argue, is why most people have a negative view of Babylon—because of the role it played in building the Bible.

CHAPTER 5

Megiddo

Armageddon. The very word strikes fear into the hearts of believers. (Either that, or you immediately see visions of Bruce Willis and Steve Buscemi blowing up a runaway asteroid hurtling toward earth.) But although Armageddon may be known in the imaginations of many as an apocalyptic battle between the forces of good and the forces of evil, the Armageddon described in Revelation 16:16 is actually a *real* place.

The Greek name Ἁρμαγεδών, or *Armageddon,* is actually the Greek rendering of two Hebrew words: *har,* meaning "mountain," and *Megiddo,* the proper name of a site at a strategic north–south *and* east–west intersection in northern Israel. Because the rough breathing mark at the beginning of the Greek word Ἁρμαγεδών has not always been preserved in transliterations into Latin, it leaves us with "Armageddon" instead of "Harmageddon."

Megiddo is significant for the building of the Bible as the location of the battle called "the great day of God the Almighty" (Rev. 16:14), an apocalyptic battle inaugurating the Day of Judgment, which reveals a lot about the cultural context in which the writers of the Bible were working. Megiddo was identified as the location of the end of the world because it had been the epicenter of armed conflict throughout Israel's history.

A Tiny Battlefield with Huge Significance

When I first stood atop Tel Megiddo and looked out over the Plain of Megiddo, my first thought was, "Well, if the armies of the world are going to meet here in a great final battle, they're going to have to squeeze in pretty close together." My colleague Eric Cline, who excavated at Megiddo from 1994 to 2014, explained that Megiddo is famous not for the size of the city or the plain below, but for its location as the strategic pass from north to south and east to west in northern Israel.

Because of Megiddo's role as the location of many ancient battles, it is a rich excavation site. In addition to the remains of the five thousand years of battles fought here, Megiddo is also home to artifacts from its settlements dating all the way back to 7000 BCE. (That's six thousand years *before* David and Solomon!) The prominent mound rises 200 feet above its surroundings, with a massive six-chambered gate and tower complex greeting you at the top of a rather steep incline that will literally take your breath away before you even enter the city. You can imagine how difficult it would have been for heavily equipped soldiers to roll their siege machinery up the hill in their attempt to conquer Megiddo. Still, despite its apparent impenetrability, the remains of at least twenty occupation levels (or "cities" that are built one on top of the other) have been discovered there, meaning the military importance of controlling this strategic pass was worth the repeated ancient efforts made to conquer it. Thus, Megiddo is famous for the ancient battles fought to control this symbolic city.

THE ARCHAEOLOGY OF ARMAGEDDON

Megiddo has produced enough important archaeological finds to fill any number of volumes. Among the best-known discoveries at Megiddo is the circular Cana'anite altar built around 2700 BCE, which was in use until approximately 1900 BCE. Cana'anite high places (Heb. *bamot*) and altars existed long before there were Israelites in Cana'an. It was altars and worship centers like these that were probably being envisioned by the authors of Exodus when God commands Moses, "You shall tear down their altars, break their pillars, and cut down their sacred poles" (34:13), and in Deuteronomy 12:2–4, which says:

> *You must demolish completely all the places where the nations whom you are about to dispossess served their gods, on the mountain heights, on the hills, and under every leafy tree. Break down their altars, smash their pillars, burn their sacred poles with fire, and hew down the idols of their gods, and thus blot out their name from their places. You shall not worship the LORD your God in such ways.*

Megiddo boasts a prominent six-chambered gate at its entrance, typically referred to as a "Solomonic Gate," because similar gates have been discovered at other sites (Lachish, Gezer, Ḥaṣor) that archaeologists have traditionally dated to the tenth century BCE, that is, the time of King Solomon. The gates are significant because they incorporate two large towers at the front, which were typically topped with archers, and chambers within the gate that could be filled with soldiers holding lances, spears, and swords to greet any enemy lucky enough to make it through the gate's door. Thus, the six-chambered gates combined a city gate with an

The six-chambered gate of Tel Megiddo.

elaborate gauntlet through which armies must progress in order to take the city.

The Megiddo ivories are also an impressive reminder of Megiddo's wealth and significance before ancient Israel existed as a nation. The ivories were recovered from the treasuries of the early thirteenth- and twelfth-century BCE palaces at Megiddo[1] and include decorated wall plaques, inlaid armrests for chairs or a throne, and game boards for ancient games known as the "Game of 58 Holes" and the "Game of 20 Squares," which are closely related to the ancient Egyptian game *senet,* the ancestor of modern backgammon.[2]

Ivory furniture inlay from Megiddo depicting naked, circumcised prisoners of Semitic origin being led before a king on his throne. Image courtesy Israel Museum.

And then there is the massive underground water system, which is perhaps the most impressive engineering achievement at Megiddo. Megiddo had a problem: it was a massive city at the top of a large tell, but its main water source—a cave hiding a spring to the southwest of the tell—is outside the city wall. Were the city ever put under enemy siege, the residents of Megiddo would not be able to get to their water, and this would lead to defeat. So instead of going to the water, the residents would bring the water to Megiddo. To do this, a monumental tunneling project was undertaken at Megiddo.

Engineers dug a 80-foot-deep vertical shaft from the top of the tell down to the bedrock. (Today, the vertical shaft is covered with modern steel steps and handrails, so that you can descend into the dark, dank belly of the mountain.)

A view of graduate student Cale Staley descending into the subterranean water system at Tel Megiddo.

Meanwhile, the engineers sealed the outside entrance to the spring's cave with a massive stone that would hide it from enemies seeking to tamper with the water supply. Then, engineers dug a 230-foot-long tunnel from the bottom of the vertical shaft toward the spring. Engineers at a later date would renovate the tunnel, sloping it slightly back toward the center of the tell, so that water from the spring would bubble into the tunnel and gravity would transport the water along the tunnel back toward the bottom of the vertical shaft. In this manner, Megiddo residents wouldn't have to descend what are now 187 steps down the vertical shaft or leave the city just to get water for dinner. Instead, they could just lower a jar at the end of a rope down into the cistern.

THE BATTLES OF MEGIDDO

Megiddo's rich archaeological finds and engineering feats reveal its complex history as a cultural center as well as the site of many battles. As mentioned earlier, the most famous reference to Megiddo comes to us from the New Testament book of Revelation, where a great apocalyptic battle "on the great day of God the Almighty" is said to take place at Armageddon. Nearly every great battle in the land variously known over time as Cana'an, Israel, Judah, or Palestine has been fought in or near Megiddo, which protects a main crossroads in the Yizre"el (Jezreel) Valley, a natural passageway connecting the inland route of the Via Maris (or "Way of the Sea") to the Mediterranean, making it a coveted strategic location. Located at the intersection of three continents (Asia, Europe, and Africa), the valley was extremely important to the ancient world, because whoever controlled Megiddo controlled the trade route between Egypt, Europe, and Mesopotamia.[3] These preferred trade routes and the epic battles fought to secure (and tax) them have shaped the history of the Holy Land and are the reason that Megiddo has the reputation it does as a famous battlefield.

The battles fought at and near Megiddo have decided local, regional, and national boundaries for four millennia. In 1479 BCE, Tuthmoses III battled against an uprising involving a coalition of local Cana'anite rulers in the Battle of Megiddo. The coalition was led by the King of Qadesh (in modern western Syria near the border with Lebanon) and included the king of Megiddo. Egypt's victory is recorded in hieroglyphics on the walls of the Temple of Amun-Re at Karnak in Upper Egypt. This battle is the best known and best documented of the many battles that took place at Megiddo prior to the presence of Israelites in Cana'an.

ISRAELITE BATTLES IN MEGIDDO

Once they were established in Israel, the Israelites recorded many other battles involving Megiddo. One such battle was between the Hebrew prophetess Deborah, working with Baraq son of 'Abino'am from Qedesh in the tribal lands of Naftali, and King Yabin of Ḥaṣor, which is recorded in Judges 4–5. The story tells how the Israelites were led to a victory by a woman, even *after* she warned the Israelite leader, "The road on which you are going will not lead to your glory, for the LORD will sell Sisera into the hand of a woman" (4:9).

The story of Deborah also contains one of my favorite biblical stories-within-a-story, which involves another heroine, Ya'el, who (inexplicably) seduces the leader of King Yabin's army, Sisera', into falling asleep in his tent with her. (I say "inexplicably," because the text never mentions any sexual advances on Ya'el's part. But c'mon, how else are you going to get the general of the enemy's army to take you into his tent and fall asleep?) Of course, after Ya'el gives Sisera' a little milk (that's what Judg. 4:19 says—go read it yourself!) and gets him to fall asleep, she gets up, grabs a nearby hammer, and drives a tent peg through Sisera"s temple, staking his head to the ground. (You can insert your own innuendo-based pun here.) Keeping with the biblical theme of women using the tools that God gave them to achieve their goals (e.g., Esther, Tamar, Rebecca, Ruth), Deborah and Ya'el led the Israelites to victory using what they had: prophecy and some hammering in the bedroom.

Another great battle at Megiddo was the one that took place in 922 BCE when Pharaoh Hedjkheperre Setepenre Shoshenq I (r. 943–922 BCE) campaigned in the Holy Land. Evidence of this battle is found in an inscription at the Bubastite Portal gate at Karnak, located to the southeast side within the precinct of Amun-Re temple complex. Most scholars agree that Pharaoh Shoshenq is one and the same as the pharaoh Shishak mentioned in 1 Kings 14:25–28.

According to 1 Kings 14:25, "In the fifth year of King Rehoboam, King Shishak of Egypt came up against Jerusalem." Whether Shoshenq *actually* came up and battled against Jerusalem and looted the Temple or whether he simply bypassed Jerusalem and campaigned against the cities to the west and north of Jerusalem is still debated among archaeologists.[4] This is because although Megiddo and several other strategically important cities are listed in an inscription on the walls of the temple in Karnak as cities conquered by Pharaoh Shoshenq, Jerusalem is *not* listed among them. The only reference to Shishak's conquest against Jerusalem is found in 1 Kings 14:25 and its parallel in 2 Chronicles 12:2–12.[5]

What we *do* know is that Shoshenq battled at Megiddo, which is corroborated not only by the inscription at Karnak, but perhaps also by a fragment of a stele discovered at Megiddo.[6] So although there will be continued debate about whether Shoshenq went up to fight against Jerusalem, there is little doubt that he battled at Megiddo, as it was strategically important to his control over trade into and out of Egypt.

The Israelite military hero Gid'on (Gideon) is also said to have fought a battle against the Midianites and the 'Amaleqites in the Jezreel Valley. Judges 6:33 says, "Then all the Midianites and the Amalekites and the people of the east came together, and crossing the Jordan they encamped in the Valley of Jezreel." So once again, we have a claim that Megiddo was the scene of a battle for the economic and political life of ancient Israel. Judges 7 tells the famous story in which YHWH argues with Gideon (who is there called Yerubba'al) that he has too *many* soldiers, puts Gideon and his army through a series of tests to whittle it down from twenty-two thousand to three hundred (the *other* "three hundred," not the Spartan three hundred), and with them defeats the Midianites and the 'Amaleqites.

But not everything goes well for Israel at Megiddo. Israel's first king, Saul, is said to have died near Megiddo:

> *The next day, when the Philistines came to strip the dead, they found Saul and his three sons fallen on Mount Gilboa. They cut off his head, stripped off his armor, and sent messengers throughout the land of the Philistines to carry the good news to the houses of their idols and to the people. They put his armor in the temple of Astarte; and they fastened his body to the wall of Beth-shan. (1 Sam. 31:8–10)*

Mt. Gilboa is at the eastern end of the Jezreel Valley. It was here that the Bible says Saul and his sons, Jonathan, 'Abinadab, and Malki-shu'a, all died (1 Sam. 31:2). Even if you interpret Saul's death as the fulfillment of prophecy allowing David to ascend to the throne of Israel without having been the one to have killed Saul, the fact that Saul dies in the Jezreel Valley only augments the legend of Megiddo as the place where all significant battles in Israel take place.

In fact, this perception of Megiddo continues to snowball. King Jehoram of Israel is killed in the Jezreel Valley in a coup d'état by his general, Jehu', who became king in his place (2 Kings 8:28–9:24). This same usurping Jehu' then orders King 'Aḥazyah (Aḥaziah) of Judah to be shot, and Aḥaziah flees to Megiddo, where he dies (9:27). Jehu' then orders that Queen 'Izebel (Jezebel) of Israel be tossed out of the palace window in Jezreel near Megiddo, where the horses trample her dead body (9:30–33). In fact, Megiddo's bloody history and strategic importance became so well known throughout the region that it became the administrative center for the Assyrian-controlled province of Samaria under King Tiglath-pileser III from about 745 to 727 BCE.

The final recorded biblical battle at Megiddo—the one that really cemented it as the place where all major battles take place—was the death of "faithful" King Josiah, recorded in 2 Kings 23:29–30 (almost as an afterthought) and retold and expanded (with a few theological apologies added) in 2 Chronicles 35:20–24. It is here at Megiddo that Josiah is said to have died in battle against Pharaoh Neko II in 609 BCE, resulting in the loss of what the Bible considers the last of the great kings of Judah.

MEGIDDO IN REVELATION

It is this history of warfare that took place in the valley below Megiddo that is responsible for so many sections of the Hebrew Bible in Joshua, Judges, Samuel, Kings, and Chronicles, and it is with this history in mind that we can perhaps understand Megiddo's most famous reference in the New Testament book of Revelation. It should come as no surprise that when John of Patmos wished to record his vision of a great apocalyptic battle between good and evil, he chose the location of *Har Megiddo* to symbolize this final apocalyptic battle: "And they assembled them at the place that in Hebrew is called Harmagedon" (Rev. 16:16). When we read the verses about the sixth angel's "bowl of wrath," the assembly of "the kings of the whole world" for battle on "the great day of God the Almighty" at "Harmagedon" (16:12–16) makes *far* more sense, once we understand that *Har Megiddo* was the obvious choice for a metaphor symbolizing a final apocalyptic battle.

Every culture has its own Armageddon. For the Greeks, it was Thermopylae, the great last stand of King Leonidas's three hundred Spartans during the Greco-Persian Wars, made famous by director Zack Snyder and, I'm told, my doppelgänger, Gerard Butler, in the movie *300*. For the Native American tribes of the Lakota, northern Cheyenne, and Arapaho, it was the Battle of the Little Bighorn, commonly known today as "Custer's Last Stand," in which the combined Native American forces in eastern Montana Territory claimed an overwhelming victory over the U.S. 7th Cavalry Regiment during the Great Sioux War of 1876. For the colonists of the Texas Revolution, the metaphor might be "Remember the Alamo" and the famous battle fought there in 1836, when about two hundred Texan soldiers were killed by the Mexican army following a siege of the historic mission. And of course, Napoléon Bonaparte had his "Waterloo" in 1815, when the French army under his command was soundly defeated by the armies of the Seventh Coalition, thereby ending Napoléon's reign as "Emperor of the French."

Ancient Jews understood the name "Har Megiddo" in the same way various groups throughout history understood the symbolic names Thermopylae, Little Bighorn, the Alamo, or Waterloo—as a great battle. Even modern battles perpetuate the legend of Megiddo as the mother of all battle sites. In fact, in 1918, British Field Marshal Edmund Henry Hynman Allenby was named 1st Viscount Allenby of Megiddo for his work leading the Egyptian Expeditionary Force (EEF) during the Sinai and Palestine Campaign. Think about that. He conquered *Jerusalem,* but he wanted the title of "Lord of Megiddo," because at the end of the day, he was a soldier, and Megiddo is the place where the *real* battles are fought and won.

THE LEGACY OF MEGIDDO

To Jewish Christians in the first two centuries CE, Armageddon needed no explanation; they knew *precisely* what it meant. The reference to Megiddo in the book of Revelation meant that despite everything that was going on—the oppression, persecution, and hopelessness Christians were experiencing on earth—behind the scenes there was about to be one *final* battle at Har Megiddo, on the Great Day of God the Almighty, in which good would overcome evil, God would be victorious over the forces of Satan, and all would be made well. Indeed, this message that God would ultimately be victorious over death is the overarching theme of the New Testament, and Megiddo is the symbol of that great victory that inspired early Christians to write down the traditions of their faith and inspires all Christians since then to keep the faith until God returns.

CHAPTER 6

Athens

We would not have Judaism as we know it without hellenization. Hellenization is the word used to describe the influence
of Greek philosophy, religion, language, rhetoric, and culture on
Judaism. Along with Mesopotamian, Cana'anite, and Persian religious traditions, Greek religion and thought made Judaism what it
is today, and Greek thought is rooted in Athens. Thus, Athens is of
great importance to the Bible. Its thought and culture were spread,
along with the Hellenistic empire of Alexander the Great, to the far
reaches of the eastern Mediterranean, including the Holy Land, and
subsequently inspired the philosophical vehicles that would transform and carry the Jewish and later Christian messages to the greater
Western world.

It was during the Hellenistic period (332–167 BCE) that Greek
philosophy and religious thought most heavily influenced Judaism,
splintering Jewish religion into various Jewish sects and expanding
the traditional Jewish focus on righteousness in *this* world to include eternal life in the next. And when Christianity, which further
incorporated Greek philosophy and religious thought, arose, it was
well suited for adoption by other Western cultures—most impor-
tantly Rome—that were predisposed to accept systems of thought
that were rooted in Athens. Therefore, Athens is a city that greatly
influenced the Bible for both Jews and Christians, as it transformed
how their religions were practiced.

CLIMBING THE ACROPOLIS

In many ways, the Acropolis of Athens is not ancient, but rather new and improved. The city of Athens, which is famous for all things ancient, needed many improvements to its infrastructure in preparation for the 2004 Summer Olympics. On a trip there last year, my wife, Roslyn, and I walked on a nearly freezing winter morning past the new Acropolis Museum, which opened in 2009. This is where the Elgin Marbles—the marble statuary taken from the Parthenon and other Acropolis buildings to London by Thomas Bruce, Seventh Earl of Elgin, between 1801 and 1805—will be housed if and when the British Museum ever repatriates the Acropolis artwork to Athens.[1]

As we wound our way to the top of the Acropolis, I couldn't help but think about how much the classical works of Greek literature, Greek history, Greek philosophy, and Greek religion all shaped what today we call "Western culture" and how *all* of that began here in the shadow of the Acropolis of Athens. The tem-

The Parthenon atop the Acropolis of Athens.

ples of this complex were both products of and the inspiration behind the thoughts and reflections upon our human experience in the world that propelled us intellectually to what we've become today. All of the debates in which we engage today about the existence and nature of God (or gods), fate and free will, ethics, politics, economics, emotions—all of it!—have already been conceived, discussed, wrestled with, and written down here. The very mountain that my wife and I were ascending symbolized the best of human civilization and intellectual development.

As we reached the top, we turned and looked out over the sprawling city of Athens, nestled between the Aegean Sea and us, and I exclaimed, "Wow! The pagan world was *really* amazing. It gave us *so much*!"

Roslyn took one large step back away from me and looked toward the sky, awaiting the lightning bolt.

I looked down to the foot of the Acropolis and saw another outcropping of rock: the Areopagus, the rock of Ares. My mind wandered to Acts 17 and Paul's sermon there. As I blocked the biting cold of the wind from my mind, I simultaneously felt small, and yet strangely proud. I felt small because I realized that Ecclesiastes 1:9 is correct: there truly is *nothing* new under the sun; every innovative, original, creative thought I had ever had had actually been thought before, and I was just the latest enlightened soul to think it. And yet I felt proud, because in a very real way I had just taken my rightful place in history as the latest in a long line of individuals who have stood on this very outcropping of rock and have been inspired to think great thoughts and do great deeds. In a very odd way, it was truly a *religious* experience (and I'm not saying that because several shrines to pagan gods were casting shadows on me). Rather, as I experienced the history of Athens, I became a part of it, and becoming *part* of the history of a special place or event is a life-changing experience that can inspire one to do wise, courageous, and amazing things. This is how travel inspires us. This is why I do what I do for a living.

THE HISTORY OF ATHENS

Athens is named after the Athena, virgin goddess of wisdom, courage, strength, justice, strategic warfare (as opposed to her brother, Ares, the bloodthirsty god of violent war), mathematics, arts, crafts, and Athenian culture in general. Athena is said to live atop Mt. Olympus, the tallest mountain in Greece. As we saw with the Ugaritic deities, who resided on top of a mountain, Mt. Ṣafon (Chapter 3), members of the Greek pantheon were said to dwell atop Mt. Olympus, overseen by Zeus, the king of the gods. Most important for us, because Athena is the patron deity of the city of Athens *and* the goddess of wisdom, law, and justice, she came to be worshipped as the patron deity of philosophy.

Athens reached its political and cultural zenith following the end of its wars with Persia in 449 BCE. Some of the most famous and influential Greek intellectuals lived during this time, including tragedians Aeschylus (525–456 BCE), Euripides (480–406), and Sophocles (497/6–406/5); the comic playwright Aristophanes (446–386); the historians Herodotus (484–425), Thucydides (460–400), and Xenophon (430–354); the "Father of Western Medicine," Hippocrates (460–370; and many others associated with him who contributed to the Hippocratic corpus); and the famed philosophers Socrates (470/69–399), Plato (428 or 423–348/7), and Aristotle (384–322).

It was also during this time that the Athenian Acropolis was rebuilt. Upon it were constructed the famed Parthenon (discussed above); other major temples, including the Propylaia, the Temple of Athena Nike, and the Erechtheion; and the Athenian sculptor Phidias's colossal 30-foot bronze statue of Athena Promachos ("Athena who fights in the front line").

Athens came to be resented for its dominance during this period, and following a series of debilitating civil wars and other internal conflicts Philip II of Macedon defeated an alliance of Greek city-states that included Athens in 338 BCE, effectively ending Athenian supremacy in the region. It was Philip II's son,

A maṣṣeboth, *or a collection of standing stones, discovered as part of a large cultic and ceremonial precinct in the upper city of Tel Ḥaṣor in northern Israel, dating from the eighteenth to sixteenth centuries* BCE. *Each stone likely represents a deity worshipped in the city, a practice later forbidden by the Bible (Deut. 16:22).*

The author removing stones from a water cistern at Tel 'Azeqah, Israel. Remains inside the cistern reveal evidence of a destruction layer from the time of the Babylonian invasion of Judah.

The last buckets of dirt excavated from the Area S2 water cistern 16½ feet below ground at Tel 'Azeqah, Israel. The cistern is plastered on the bottom and all sides to prevent water loss.

A close-up of the Akkadian cuneiform text of the law code of Babylonian King Hammurabi.

A view of the descent into the water system at Tel Megiddo. The tunnel is 115 feet deep and 230 feet long.

A view of graduate student Cale Staley descending into the subterranean water system at Tel Megiddo.

The view of the Temple of Hephaestus, Greek god of fire, volcanoes, blacksmiths, and craftsmen, from atop the Acropolis, with the ancient Agora of Athens in the foreground and the modern city of Athens in the background.

A view of the Areopagus of Athens mentioned in Acts 17 as seen from atop the Acropolis, with the modern city of Athens in the background.

The author doing his best Apostle Paul impression on the Areopagus of Athens. Several of the monuments to various Greek deities (under restoration) are easily visible on the Acropolis in the background.

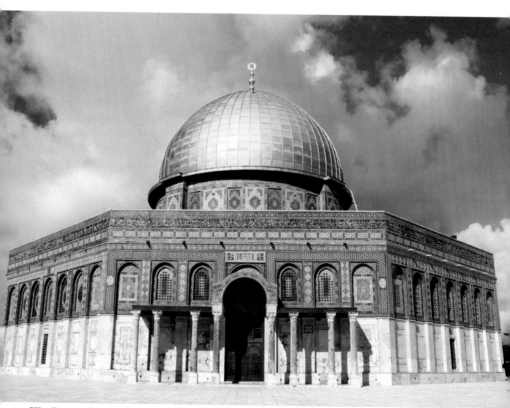

The Dome of the Rock in Jerusalem stands where the Jewish Temple likely once stood. The present shrine was built in 691 CE and commemorates the Muslim Prophet Muḥammad's traditional Isrā' and Mi'rāj, or Night Journey into the heavens.

The Western Wall in Jerusalem, the holiest place in Judaism.

A panel from the Arch of Titus depicts a processional of treasures taken from the Jerusalem Temple as the spoils of war following Rome's Siege of Jerusalem in 70 CE. Visible are the golden Menorah (Exod. 25:31–40), trumpets (Num. 10:2), and a ceremonial table, likely the Table of the Bread of the Presence (Exod. 25:30).

The Mount of Olives across the Qidron Valley east of Jerusalem as seen from the top of the Temple Mount walls.

The famous Cave 4 at Qumran, as seen from the visitor's viewpoint south of the Khirbet
Qumran settlement.

A view of the Qumran plateau visitor's lookout from inside Cave 4.

The author inside Cave 4 at Qumran.

The Door of Humility, the entrance to the Church of the Nativity in Bethlehem, West Bank, built to commemorate the traditional birthplace of Jesus of Nazareth.

The "Pilate Stone" on display in the Israel Museum in Jerusalem. Discovered at Caesarea Maritima, the Latin inscription preserves the line "[PO]NTIVS PILATVS ... [PRAEF]ECTVS IVDA[EA]E," or "Pontius Pilate ... Prefect of Judea." Pilate served in the position from 26 to 36 CE.

The iconic Flavian Amphitheater, commonly known as the Colosseum of Rome, built from 72 to 80 CE.

The inside of the Colosseum in Rome depicting the hypogeum, *the labyrinth of passages and storage chambers that sat beneath the Colosseum floor.*

Alexander "the Great," who went on to spread Greek thought and literature to the greater Near East, bringing Hellenism to cities that were still shaping the Bible.

ALEXANDER'S CONQUEST
AND THE DIADOCHOI

Greek culture influenced the Bible because of one man: Alexander the Great. His conquest of the Mediterranean and Near East introduced Greek culture to Jerusalem, which was at the time the center of the Persian province of Yehud (which would become Judea).[2] Alexander's victory at the Battle of Issus (near the present-day Turkish city of Iskenderun) in 333 BCE and the Battle of Gaugamela (near Nineveh) in 331 BCE meant that Alexander's Hellenic armies controlled the eastern Mediterranean. But following the unexpected death of Alexander the Great in 323 BCE, his kingdom was divided up among a number of his generals, family members, and close friends. These are referred to as the Diadochoi, or "the successors."

Two of the Diadochoi, both generals under Alexander, are important for the composition of the Bible: Ptolemy I Soter (or "Savior," 367–283 BCE) and Seleucus I Nicator (or "Victor," 358–281 BCE). Ptolemy I took control of Egypt. He named himself pharaoh in 304 BCE, and it was from Egypt that the Ptolemaic dynasty ruled Jerusalem and Judea. Under the Ptolemies, Jerusalem had de facto control over its own affairs. Residents were allowed to choose their own high priest and enjoyed relative autonomy.

However, after the Battle of Panium (biblical Caesarea Philippi and modern Banias) in 199 BCE, when the rival Seleucids ruling from Syria defeated the Ptolemies for control of the eastern Mediterranean coastal lands, the Seleucids imposed much harsher hellenizing policies on Jerusalem. Under the rule of Antiochus IV Epiphanes (or "God Manifest," 215–164 BCE), life became intolerable for conservative religious Jews. Antiochus IV's aggressive program of hellenization not only introduced Greek thought, religion, philosophy, and language to the Jewish people, but it also banned Jews from many traditional Jewish religious rites like sacrifice and circumcision. Antiochus IV's actions led to the Maccabean Revolt, in which conservative religious Jews led by Mattathias and his son, Judah Maccabee, his brothers, and their descendants threw off their Greek Seleucid overlords and established an approximately one-hundred-year period of Jewish self-rule under their own Hasmonean dynasty.

We'll discuss the significance and results of hellenization in the next chapter on Alexandria, but it is important to note that one book of the Hebrew Bible directly mentions the Greek conquest of the eastern Mediterranean—and specifically the actions of Antiochus IV. This book is Daniel, which cleverly chronicles the conquest by the Greek Seleucids not as history, but as a prophecy.

HELLENIZATION IN DANIEL

Chapter 8 of the canonical book of Daniel describes the rise and fall of Alexander the Great as well as the rise of Antiochus IV using metaphorical, apocalyptic language as the literary vehicle of the vision. Apocalyptic is a style of writing that incorporates wildly vivid, yet meticulously symbolic visions set as prophecy usually of the end times, but is actually a commentary about the author's *present* situation and his hopes for tomorrow. The second half of Daniel is unique in that it is apocalyptic prophecy actually set in the past, meaning that the author is "foretelling" things that appear to have already happened. In doing so, Daniel 8 preserves an encoded commentary on the rise of Antiochus IV and his oppressive policies in Jerusalem.

Let's take a look at a few select passages of Daniel to see how these events are described. Daniel 8:1–2 recounts the history of Jerusalem and the greater Near East from the Neo-Babylonian Empire to the reign of the Seleucid king Antiochus IV. Then

8:3–4 describes the rise of the two-horned ram, representing the initially dominant Medes and the Achaemenid Persians who later overtook the Medes, and its conquest along the Fertile Crescent of the Neo-Babylonians to the west, its conquest north up the Tigris and Euphrates Rivers, and its campaign southward into Cana'an:

I looked up and saw a ram standing beside the river. It had two horns. Both horns were long, but one was longer than the other, and the longer one came up second. I saw the ram charging westward and northward and southward. All beasts were powerless to withstand it, and no one could rescue from its power; it did as it pleased and became strong.

Daniel 8:5–8 discusses the rise and fall of a male goat with one horn (yes, a unicorn goat), representing Alexander the Great, and his conquest of the Median-Persian two-horned ram (vv. 6–7). In antiquity (and in apocalyptic symbolism), horns represent power. Thus, as Alexander the Great was a single conqueror, he is represented by a powerful single-horned animal. Verse 8 then describes the death of Alexander and the rise of the "four prominent horns," representing the Diadochoi, the successors to his divided kingdom:

As I was watching, a male goat appeared from the west, coming across the face of the whole earth without touching the ground. The goat had a horn between its eyes. It came toward the ram with the two horns that I had seen standing beside the river, and it ran at it with savage force. I saw it approaching the ram. It was enraged against it and struck the ram, breaking its two horns. The ram did not have power to withstand it; it threw the ram down to the ground and trampled upon it, and there was no one who could rescue the ram from its power. Then the male goat grew exceedingly great; but at the height of its power, the great horn was broken, and in its place there came up four prominent horns toward the four winds of heaven.

Daniel 8:9–12 discusses the rise of the "little horn that grew exceedingly great," which represents Antiochus IV, and gives an apocalyptic description of Antiochus IV's actions against Jerusalem, including interfering with the Jerusalem priesthood and halting the sacrifices at the Temple:

Out of one of them came another horn, a little one, which grew exceedingly great toward the south, toward the east, and toward the beautiful land. It grew as high as the host of heaven. It threw down to the earth some of the host and some of the stars, and trampled on them. Even against the prince of the host it acted arrogantly; it took the regular burnt offering away from him and overthrew the place of his sanctuary. Because of wickedness, the host was given over to it together with the regular burnt offering; it cast truth to the ground, and kept prospering in what it did.

Daniel 8:13–14 adds a time component pertaining to Antiochus IV's reign: "'For how long is this vision concerning the regular burnt offering, the transgression that makes desolate, and the giving over of the sanctuary and host to be trampled?' And he answered him, 'For two thousand three hundred evenings and mornings; then the sanctuary shall be restored to its rightful state.'" The reference to 2,300 days (1 day is one evening and one morning)[3] adds up to a little over six years on a 365-day calendar or half of that if the evenings and mornings are being counted separately. However it is counted, the period is intended as a comment about the duration of Antiochus's policies.[4]

Thus, Daniel 8 preserves a commentary of the rise of Antiochus IV and his oppressive regime in Jerusalem. But although Antiochus IV's brand of Hellenism was harsh, the general spread of Greek thought was ubiquitous and Jews living in antiquity far more readily accepted and adopted aspects of Greek culture than rejected it. And nowhere is this more evident than with regard to Greek philosophy.

GREEK PHILOSOPHIES
THAT INFLUENCED THE BIBLE

With the advent of Hellenism and particularly Greek thought in the lands where Jews were living, it was inevitable that Greek philosophy would influence both the Old and New Testaments of the Bible. But before we look at how Greek philosophy helped shape the Bible, we should discuss a few of the philosophical schools that are mentioned by name or whose teachings are found in the Bible.

STOICISM

Stoicism was a school of Greek philosophy founded in Athens by Zeno of Citium early in the third century BCE. Stoics were characterized by their lack of expression of emotions they considered to be destructive, like anger, jealousy, and pride. They believed these emotions were the result of errors of thought, and therefore those who rid themselves of these emotions could achieve moral and intellectual perfection. Imagine Mr. Spock from *Star Trek* (or Commander Data for you *The Next Generation* fans) when thinking about Stoics. But far from being dour, Stoics actually sought to cultivate joy through mental discipline and virtuous living. Famous Stoics include statesman and dramatist Seneca the Younger (4 BCE–65 CE), Epictetus (55–135 CE), and the Roman emperor Marcus Aurelius (r. 161–80 CE). The apostle Paul is said to have debated with Stoic philosophers in Acts 17:18.

CYNICISM

The founding of Cynicism as a school of Greek philosophy is credited to Antisthenes (445–365 BCE), who was a disciple of Socrates (470/69–399 BCE). Cynics believed in living a virtuous life in agreement with nature, which they interpreted as the rejection of vanity, fame, power, cultural sophistication, sex, wealth, and personal possessions. They praised the "simple lifestyle" and a life consisting only of the bare necessities for survival. Cynics are so named after the Greek word for "dog" (κύων, think "canine") because of their doglike behavior: they eat, sleep, pee, and poop anywhere and have a penchant for "barking" at others (i.e., preaching their message) in the public square.

Perhaps the most famous Cynic was Diogenes of Sinope (412 or 404–323 BCE), who is said to have lived in a large *pithos,* or ceramic storage vessel, in the alleys of Athens. Several scholars have argued that Jesus and Paul's critique of wealth, earthly power, and pride and their promotion of a life spent in pursuit of the virtue of poverty were at the very least influenced by Cynicism.

EPICUREANISM

Epicureanism was a school of Greek philosophy founded by Epicurus (341–270 BCE) at the very end of the fourth century BCE. Epicurus taught that seeking what he called "pleasure" was the ideal in life. Many Christians have mischaracterized Epicurean pleasure as a hedonistic philosophy seeking "all pleasure and no pain," one that is obsessed with sexual excess, gluttony, drunkenness, decadence, and cowardice, but this is a common rhetorical misrepresentation. In fact, Epicurus defined pleasure as the absence of fear (mental stress) and pain (physical stress) and taught that frugal, modest living, personal sacrifices for the long-term good, and the lifelong pursuit of knowledge were the best means by which to achieve such pleasure.[5] The motivation behind the Christian mischaracterization of Epicureanism is more likely due to the fact that Epicureans regularly critiqued theistic religions and superstition. Famous Epicureans include the Roman poet Lucretius, whose poem *On the Nature of Things* is said to be the best summary of Epicurean thought in antiquity. The apostle Paul is also said to have debated with Epicurean philosophers in Acts 17:18.

PLATONISM

Platonism is the philosophical school associated with one of the best-known classical philosophers in history, Plato (428 or 423–348/7 BCE). Plato founded his Academy in Athens in 387 BCE, which is considered the first institution of higher learning in the world. The Academy influenced Western thought, culture, and science, and its legacy continues to this day. Plato's famous theory of Forms postulates that material objects we encounter on earth have an idealized, nonmaterial "form" in a higher realm and that the objects we experience with our senses on earth are but mere reflections of these idealized forms. This dualist theory is explained by Plato using the Allegory of the Cave, which suggests that while on earth we see only shadows on the walls of the cave (in which we live) of *real* objects that exist outside the cave (representing their existence in the world of forms). It is this idea of two worlds that the later Neoplatonists would adopt into Christianity and use to explain the world as divided into the ideal heavenly realm, in which God operates, and our physical realm, which is merely a reflection of it (cf. 1 Cor. 13:12; Heb. 1:3).

NEOPLATONISM

The Platonist philosopher Plotinus (204–70 CE) added mystical elements to Platonism in the third century CE and founded what scholars today call Neoplatonism. Although it is difficult to describe beyond calling it "mystical Platonism," Plotinus argued that all of reality was created by and exists because of a single, indescribable, unknowable principle he called "the One." Ironically, Neoplatonists were originally opposed to Christianity; Plotinus's student, Porphyry of Tyre, wrote a work called *Against the Christians,* which was one of the earliest refutations of Christianity.[6] The Roman emperor Constantine the Great (272–337) banned every copy, as did Emperor Theodosius II (401–50), who ordered the burning of any existing copy of *Against the Christians* in 435 and again in 448.

However, given its belief in a single, divine source of all things and its dualistic worldview, one can see how Christians could be attracted to an altered form of Neoplatonism, which is exactly what happened when St. Augustine of Hippo (354–430) reinterpreted "the One" of Neoplatonism as the *logos* in the first chapter of the Gospel of John. Since that time, many Christians have attempted to conflate what they believe to be Platonist, Neoplatonist, and Second Temple Jewish apocalyptic thought with Christian thought, producing many of the popular Christian worldviews we have today, like the belief that a spiritual battle is taking place in another realm that can occasionally affect the lives of those in this *earthly* realm.

GREEK PHILOSOPHY IN QOHELET (ECCLESIASTES)

Hellenization was so pervasive in the ancient Jewish world that it seems inevitable that we would find some Greek philosophical influence within the pages of the Bible. One of the prime examples of Greek philosophy in the Hebrew Bible is found in the book of Qohelet (Ecclesiastes).[7] Scholars have long considered Qohelet to contain elements of Greek philosophy, including Cynic, Stoic, and Epicurean ideals. This is because peppered throughout Qohelet is philosophy that doesn't necessarily match up with the theology of the rest of the Bible.

Qohelet never refers to God as YHWH, but instead often uses the term "the God" (האלהים, *ha-'elohim*) with the definite article, to refer to the deity almost impersonally. This impersonal approach is consistent with the skeptical nature of the arguments of the book.

Qohelet begins with the famous line, "Vanity of vanities, all is vanity." Other versions translate "vanity" as "meaningless" (NIV) or "futility" (JPS). In fact, the opening eleven verses of Qohelet appear at first glance to be so foreign to the rest of the Bible that the early rabbis actually debated in the Mishnah (the first written edition of

Jewish oral traditions, also known as the "Oral Torah") whether Qohelet was "inspired" and should be allowed in the canon![8]

Qohelet is full of lines that appear to reflect Cynic and Epicurean philosophy:

> *I said in my heart with regard to human beings that God is testing them to show that they are but animals.* For the fate of humans and the fate of animals is the same; as one dies, so dies the other. *They all have the same breath, and* humans have no advantage over the animals; for all is vanity. All go to one place; *all are from the dust, and all turn to dust again.* Who knows whether the human spirit goes upward and the spirit of animals goes downward to the earth? *So I saw that there is nothing better than that all should enjoy their work, for that is their lot. (3:18–22)*

> *And I thought the dead, who have already died, more fortunate than the living, who are still alive; but* better than both is the one who has not yet been, *and has not seen the evil deeds that are done under the sun. (4:2–3)*

> *Do not all go to one place? (6:6)*[9]

Qohelet's theology appears to be so different from that of the remainder of the Hebrew Bible that many scholars believe it to be a *critique* of the predominant "vending machine" theology found in Deuteronomy—which rewards those who keep God's law and punishes those who do not. In fact, this may be the genius behind the book and of those Jewish leaders who voted to retain it as part of the canon. The organizers of the Hebrew Bible were smart enough to realize that the Jewish experience during the Hellenistic and late Second Temple periods was different for different Jews. Some strands of the Jewish experience had, in fact, gone beyond the idealized Deuteronomistic theology of the exilic and Persian periods and were now better expressed by the teachings of various Greek philosophical schools. Thus, we should expect that some Jewish authors during the Hellenistic period incorporated various Greek philosophies into Judaism in an attempt to better express their own Jewish reality. It is to Judaism's credit that it preserved these diverse traditions in its canon instead of banishing and burning those books that did not fit the narrow dogmas defined by certain religious leaders, as was done in later religions. (I'm looking at you, church fathers and early Christianity.)

GREEK PHILOSOPHY
IN THE NEW TESTAMENT

The Hebrew Bible isn't the only part of the Bible that experienced Greek influence. Because the sect of Jews that believed Jesus of Nazareth to be the promised Messiah (later called "Christians") was a thoroughly hellenized Jewish movement, we should not be surprised that the New Testament in several places exhibits examples of Greek thought.

Greek deities and otherworldly places make several appearances in the New Testament. "Gehenna"[10] became the term used most often in the New Testament for the fiery underworld abode that came to be known as "hell,"[11] but two other Greek words are used to reference this place of unquenchable fire as well. The first is Hades (Gk. ᾅδης), the Greek god of the underworld, whose name became synonymous with the abode of the dead.[12] The second is Tartarus (Gk. Τάρταρος; 2 Pet. 2:4), the deep dungeon of torment beneath Hades reserved for the vilest of criminals, where they are punished for eternity. Famous residents of Tartarus in Greek mythology include Tantalus, who sacrificed his son, Pelops, and served him at a banquet to the gods, who punished him by standing him in a pool (whose water he could never drink) beneath an abundant fruit tree (whose fruit he could never eat), giving us the word "tantalize"; and Sisyphus, who tricked Death into chaining himself in Tartarus, for which he was punished by being eternally forced to roll a boulder up a hill, only to watch it roll back down and have to begin again. It is the idea of Tartarus that became the popular image of hell as a place of eternal punishment in the Christian tradition.

But Greek influence on Christianity wasn't limited to the concept of hell. The idea of an independent *soul* (ψυχή, *psyche*) that exists apart from the body is a Greek contribution to very late Jewish and then Christian theology. Prior to the hellenization of Judaism, the Hebrew word *nefesh* (נפש) simply designated something that was alive; that is, in the early Hebrew Bible, *nefesh* meant simply "life" or "living," and it was lost when living beings died.[13] Throughout the Hebrew Bible, when a person died, he or she was said to go to a place called *she'ol* (Heb. שאול), which is where all living beings went when they died.[14] There is no concept of life after death in the Hebrew Bible until we begin to see it appear in books that were written at a very late date (like Daniel), and even then the life after death described there involved *resurrection* from the dead, not the transcendence of an immortal soul.[15] It was only much later, following a period of sustained, invasive hellenization, that the word *nefesh* would come to be used as equivalent to the Greek idea of the soul,[16] something that would transcend your body and live beyond your physical life—a concept that was then adopted by early Christianity.

Greek influence on the New Testament is not limited to a few borrowed words and concepts. Rather, the New Testament preserves numerous quotes from many famous Greek writers (usually without attribution). On many occasions in the New Testament, Paul's letters employ the writings of Greek authors as a rhetorical device to convince Greek listeners that the gospel Paul was preaching was similar to the great teachings of those legendary Greek philosophers. Thus, much of what Paul wrote was either inspired by classical philosophers or taken directly from their writings. The New Testament may have been written by "inspired men," but precisely where that inspiration may have come from is debated by scholars.

Of course, Paul *says* that he dislikes philosophy, preferring the "folly" of the Christian message (see 1 Cor. 1:18). This stands in opposition to many Jewish attempts to make the Jewish faith as palatable to Romans as possible by recasting Jewish religion and literature as Hellenistic philosophy. Both Philo of Alexandria (25 BCE–50 CE) and Flavius Josephus (37–100 CE) did this in their writings. Paul chastises Greek "wisdom" in 1 Corinthians 1:18–31, and Colossians 2:8 offers a full-blown warning against philosophy: "See to it that no one takes you captive through philosophy and empty deceit, according to human tradition, according to the elemental spirits of the universe, and not according to Christ."

However much Paul may rail against the content of Greek philosophy, especially when it is at odds with his gospel, he nonetheless references the pagan Greek philosophers and utilizes classical forms of rhetoric in his preaching. This may come as a shock to some readers, but a quick look at a few obvious examples will demonstrate Paul's use of Greek philosophy.

For instance, Paul states in 1 Corinthians 15:33: "Do not be deceived: 'Bad company ruins good morals.'" Many scholars attribute this quote to the dramatist Menander (342–290 BCE), from his comedy *Thaïs,* which he, in turn, likely quoted from the Greek tragedian Euripides (480–406 BCE).[17] The church historian Socrates of Constantinople (380–439 CE) attributes the quote to Euripides in his *Ecclesiastical History:* "Again this sentence, 'Evil communications corrupt good manners,' is a sufficient proof that he was conversant with the tragedies of Euripides" (3.16). Thus, Paul is quoting an existing Greek saying without actually crediting the author.[18]

In Titus 1:12, we read an interesting passage attributed to Paul (likely an author claiming to be Paul) written to Titus, who oversees a church in Crete, regarding some rabble-rousers who are essentially not teaching what Paul taught. In the midst of the author's instruction to censor these false teachers, he states, "It was one of them, their very own prophet, who said, 'Cretans are always liars, vicious brutes, lazy gluttons.'" Here the author acknowledges that he is quoting an unnamed "prophet" who is believed to be Epimenides of Knossos

according to Socrates of Constantinople.[19] A Greek poet and scholar
at the Library of Alexandria, Callimachus of Cyrene (310 or 305–240
BCE), also appears to cite the line in his *Hymn to Zeus:*

> *O Zeus, some say that thou wert born on the hills of Ida; others,*
> *O Zeus, say in Arcadia; did these or those, O Father, lie? "Cretans*
> *are ever liars." Yea, a tomb, O Lord, for thee the Cretans builded;*
> *but thou didst not die, for thou art for ever.*[20]

The apostle Paul also appears to have alluded to (if not quoted
outright) Plato on at least a couple of occasions. Paul writes in
Philippians 1:21, "For to me, living is Christ and *dying is gain.*"
Plato said almost identically, "Now if death is like this, *I say to
die is gain.*"[21] On another occasion, Paul writes, "See that none of
you repays evil for evil, but always seek to do good to one another
and to all" (1 Thess. 5:15). Plato writes something similar at least
four hundred years earlier when he recounts Socrates's statement:
"Then we ought neither to requite wrong with wrong nor to do
evil to anyone."[22] In 1 Corinthians 9:24, Paul writes, "Do you not
know that in a race the runners all compete, but only one receives
the prize? Run in such a way that you may win it." He appears yet
again to be channeling Plato's most famous work, the *Republic,* in
which Plato writes, "But the true runners when they have come to
the goal receive the prizes and bear away the crown."[23]

Paul may also have been familiar with the teachings of
Aristotle. In Galatians 5:23, Paul utters the line, "*There is no law
against such things.*" He dictates a similar line in Romans 2:14,
when he says, "When Gentiles, who do not possess the law, do
instinctively what the law requires, these, though not having the
law, *are a law to themselves.*" Both lines seem to echo the words of
Aristotle, who four hundred years earlier wrote in *Politics,* "but
there can be no law dealing with such men as those described,
for they are themselves a law."[24] Again, we see that Paul uses the
rhetoric and popular lines, in this case, of Aristotle to make
his argument.

Perhaps one of my favorite instances of Paul's incorporation of the work of a classical Greek author is in Acts 26:14–15. Here Paul recounts his conversion experience on the road to Damascus as part of his trial before Herod Agrippa II and states that he heard Jesus speak to him from the heavens:

> *When we had all fallen to the ground, I heard a voice saying to me in the Hebrew language, "Saul, Saul, why are you persecuting me? It hurts you to* kick against the goads*." I asked, "Who are you, Lord?" The Lord answered, "I am Jesus whom you are persecuting."*

In the expression "kick against the goads" (KJV: "kick against the pricks"),[25] "goads" are spurs used to prod horses and other animals to move along. "Kicking against the goads" is what an animal does when it's being stubborn; hence Jesus's comment to the stubborn Paul. What is interesting is that this expression actually comes from the play *Agamemnon* by the Greek tragedian Aeschylus (525–456 BCE). In the play, the antagonist, Aegisthus, who was sleeping with Agamemnon's wife, Clytemnestra, says the following, "Kick not against the pricks, lest thou strike to thy hurt."[26]

So we have evidence either that Jesus loved Greek tragedies and recited Hebrew translations of his favorite lines from heaven or that Paul may have been attempting to impress the Roman procurator at the time, Porcius Festus, who oversaw Paul's trial (Acts 25:24), by attributing to Jesus an expression from a popular Greek play (which was *left out* of the account of the same conversion experience in Acts 9:3–9) or to impress King Herod Agrippa II by claiming Jesus uttered the line *in Hebrew*.[27] Regardless, the fact that Jesus is said to utter a line from a Greek tragedy should not be lost to careful readers.

PAUL IN ATHENS

But Paul's most obvious incorporation of Greek philosophy and classical writings comes from his famous "Areopagus Sermon" in Athens, recorded in Acts 17:16–34. The book of Acts suggests that the beginnings of Christianity reached Athens via the apostle Paul, who the Bible says visited the city on his second missionary trip.

Paul's famous sermon on the Areopagus in Athens has long been cited as an example of Paul's (or the author of Acts's) skilled rhetoric. Rather than lashing out at the Athenians for worshipping gods other than YHWH, as the Hebrew prophets of old had done against idolators, Paul is said to have praised the Athenians' religiosity in order to hold their attention as he introduced his gospel to them.

The speech begins in Acts 17:16–18:

> *While Paul was waiting for them in Athens, he was deeply distressed to see that the city was full of idols. So he argued in the synagogue with the Jews and the devout persons, and also in the marketplace every day with those who happened to be there. Also some Epicurean and Stoic philosophers debated with him. Some said, "What does this babbler want to say?"*

The author of Acts sets Paul on equal footing with the Epicureans and Stoics and then uses the well-attested culture of debate at the Areopagus (17:19) as the setting for Paul's testimony to the Jewish God and Christ's role in this tradition. As Roslyn and I gazed down upon the Areopagus from atop the Acropolis, we imagined Paul preaching below.

Acts 17:22–23 follows:

> *Then Paul stood in front of the Areopagus and said, "Athenians, I see how extremely religious you are in every way. For as I went through the city and looked carefully at the objects of your worship, I found among them an altar with the inscription, 'To an*

unknown god.' What therefore you worship as unknown, this I proclaim to you."

Note how Paul cleverly uses the presence of the many architectural monuments to various deities atop the Athenian Acropolis looming in the background to invite those listening to hear about a god they did not yet know about.

Paul continues by giving a summary of the Jewish faith, arguing first that "the God who made the world and everything in it, he who is Lord of heaven and earth, does not live in shrines made by human hands" (17:24). Paul's phrase "does not live in shrines made by human hands" may actually be a reference to the work *On Benefits* by the Roman Stoic philosopher Lucius Annaeus Seneca "the Younger" (4 BCE–65 CE), who lived during the time of Jesus and whom the church father Tertullian (155–240 CE) called "our Seneca."[28] Seneca wrote, "The whole world is the temple of the gods,"[29] and is quoted by Lactantius (250–325 CE) as having said, "Temples are not to be built to God of stones piled on high. He must be consecrated in the heart of every man,"[30] echoing the same sentiment.

Paul's statement in Acts 17:25, "Nor is he served by human hands, as though he needed anything, since he himself gives to all mortals life and breath and all things," sounds a lot like another of Seneca's statements from his *Moral Letters to Lucilius:* "For God seeks no servants. Of course not; he himself services mankind, everywhere and to all he is at hand to help."[31]

Seneca also stated in the same letter, "We are the parts of one great body. Nature produced us related to one another, since she created us from the same source and to the same end."[32] Paul seems to have had this in mind when he argues in 17:26, "From one ancestor he made all nations to inhabit the whole earth," perhaps adapting Seneca's quote to fit with his own belief in a historical Adam.

Paul then appears to reference Seneca's *Moral Letters* once again when he states in 17:28, "In him we live and move and have our being." This is quite similar to Seneca's claims that "God is at hand

A view of the Acropolis of Athens from the Areopagus. Note that several of the monuments to various Greek deities (under restoration) are easily visible from the Areopagus.

A view of the Areopagus of Athens mentioned in Acts 17 as seen from atop the Acropolis, with the modern city of Athens in the background.

everywhere and to all men. . . . God is near you; he is with you; he is within you"[33] and that "a holy spirit indwells within us,"[34] demonstrating that Paul was well versed in Seneca's writings.

Paul follows this by acknowledging in Acts 17:28 that he, in fact, *is* referencing Greek authors: "Even as some of your own poets have said, '*For we too are his offspring.*'" This is a direct (but unattributed) reference to the Greek poet Aratus of Soli (315 or 310–240 BCE), who in his *Phaenomena* ("Appearances") wrote *of Zeus:* "We all have need of Zeus always! *For we are also his offspring;* and in his kindness to men he gives favorable signs and awakens the people to work, reminding them of livelihood."[35] Again, Paul appears to be lifting out of context individual phrases from well-known Greek works in a rhetorical attempt to make the Hebrew God appear more acceptable to Greek Hellenistic philosophers. Paul argues that the Greeks are correct in arguing that we are all the offspring of the same deity, but this deity is YHWH, not Zeus.

Finally, in Acts 17:29, Paul returns to channeling Seneca's *Moral Letters* when he says, "Since we are God's offspring, we ought not to think that the deity is like gold, or silver, or stone, an image formed by the art and imagination of mortals." This again echoes the writings of Seneca: "And fashion yourself worthy of God.[36] This fashioning will not be done in gold or silver; an image that is to be in the likeness of God cannot be fashioned of such materials."[37]

Thus, we can conclude that at just about every point in Paul's classic Areopagus speech, he is making allusions and direct references to the works of classical Greek authors, which would have served the rhetorical purpose of making his gospel of Jesus sound more like traditional Hellenistic philosophy, with the hope that it would sound familiar to the men on the Areopagus and therefore be more convincing to them. It is also further evidence that Greek thought and literature *directly* impacted the words of the apostle Paul, who cited and referenced them specifically. This means that the words of the Greek philosophers and writers directly contributed to the composition of the Bible itself, as many sentences that form the "Word of God" are actually famous lines from classical Greek authors.

THE LEGACY OF ATHENS

Athens is far more important to the Bible than the few brief mentions within its pages. Athens was the center of the very Greek philosophy, religious ideas, language, and culture that were conveyed to the Holy Land following Alexander the Great's conquests. This Greek culture would later integrate with and redefine Second Temple Judaism, transforming the Jewish and later Christian beliefs that would go on to shape the Western world. Paul's recasting of Judaism and the Christian message in the language of Hellenistic and Roman philosophy allowed it to be welcomed beyond the borders of Judea. In fact, it can be said that without Athens and hellenization, Judaism and Christianity would have never left Roman Palestine.

Because Greek philosophy and religious thought—particularly views of an independent soul and the afterlife—so heavily influenced Judaism during the Hellenistic period, Judaism and Christianity came to be concerned with right living in *this* world as the means of achieving eternal life in the *next*. Thus, it can be said that Athens literally contributed the "soul" to both Judaism and Christianity.

CHAPTER 7

Alexandria

In Chapter 1 we discussed Egypt's most famous export (other than Pyramid souvenirs and mummy movies), namely, papyrus, the forerunner to modern paper, which was originally made from the pith of the papyrus plants found along the banks of the Nile. The plant fibers were layered and pressed into flexible, smooth sheets that could be sewn together to form a scroll and written upon.[1]

Most people are familiar with the modern capital city of Egypt, Cairo. They know about the famed Pyramids of Giza and the Sphinx and recall vividly when the *Raiders of the Lost Ark* character Sallah belted out the line, "Cairo, city of the living!" in his distinctive voice. But many may not realize that the center of the Egyptian world in the first millennium CE was not in Cairo, but a

The Great Sphinx of Giza with the Great Pyramid of Khufu in the background.

Mediterranean coastal city that is never mentioned in the Hebrew Bible and only referenced in passing in the New Testament; this is the city of Alexandria.[2]

The importance of Alexandria to the Bible stems from the fact that it is where the Hebrew Bible was translated from Hebrew (and Aramaic) into Greek, and where many of the books that comprise the Apocrypha were created. Thus, it must be said that Alexandria made it possible for the Hebrew Bible to live beyond Persian-period Judaism, as it made the Bible accessible to a Jewish population that increasingly favored Greek and Aramaic as its primary languages. This transition to a Greek Bible allowed Judaism to become a viable religion and philosophy in the ever-expanding Greco-Roman world.

THE LIBRARY OF ALEXANDRIA

Founded on the westernmost edge of the Nile Delta by its name-sake in 331 BCE, Alexandria was transformed by Alexander the Great from a major Egyptian port town into the seat of the Ptolemaic rulers of Egypt. Alexandria remained the capital of Hellenistic, Roman, and Byzantine Egypt until the Muslim conquest of Egypt in 641 CE. Alexandria also became the center of knowledge of the Western world. It was famous in antiquity for its lighthouse (Gk. Φάρος, or Pharos), one of the seven wonders of the ancient world, and of course for its library.

Roslyn and I found that getting to Alexandria can be a nightmare and is not recommended for travelers who are elderly or claustrophobic, have motion sickness, or dislike heavy smoking, body odor, or live poultry on overcrowded trains. The city of Alexandria also suffers from significant infrastructural problems, which have only been exacerbated by two full-scale Egyptian revolutions in the past five years. Pollution, insufficient city planning, traffic congestion, and consistently slow response from governmental service agencies all detract from this otherwise popular tourist destination. In October of 2015, rainfall from severe storms flooded the city, leading to the deaths of at least seven people, five of whom were electrocuted when a live power line broke and fell into a flooded street on which they were standing.[3] Walking through the streets of modern Alexandria it is sometimes hard to imagine that this was once the center of the intellectual world.

Of course, as you work your way toward the Alexandrian waterfront, you will eventually happen upon the Bibliotheca Alexandrina—the *new* Library of Alexandria—a beautiful, modern architectural tribute to the original Library of Alexandria, which was mysteriously destroyed long ago and to which we now turn.

The Royal Library of Alexandria was the center of the intellectual world twenty-two hundred years ago. Back then, libraries weren't just places to read books (which were rare enough on their own), but were centers of learning that more closely resemble the colleges and universities we have today. Scholars and

Inside the new Bibliotheca Alexandrina in Alexandria, Egypt. Photo by Stewart Perkins.

philosophers would travel to Alexandria and take up residence
for an extended period of time not just to read the books that were
present there, but also to discuss intellectual matters with other
scholars. It was essentially *the* real-time, crowd-sourced mechanism for scholarly collaboration and peer review two thousand
years before the Internet.

The library was built in the third century BCE and is traditionally credited to Ptolemy I, who, as we learned in the last chapter,
ruled over Egypt with Alexandria as its capital after Alexander's
death in 323 BCE. His Ptolemaic dynasty ruled Egypt until the
Roman conquest in 30 BCE. In addition to collections of books,
the library possessed lecture halls, meeting rooms, and gardens. It
was part of a larger research institution called the "Musaeum of
Alexandria," where many of the most famous thinkers of the ancient world studied. The Library of Alexandria was dedicated to
the Greek *Mousai* (Μοῦσαι), or Muses, the nine patron goddesses
of the arts. In fact, we get our English word "museum" from the
muses (hence "Musaeum"), who were actually the personifica-
tion of the arts, or the nine applications of knowledge at the time.
They were responsible for song and dance and all of the different
forms of music and poetry.[4]

Unfortunately, the Library of Alexandria met a terrible fate,
although who actually burned down the famed library is still a
mystery. Plutarch wrote that a fire during Julius Caesar's Civil War
in 48 BCE, which included the Siege of Alexandria, is responsible for
the accidental burning of the library.[5] Others say it occurred during the attack of the Roman emperor Lucius Domitius Aurelianus
(Aurelian) over three hundred years later, sometime between 270
and 275 CE, when the Brucheion (the Royal Quarter in Alexandria
where the library stood) was burned to the ground.

Others suggest it might have been Pope Theophilus, the
twenty-third pope of the Coptic Orthodox Church of Alexandria,
who in 391 CE legalized and endorsed state persecution of pagan-
ism, leading to the destruction of all of the "heathen temples,"
buildings, and "pagan" monuments in Alexandria. One of these

"pagan" centers may have been the Library of Alexandria, which housed writings that contained centuries of pre-Christian (and therefore "non-Christian," and therefore "heretical" or "pagan") thoughts and beliefs.[6]

However, the answer to the question of who destroyed the Library of Alexandria may be a lot less dramatic. Beginning in the early second century BCE, many scholars began to leave Alexandria for less politically volatile locations, and in 145 BCE Ptolemy VIII Eugeretes II (nicknamed "Physcon," meaning "sausage" or "potbelly," by the people because of his obesity) expelled all foreign intellectuals from Alexandria as part of a campaign of revenge against those who had opposed him politically.[7] This led to the gradual demise of the Library of Alexandria, whose fate was more than likely a steady descent into disrepair and neglect rather than one single great conflagration.

Most of the books were kept as papyrus scrolls, and though it is unknown how many such scrolls were housed at any given time, their combined value was incalculable. The Library of Alexandria thus was not only the greatest repository of the Western and Near Eastern world's knowledge, but became a symbol for knowledge that is wise, meaningful, and worthy of retention throughout history.

So one can understand the embarrassment many Jews may have felt when they realized that there was no copy of their Hebrew Scriptures in the Library of Alexandria. Judaism was becoming increasingly hellenized during the third and second centuries BCE, and yet a record of Jewish history and religious beliefs was not deemed worthy of inclusion among the world's great literature. It is likely that as Jews began speaking (and reading and writing) Greek, learned Jewish scribes slowly began translating the Hebrew Scriptures into Greek, giving us what we today call the Septuagint, which is abbreviated using the Roman numerals for seventy, or LXX.[8] The creation of an official Greek translation of the Hebrew Bible was significant, because it quickly became the standard Bible for all Jews throughout Egypt and Palestine.

As with many translations of important documents, the problem became whether Jews could trust a new, Greek translation of the Hebrew Scriptures. Remember, we're not talking about translating just *any* book like a treaty or a book of medicinal remedies, but *the* collection of "Scripture"—sacred texts narrating the creation of the earth, tales of the patriarchs, the religious laws to be followed by Jewish people, Jewish prophecy, and the very *words of God*—now being read in Greek, *not* Hebrew. This wasn't an easy shift for some Jews of the first few centuries BCE who felt the integrity of their beloved Hebrew Bible might be threatened by invasive Greek ideas present in a Greek translation. Greek-speaking Jews needed assurances that the Greek Bible they were reading was the *actual* word of God, as they believed their Hebrew Bible to be. And this reassurance came in the form of the *Letter of Aristeas*.

THE SIGNIFICANCE OF TRANSLATION:
THE *LETTER OF ARISTEAS*

It is incredibly difficult to change religious tradition. Heck, I can't stand it when the words to a *hymn* are updated! (It's "bind us together with *chains*," not "*cords*"!) It goes for skeptics and saints alike; we simply do not like it when things we consider "holy" are altered. (And may heaven forgive U2 for attempting to add a verse to "All Along the Watchtower." We do not mess with the words of God or Bob Dylan!)

Likewise, anyone raised with a particular version of the Bible knows how skeptical one becomes when a different version of Scripture is being used. Is the new translation accurate? Does it support a theology with which I don't agree? Why should I trust a new translation? I like the one I have, thank you very much.

This is not a new problem. The Jews of the first three centuries BCE experienced an even more harrowing threat to their beloved Hebrew Bible. It came in the midst of a culture war in which the ever-expanding influence of Greek culture, religion, philosophy, government, and the Greek language reached Jewish centers in Alexandria and Judea. Because activities in most areas of society—business, education, law—were now being conducted in Greek, and Jewish children were learning Greek so that they could survive in the new hellenized economy, there came a point where Aramaic-speaking Jews began to learn and know Greek better than the Hebrew they learned as children. Ultimately, Hebrew came to be used only when reading the Bible; everything else of importance was written in Greek.[9] Thus, the Hebrew Bible needed to be translated into Greek in order for it to be read and understood and remain relevant in the modern Jewish world of the Second Temple period.

The problem, of course, is that some don't readily trust new translations of their Bible, especially when it is being translated into the language of the foreign power occupying their land and running the government. Even in antiquity individuals realized, "There is no such thing as translation without interpretation," because translators inevitably must choose between similar competing words in the destination language, and each word may have slightly different connotative meanings. As Sirach says in its prologue, "What was originally expressed in Hebrew does not have exactly the same sense when translated into another language."

This posed a problem for Jewish leaders who wanted to promote a new Greek translation of the Hebrew Bible: How do we get our fellow Jews to accept a Greek Bible? The solution became the *Letter of Aristeas,* a forged document written in the second century BCE. It claims to be a letter from a man named Aristeas, a pagan member of the court of the Egyptian king Ptolemy II Philadelphus (285–246 BCE), to his brother, Philocrates, that tells the tale of how the Hebrew Scriptures came to be translated into Greek. However, as the late Princeton Theological Seminary biblical scholar Bruce Metzger states, "The author cannot have been the man he represented himself to be but was a Jew who wrote a fictitious account in order to enhance the importance of the Hebrew Scriptures by suggesting that a pagan king had recognized their significance and therefore arranged for their translation into Greek."[10] Thus the *Letter of Aristeas* was likely composed some time closer to 125 BCE.[11]

Indeed, the principal purpose of this letter was twofold. First, it needed to convince Jews that this new, Greek translation of the Bible was credible and trustworthy. This meant offering some sort of evidence that the translation was a *perfect*—trustworthy and accurate—translation of the perfect word of God. It accomplished this task by recounting the miraculous tale of seventy-two scribes in pairs (six from each of the twelve tribes) taking (coincidentally) seventy-two days to translate the Torah (*Let. Arist.* 307) and producing thirty-six copies that were identical down to the letter.

This, of course, is a complete fable, as anyone who has ever set a copy of the Septuagint next to a copy of the Hebrew Bible will immediately see. There are differences between the two documents in length due to omissions of portions of the Hebrew text and the addition of Greek interpretations as well as in the arrangement of the text at the verse, chapter, and even book level; also, books appear in the Septuagint that are not in the Hebrew canon! And all of this is in addition to the mistranslations, mistakes, and deliberate alterations that were made by the Greek translators, which we'll discuss later in this chapter. Thus, although the *Letter of Aristeas* tried to convince Jews that the Septuagint was a perfect translation of the Hebrew Scriptures, the reality is that the Septuagint was the product of over 150 years of translation, beginning about 250 BCE, by multiple authors, which produced a *relatively* accurate version of the Hebrew Bible (in most places).

The second goal of the *Letter of Aristeas* was to couch the Jewish faith in a philosophical framework that was palatable to Hellenistic philosophers and other Greek aristocrats. In much the same way that Flavius Josephus attempted to recast the Jewish faith as Hellenistic philosophy that was acceptable to Roman authorities (see Chapter 11), the *Letter of Aristeas* was written to make the

Hebrew Bible and Jewish faith look more "Greek," in the hope
of stemming Greek persecution of Jews and the loss of the Jewish
faithful through attrition. In fact, Josephus appears to have knowledge of and to rely heavily upon the *Letter of Aristeas* to summarize
the justification of Judaism to his Roman audience.[12] Similarly, the
Jewish author Philo of Alexandria also tells the story of the translation of the Bible into Greek, adding that the thirty-six translations
were identical because they "had been divinely given by direct
inspiration."[13] Simply put, Greek philosophy and culture were in
vogue, and the *Letter of Aristeas* wanted to make the Hebrew Bible
and Jewish thought look as Greek as possible.

Thus, the letter opens with a rationale for why the Greek
king would want a copy of the Hebrew Bible in his Library of
Alexandria. *Letter of Aristeas* 10–11 recounts a supposed conversation between the king and Demetrius of Phalerum, the president
of the king's library. Demetrius suggests to the king, "I am told
that the laws of the Jews are worth transcribing and deserve a place
in your library." Demetrius explains that the Jewish Scriptures
must be translated, and in response the king orders that a letter
be written to the Jewish high priest to ask for a translation of the
Hebrew Scriptures.

The *Letter of Aristeas* begins with a decree from none other
than the Greek king himself that the text of the Hebrew Bible
be translated into Greek.[14] The purpose of this introduction is to
convince Jewish readers that the Greek king genuinely appreci-
ates the Jews and their Scriptures, and that the Greek translation
of the Bible has been authorized at the highest levels of both
Greek and Jewish authority.

Following lists of the names of the translators, the materials
collected to produce both the translation and the luxurious place
the translations would be made, and even descriptions of what
the high priest wore to oversee the process (96–99), the *Letter of
Aristeas* offers a lengthy philosophical exchange on the interpretation of Jewish law by the high priest (121–71), again reassuring
the readers that he was well versed in both Hebrew Scripture

and its interpretation and that by proxy his chosen translators were "men who had not only acquired proficiency in Jewish literature, but had studied most carefully that of the Greeks as well" (121).

Following the description of a congratulatory banquet hosted by the Greek king, *Letter of Aristeas* 310–11 declares the outcome of the translation process:

> *After the books had been read, the priests and the elders of the translators and the Jewish community and the leaders of the people stood up and said, that since* so excellent and sacred and accurate a translation had been made, it was only right that it should remain as it was and no alteration should be made in it.[15]

Note that the *Letter of Aristeas* makes sure to pronounce the resulting Greek translation as "excellent," "sacred," and, most important, "accurate," which was one of the two primary goals of the entire letter: to reassure faithful Jews that the Septuagint is a faithful translation of the Hebrew Bible.[16]

One final assurance is achieved in 312:

> *When the matter was reported to the king, he rejoiced greatly, for he felt that the design which he had formed had been safely carried out. The whole book was read over to him and* he was greatly astonished at the spirit of the lawgiver. *And he said to Demetrius,* "How is it that none of the historians or the poets have ever thought it worth their while to allude to such a wonderful achievement?" *And he replied, "Because the law is sacred and of divine origin."*[17]

By placing the final affirmation of the philosophical sophistication of the Hebrew Scriptures in the mouth of the Greek king himself, the *Letter of Aristeas* simultaneously convinces both Greek and Jewish readers that Judaism is no threat to the Greek

overlords and that the Jewish people are noble and philosophi-
cally sophisticated.

The forged *Letter of Aristeas* accomplishes both of its propagandistic goals and answers the question of why the great Greek poets
and philosophers had not yet alluded to the Hebrew Scriptures:
they hadn't been able to read them. Thus, for Jews of the Second
Temple period, the *Letter of Aristeas* was the reassurance they
needed that the Greek Bible was a trustworthy translation.

THE ROLE OF THE SEPTUAGINT

The Septuagint became the de facto Bible of Jews in the first centuries BCE and CE. This means it was the version of the "Scriptures"
that was more often than not cited by the various authors of the
New Testament.[18] It was also the Bible of choice for Josephus,
Philo of Alexandria, and most of the church fathers, who favored
it over the Hebrew version. The Jewish use of the Septuagint did
not begin to wane until the second century CE. This was due to
the gradual displacement of Greek by Latin as the lingua franca
following the rise of Rome in the east, but also as a response to
Christians, who had become fond of this "less Jewish" version
of the Hebrew Scriptures. The waning of Jewish interest in the
Septuagint coincided with a rekindled interest in preserving
the Jewish religious traditions following the destruction of the
Temple in 70 CE on the Jewish side, and the Septuagint was ultimately replaced on the Christian side by the Latin version of
the Bible.[19]

But while the Septuagint was at its height of popularity, New
Testament authors found that it often provided the textual support they needed to introduce many new interpretations of the
Hebrew Scriptures—interpretations that the Hebrew authors
had neither intended nor considered prior to the creation of the
Septuagint—that would both favor Christianity over Judaism
and further distinguish Christians from Jews.

Let's look at two examples of how the Septuagint differed from
the original Hebrew Scriptures it claims to have been translating,
and how one of those peculiar translations ultimately led to new
interpretations of Hebrew Scripture that Christians used to make
a fascinating new claim about Jesus.

THE "RED" SEA

One well-known questionable translation in the Septuagint that
has led to much confusion in the Bible comes from the story of
the exodus of the Israelites from Egypt in Exodus 13–15. Although
many believe the Hebrews crossed the *Red* Sea, the large seawater
inlet separating Africa from the Arabian Peninsula, the Hebrew
name for the body of water that was crossed is *yam suf* (יַם־סוּף),
or "Sea of *Reeds*," as *suf* in Hebrew means "reed" (cf. Exod. 2:3),
not "red."

So why do most people call it the *Red* Sea? The problem stems
from the Septuagint's translation of *yam suf* as *erythran thalassan*
(Gk. ἐρυθρὰν θάλασσαν), or "*Red* Sea," in Exodus 13:18 and multiple other locations.[20] This translation is not due to ignorance on
the translator's part; when the Septuagint translates the word for
actual *reeds* on the bank of the river in another passage in Exodus
(2:3), the Septuagint satisfactorily translates the Hebrew word *suf*
as *helos* (ἕλος), the Greek word for "marsh" or "backwater," where
one would find reeds. Likewise, when Isaiah asks, "Why are your
robes *red?*" (63:2), using the Hebrew word *'adom* (אדם) for the
color red, the Septuagint employs an appropriate Greek word for
the color red (*erythros*). So the Septuagint translators know that
suf means something related to "reeds" and knows the difference
between reeds and the color red. So why does the Septuagint constantly refer to the Sea of Reeds as the Red Sea?

The Septuagint translators employ the phrase *erythran thalassan,*
or "*Red* Sea," because by the time of the creation of the Septuagint
(ca. 250 BCE) the Red Sea was already well known as the body of
water separating Egypt from the Sinai Peninsula. For example,

in his play *The Birds* (414 BCE), Greek poet Aristophanes (446–386 BCE) refers to the name of this body of water as the "Red Sea."[21] Furthermore, the fact that Josephus (37–100 CE) claims in *Antiquities* (1.1.3 [1:39]) that the Tigris and Euphrates flow into the *Erythran thalassan* ("Red Sea") does not necessarily mean that he was mistaken, but may indicate that he understood the entire Arabian Sea, including the Persian Gulf *and* the Red Sea and its two gulfs (the Gulf of Suez to the west and the Gulf of 'Aqaba to the east) *all* to be the Red Sea according to the nomenclature of the time. As early as the fifth century BCE, Herodotus (484–425 BCE) refers to the Persian Gulf as the *Erythrēs thalassēs* ('Ερυθρῆς θαλάσσης), or "Red Sea," twice in his *Histories* (1.1.1; 1.180.1), indicating that all of the waters south and southeast of western Asia may have been known as the Red Sea.

The Septuagint's translation of the Bible, therefore, gave us the legendary "crossing of the Red Sea." But why did the translators of the Septuagint say the Israelites crossed the *Red* Sea if they knew the Hebrew Bible clearly said *Reed* Sea? By associating the exodus with the Red Sea as opposed to the Reed Sea, the miracle became a far more impressive feat, as crossing a well-known massive body of water is far more remarkable than crossing a marshy, shallow swamp fed by the waters of the eastern Nile Delta, somewhere between the northern end of the Gulf of Suez and the Mediterranean coast. It is also quite possible that the translators of the Septuagint simply did not know what or where the "Sea of Reeds" was and therefore chose the nearest identifiable body of water, which just so happened to provide the additional benefit of aggrandizing the miracle into what we see in the movies today.

THE VIRGIN BIRTH

Of course, one of the most famous examples of a biblical tradition that may have been created by a (mis)translation in the Septuagint is the story of the virgin birth of Jesus by his mother, Mary.[22] Most Christians are familiar with the story of the virgin birth, how Jesus was said in the Gospels of Matthew (1:23) and Luke (1:27, 34) to have been born to Mary, a "virgin" (Gk. παρθένος). But many scholars point out that the entire story of the virgin birth may have been the result of the Septuagint's mistranslation of a single word in Isaiah 7. Regardless of whether that is true, we *can* say for certain that the *citation* of the prophecy of Isaiah 7 in Matthew 1:23 *is* the result of the Septuagint's translation of Isaiah 7:14.

Recall that the Gospel of Mark does not mention the birth of Jesus and that the Gospel of John begins not with Jesus's physical birth, but with a beautiful philosophical introduction stating that Jesus existed as the *logos* (Gk. λόγος), or "word," which Greek philosophers like the Stoics traditionally used to describe "divine reason." Matthew and Luke desired to remedy the problem of Jesus's absent childhood by including birth narratives that would demonstrate Jesus's divine origin and support claims that he was the Jewish messiah *and* the Son of God. (We'll look at the birth narratives more closely, including their differences, in Chapter 10, where we discuss Bethlehem and Nazareth.)

Matthew 1:22–23 appeals specifically to a prophecy from Isaiah 7 to portray Jesus as a fulfillment of prophecy. However, because both Matthew and Luke tell stories of the divinely facilitated impregnation of Jesus's mother, Mary, it is evident that both relied on the Septuagint's version of Isaiah 7 and not on the original Hebrew version. This is because both authors not only describe Mary as the "young woman" Mary (as in the Hebrew version), but also use a word that specifically describes a woman who has not yet had sex (as in the Greek version) and who therefore must have been miraculously impregnated by God, making the birth of Jesus all the more auspicious. However, the tradition of the virgin birth is the result of not only a questionable translation on the part of the Septuagint, but also the recycling of an expired prophecy that initially involved another king of the Jews: Hezekiah.

Context is important. The context of the prophecy in Isaiah 7:14–16 is actually the threats against Jerusalem coming from the north in the late eighth century BCE. King 'Ahaz, Hezekiah's father, feared Jerusalem would be lost to an alliance between King Peqaḥ of Israel and King Reṣin of Aram-Damascus around 732 BCE (2 Kings 16:5). Although Jerusalem was ultimately spared during the time of Ḥezekiah's father, Jerusalem again came under threat around 701 BCE during the reign of King Ḥezekiah of Judah, who had rebelled against Assyria. Not liking that Ḥezekiah broke the terms of their deal, the Assyrian king Sennacherib laid siege to Jerusalem (see Chapter 3). When things looked bad, Isaiah was called in to advise.[23]

This is the original context of the prophecies in Isaiah 7:14–16 and 37:30–32. They deal *specifically* with threats against Jerusalem in the late eighth century BCE. These prophecies offer reassurance to the residents of Jerusalem that the city would survive, as it would be of little consolation for Isaiah to have prophesied, "I know that we are under threat of annihilation by our enemies and you are scared, but fear not, in 730 years it will all be made better." Isaiah's prophecy wasn't about something that would happen seven centuries later; it was made as reassurance that Israel would survive the *immediate* threat of destruction.

First, the prophet Isaiah goes to speak to King 'Aḥaz (7:1–6) and delivers the following words (7:14–16) on behalf of God regarding the threat from the alliance between the Northern Kingdom, Israel, and Aram-Damascus:

> *Therefore the Lord himself will give you a sign. Look, the* young woman (Heb. עלמה, 'almah) *is with child and shall bear a son, and shall name him Immanuel (*עמנו אל, *'Immanu 'El). He shall eat curds and honey by the time he knows how to refuse the evil and choose the good. For before the child knows how to refuse the evil and choose the good, the land before whose two kings you are in dread will be deserted.*

This prophecy is explicit, as it provides the unmistakable context *and* interpretation of the comment about the young woman. In response to the threat from the northern coalition and questions about whether YHWH will deliver the people from annihilation, Isaiah says that a young woman is pregnant with a son who will be named "Immanuel," or "God is with us," answering the question about whether God would be handing Judah over to Israel and Aram-Damascus or saving it. Isaiah continues by essentially saying, "A young woman is with child now, and by the time he knows good from evil (i.e., reaches adulthood), life will be good for him, and he will be eating curds and honey from our own land."

Isaiah's prophecy is a poetic way to communicate to the king that Judah will survive this *present* threat and that a child born this year will soon enjoy not just the fruits of his homeland, but an agricultural bounty, as honey requires bees, which require established orchards full of flowering plants, and curds require dairy animals, which require pasturelands. Milk and honey are symbols of long-term agricultural prosperity. The prophecy is explicit: Isaiah is claiming that Jerusalem will not be conquered and will be prosperous in about twelve years (the period between birth and adulthood for Jewish males).

And if that is not explicit enough, Isaiah explains his own prophecy in vv. 16–17: "Before the child knows how to refuse the evil and choose the good, *the land before whose two kings you are in dread will be deserted*." The prophecy *explicitly* mentions the two kings—King Reṣin of Aram-Damascus and Peqaḥ son of Remaliah in Samaria, the capital of the Northern Kingdom (cf. 7:4–9)—who had joined forces to assail Judah. Isaiah's prophecy was not about some event that would take place seven centuries later; it was about the present threat from Israel and Aram-Damascus—Isaiah says so himself!

Some scholars have even suggested that the child referred to in the prophecy is none other than the messianic king from the line of David who would deliver his people from a later threat—that's right, Hezekiah! This is because Isaiah uses another agricultural metaphor in a prophecy to Hezekiah when the Assyrian army besieged Jerusalem around 701 BCE, essentially saying that Judah will eat the produce of its own lands because

Assyria will not defeat it (37:30–32). Of course, both predictions came to pass, and Jerusalem was spared from both threats in the late eighth century BCE.

Thus, not only are Isaiah's prophecies about Jerusalem's *immediate* salvation from the *immediate* threats from foreign kingdoms to the north, but the child, whose name means "God is with us," appears to be Ḥezekiah, the king of Judah, to whom God listened when he prayed and delivered Jerusalem from King Sennacherib of Assyria (Isa. 37:21). However, during the first centuries BCE and CE, many Jews were living in a Jerusalem that was occupied by oppressive Greek and later Roman forces. They began to look back to the books of the prophets to see if any word of consolation or deliverance could be found regarding *their* present situation. They reread some of their prophets' expired prophecies, that is, prophecies that had predicted an outcome in the *past* that had already come to pass (like the deliverance of Jerusalem in the late eighth century BCE), and began to reinterpret them as speaking to *their* time and struggle.

This is precisely what happened to Isaiah's prophecy in Isaiah 7. Isaiah 7:14–16 began to be read not as something that foretold Jerusalem's deliverance seven hundred years earlier, but as an ancient prediction that *another* messianic deliverer of the line of David would come *again* to deliver the Jews. And because at this time Jews and Christians were reading the Septuagint, a new tradition would be made possible by Isaiah 7:14–16.

Once again, the Hebrew version of Isaiah 7:14 reads: "Therefore the Lord himself will give you a sign. Look, the *young woman* (Heb. עלמה, *'almah*) is with child and shall bear a son, and shall name him Immanuel." However, in the Septuagint, the Hebrew word *'almah* (עלמה), meaning "young woman" or "marriageable girl," was translated as the Greek word *parthenos* (παρθένος), which means "young woman" or "maiden," but also a woman who has not yet had sex, that is, a "virgin."

The choice of the word *parthenos* in Isaiah 7:14 was peculiar to say the least. Had the Hebrew word been *betulah* (בתולה), meaning explicitly "virgin,"[24] then *parthenos* would have been the correct and expected translation. However, since the Hebrew word was *'almah,* which is simply one synonym for "young woman of marriageable age," *parthenos* is unexpected, especially since the Septuagint translates other instances of the word *'almah,* with a different synonym for "young woman" like *neanis* (Gk. νεᾶνις) in Exodus 2:8 or *neotēti* (Gk. νεότητι) in Proverbs 30:19.[25]

However, since *parthenos* can mean "virgin," and is translated as such by the Septuagint in Isaiah 7:14, Matthew interpreted the text in *that* fashion, understanding and implying a miraculous conception without conventional sex—an interpretation only made possible by the Septuagint's translation. Thus, the author of Matthew used the verse from the Septuagint's version of Isaiah 7:14 to describe Mary, whom he believed had miraculously conceived and was giving birth to Immanuel, "God is with us," or the incarnation of God.

Objections to the virgin birth appear in literature relatively early on in Christian history. In his *Dialogue with Trypho,* the second-century Christian apologist Justin Martyr records a supposed conversation with a Jew named Trypho, who objects to the Christian story of the virgin birth:

> And Trypho answered, "The Scripture has not, 'Behold, the virgin shall conceive, and bear a son,' but, 'Behold, the young woman shall conceive, and bear a son,' and so on, as you quoted. But the whole prophecy refers to Hezekiah, and it is proved that it was fulfilled in him, according to the terms of this prophecy. Moreover, in the fables of those who are called Greeks, it is written that Perseus was begotten of Danae, who was a virgin; he who was called among them Zeus having descended on her in the form of a golden shower. And you ought to feel ashamed when you make assertions similar to theirs, and rather [should] say that this Jesus was born man of men. And if you prove from the Scriptures that He is the Christ, and that on account of having led a life conformed to the law, and perfect, He deserved

the honor of being elected to be Christ, [it is well]; but do not
venture to tell monstrous phenomena, lest you be convicted of
talking foolishly like the Greeks."[26]

Despite the fact that Justin rejects Trypho's skepticism concerning the virgin birth, the fact that Justin's *Dialogue* appears in the
middle of the second century CE demonstrates that the objection
to the Christian reinterpretation of Isaiah's prophecies, which
were used to support the Christian claim of Jesus's virgin birth,
was well known in early Christianity.[27]

So we see that the translations made by the Septuagint were
not always perfect and led to some major changes in the way the
Hebrew Scriptures were interpreted. There are literally hundreds of differences between the Hebrew Bible and the Greek
Septuagint, including additions, omissions, theological alterations, and poor translations—all of which affected the way the
Hellenistic Jews and Christians interpreted the Bible.

But it was not just the canonical Hebrew books that were translated into Greek in Alexandria. The Septuagint also included a
number of texts that were ultimately excluded from the canon of
the Hebrew Bible. This assortment of books omitted from the
canon is collectively called the Apocrypha.

THE APOCRYPHA

The Apocrypha is the common term for the books that are present
in the Septuagint, but were left out of the canonical Hebrew Bible
for reasons that are debated to this day. These books include Tobit,
Judith, the Additions to Esther, Wisdom of Solomon, Sirach (also
called Wisdom of Jesus the Son of Sirach, as well as Ecclesiasticus),
Baruch, the Letter of Jeremiah, the Prayer of Azariah and the
Song of the Three Jews, Susanna, Bel and the Dragon, the Prayer
of Manasseh, Psalm 151, 1 Maccabees, 2 Maccabees, 3 Maccabees,
4 Maccabees, and 1 Esdras.

Some readers may recognize some of these books, while others may suspect I made a bunch of them up. But rest assured, each of the above books was preserved in the Septuagint. What's more, many of the books of the Apocrypha echo themes that are consistent with stories that were written later in the Hebrew Bible, like Daniel and Esther. This is significant because it reveals to us some of the specific issues Jews were dealing with in the late Second Temple period, like resistance against foreign occupation and avoiding idolatry. Let's take a quick survey of the apocryphal books.

TOBIT

Tobit is a lengthy tale of characters similar to those found, for instance, in the biblical book of Esther, the stories of Samson and Deborah in the book of Judges, or the stories of the prophets 'Eliyahu (Elijah) and 'Elisha' (Elisha) in the books of Kings. Tobit is a righteous Israelite who became blind and prayed to God for a death that would come soon. He sent his son, Tobias, to complete an errand. Along the way, Tobias runs into Sarah, who was also praying for death out of her grief because she had lost seven different husbands on her seven respective wedding nights; the demon Asmodeus would kill each new husband before the marriage could be consummated.

If this sounds a lot like the plot of Mike Myers's *So I Married an Axe Murderer* (one of my all-time favorites!), keep in mind that Tobit 3:8 (and 6:14) is also the likely source for the challenge to Jesus brought by the Sadducees who questioned Jesus's teaching about the afterlife. Matthew 22:25–28[28] reads:

> *Now there were seven brothers among us; the first married, and died childless, leaving the widow to his brother. The second did the same, so also the third, down to the seventh. Last of all, the woman herself died. In the resurrection, then, whose wife of the seven will she be? For all of them had married her.*

This question may not be the absurdly hypothetical impossibility it seems to be at first. The Sadducees may have been appealing to the well-known Jewish story of Sarah in the book of Tobit.

God ultimately had mercy on both Tobit and Sarah, and the story concludes with a happy ending when Tobias and Sarah finally marry. The story of Tobit was popular in the Second Temple period, because it provided hope and joy for Jews suffering under foreign (Seleucid) occupation.

JUDITH

Readers of the story of Judith will quickly see parallels to the story of Ya'el and Sisera' in Judges 4. Judith is a beautiful Jewish widow turned assassin who seduces and then decapitates the enemy Assyrian general, Holofernes. The book is considered by nearly all scholars to be historical fiction (due to many historical inaccuracies preserved in the text beginning with the very first verse, which describes Nebuchadnezzar II as the king of *Assyria*, not Babylonia) that serves as an extended parable about resistance against a foreign occupying army. This "salvation story" was likely composed as a model of bravery and deliverance during the Seleucid occupation of ancient Judah to both entertain and encourage Jews who found themselves discouraged and struggling under occupation.

ADDITIONS TO ESTHER

The Additions to Esther is exactly what it sounds like, a series of six extra sections added to the canonical text of Esther to solve a specific problem, the fact that the book of Esther, unique among the books of the Hebrew Bible, never mentions God, either by name (YHWH) or generically ('Elohim). If fact, many scholars believe this is the reason that no copy of Esther was discovered among the Dead Sea Scrolls. The Additions to Esther remedies God's absence in the book of Esther by adding prayers and narratives that explicitly mention God and filling in some details that the author of the Additions to Esther felt provided further explanation.

WISDOM OF SOLOMON AND SIRACH

The Wisdom of Solomon and Sirach (Ecclesiasticus) are considered "wisdom" books; they record a litany of wisdom sayings and pithy aphorisms and read much like the canonical book of Proverbs. But unlike general collections of wisdom sayings, both books are theologically Jewish and define true wisdom as obedience to YHWH and the Torah.

BARUCH

Baruch (which is technically 1 Baruch to distinguish it from the later 2, 3, and 4 Baruch) is supposedly written by the prophet Jeremiah's scribe, Baruch ben Neriah (Jer. 36:4). A short text on the themes of exile and return, Baruch is primarily concerned with articulating in great detail how the exile to Babylon was the fault of Jews who were unfaithful to YHWH and not due to God's negligence or impotence. The book ends on a word of hope, reflecting the return from exile under the Persian Empire.

THE LETTER OF JEREMIAH

In Jerome's Latin Vulgate (his translation of the Bible into Latin), the Letter of Jeremiah is actually appended as the sixth chapter of Baruch, but in the Septuagint it is a separate letter. The oldest extant copy of the Letter of Jeremiah is a Greek copy from Cave 7 at Qumran (7Q2) dating to at least the first century CE. Bruce Metzger argues that the Letter of Jeremiah is a short satire on a single verse in the book of Jeremiah (10:11). This single verse is peculiar because it is written in Aramaic, not in Hebrew, the language that is used throughout the remainder of Jeremiah. In fact, it is the only Aramaic verse in the Hebrew Bible outside of the texts of Daniel and Ezra.[29]

This singular verse in the middle of Jeremiah 10 is a warning against idolatry and includes a quite appropriate Aramaic wordplay involving the worship of idols. Jeremiah 10:11 says in Aramaic, "Thus shall you say to them: The gods who did not make the heavens and the earth shall perish from the earth and from under the heavens." This verse is an Aramaic pun because the word for "make" used here is the Aramaic word *'avadu* (עָבַדוּ), while the word for "perish" in Aramaic is the similarly sounding *ye'vadu* (יֵאבַדוּ).[30]

Thus, the Letter of Jeremiah is an extended warning against the worship of idols stemming from an anomalous Aramaic verse. It includes some rather graphic and even comical portrayals of idol worship, including my favorite in vv. 20–23: "They do not notice when their faces have been blackened by the smoke of the temple. Bats, swallows, and birds alight on their bodies and heads; and so do cats. From this you will know that they are not gods; so do not fear them." Essentially, if idols can't stop cats from sleeping and birds from pooping on them, they're probably not real gods.

PRAYER OF AZARIAH AND THE SONG OF THE THREE JEWS

Prayer of Azariah and the Song of the Three Jews are actually two separate, yet closely related stories pertaining to the fiery furnace story from Daniel 3. In the canonical story, three of Daniel's Jewish friends, Shadrach (Ḥananiah), Meshach (Misha'el), and 'Abednego ('Azariah; 1:7), refuse to bow down to an idol, so they are thrown into a fiery furnace and then saved from death by an angel of God.

In Jewish literature composed during the Second Temple period, we consistently find that those desiring deliverance from God must first pray to God for help, confess their sins, beg for forgiveness, and then offer a promise of praise after God delivers them. Apparently, because the canonical text of Daniel 3 proceeds directly from the descent of the three faithful Jews into the furnace

to God's miraculous intervention on their behalf *without* so much
as a cry for help from them, the author of the Prayer of Azariah
felt it necessary to "supplement" the story with the prayer that
was "omitted" from the original text of Daniel 3. Thus, the text
of the Prayer of Azariah is exactly that: the text of a supposed
penitential prayer of 'Azariah ('Abednego).

The Song of the Three Jews is the text of a hymn sung by
Shadrach, Meshach, and 'Abednego as they realized that God was
saving them from the flames of the fire.

SUSANNA

The book of Susanna is a wonderful story again featuring Daniel
as the wise hero who essentially provides a *Law & Order*–style
prosecution and cross-examination of two creepy, corrupt, elderly
voyeurs who peep at Susanna, the wife of a righteous man, as she
bathes in her garden. And once again, the story features a prayer
of petition asking God to deliver Susanna from the near-death
situation in which she found herself.

After Susanna refuses to sleep with two of the city's respected
elders, they falsely accuse her of adultery. Knowing that she
would not be believed, Susanna prays to God for justice, causing God to rally the story's hero, Daniel, to her defense. Daniel
chastises the people of the city for condemning Susanna without
evidence (v. 48) and accuses the two elders of false testimony—a
crime equally punishable by death if convicted. Daniel traps the
two elders into offering conflicting accounts in their testimony,
and Susanna is exonerated. The book of Susanna encourages Jews
to refrain from sin even in the face of false accusations and certain
death, because God will ultimately save the righteous.

BEL AND THE DRAGON

Bel and the Dragon is yet another narrative doublet starring Daniel
that criticizes the practice of idolatry. Daniel is placed in two separate

life-threatening situations for refusing to worship Babylonian idols. In the first story, Bel (an Akkadian and Babylonian title meaning "lord" or "master," similar to the Cana'anite Ba'al) is the name of an idol that Daniel refuses to worship. He successfully demonstrates that the priests of Bel are eating the sacrificial food placed nightly before the idol, and the king kills the priests instead of the faithful Daniel. In the accompanying story of the Dragon, Daniel again faces death for refusing to worship a great dragon that the Babylonians revered. Daniel destroys the idol and faces six days in a den of seven lions in retaliation, which Daniel survives with God's help.

Interestingly, in the stories of Bel and the Dragon, Daniel is ordered to worship the idol by "Cyrus the Persian" (v. 1), who ultimately converts to the worship of Daniel's God (YHWH), uttering in v. 41, "You are great, O Lord, the God of Daniel, and there is no other besides you!" Thus, in addition to serving as a humorous polemic against idolatry, Bel and the Dragon provides an apology for the problematic text of Isaiah 45:1, where the Persian king Cyrus is referred to as God's *messiah*. Bel and the Dragon offers a solution to the problem of a foreign king being named as the messiah: King Cyrus *converted* and therefore allowed his fellow Jewish "brothers" to return to Jerusalem.

Prayer of Manasseh

The Prayer of Manasseh is yet another book of the Apocrypha that serves an apologetic purpose by supplying the text of a prayer the author felt was missing from the canonical text of the Bible. In 2 Chronicles 33:12–13, one of the most idolatrous kings of Judah, King Menasheh (Manasseh), is said to have uttered a prayer to God, but the words of the prayer are not given. Therefore, the author of the Prayer of Manasseh provides the supposed words of the prayer. This serves an apologetic role because the text of 2 Chronicles 33:1–20 itself contains an apology added to its parallel text of 2 Kings 21:1–18 in the form of a report of Manasseh's repentance.

In 2 Kings 21:1–18, we are told of the great evils that King Manasseh did in Judah, but there is not a word of repentance mentioned anywhere in the passage. However, the parallel retelling of this episode in 2 Chronicles 33:1–20 says King Manasseh was exiled to Babylon, where he repented of his evil ways, prompting God to return him to his throne to rule out the rest of his days in Jerusalem—fifty-five years, longer than any other king of Judah.

The archaeological record suggests that Manasseh was a loyal Assyrian vassal, which would certainly have been the reason for his condemnation in the biblical text.[31] But we are left with the discrepancy between 2 Kings 21, which depicts Manasseh as an unrepentant, evil king, and 2 Chronicles 33, which says he was exiled, repented, and was returned to his throne in Jerusalem to live out his years. Second Chronicles 33:15–16 further describes the righteous deeds of King Manasseh after his repentance, thus providing a reason why God allowed him to stay on the throne. However, we have no record of what Manasseh actually said—a problem that is exacerbated in 33:19, where the text specifically states that the text of his prayer was written in the "records of the seers."

Enter the Prayer of Manasseh, which offers the short text of the "missing" prayer purportedly offered to God by Manasseh while in Babylon. The short Prayer of Manasseh supplies the text of Manasseh's prayer, and in doing so further repairs the discrepancy between 2 Kings 21 and 2 Chronicles 33 by elaborating upon Manasseh's repentance and justifying his longevity.

PSALM 151

Many readers may not know that there were far more psalms than the 150 canonical psalms contained with the Hebrew Bible's book of Psalms. Several additional psalms were discovered, for instance, among the Dead Sea Scrolls (11QPs[a] = 11Q5), including Psalm 151. This psalm is found immediately after Psalm 150 (the final canonical psalm) in the Septuagint, and the superscript of Psalm 151 tells us exactly what the psalm is about: "This Psalm is ascribed to David and is outside the number.[32] When he slew Goliath in single combat." The psalm appears to be a composite of David and Goliath traditions.

1–2 MACCABEES

Simply put, the books of 1 and 2 Maccabees are propaganda for the Hasmonean dynasty, the Jewish line of kings who ruled following the Maccabean Revolt. Written sometime in the late second or early first century BCE, 1–2 Maccabees are used by scholars as a record of what the Hasmoneans wanted people to know about their rise to power beginning with the end of the rule of the Seleucid king Antiochus IV Epiphanes (167 BCE) up to the end of Simon's reign (134 BCE) and the ascension of John Hyrcanus to the throne. Second Maccabees is essentially a prequel to 1 Maccabees (think *Star Wars: Episode I—The Phantom Menace*), narrating history from the rise of Hellenism in Judea and highlighting the Maccabean Revolt against Antiochus IV, led by the revolt's namesake, Judas Maccabeus.

3 MACCABEES

Third Maccabees is very different from 1–2 Maccabees. Written sometime between 80 and 15 BCE in Greek (likely in Alexandria), the book appears to be missing its original beginning. The first part of 3 Maccabees (chaps. 1–2) is two episodes; first, the text recalls a story of how the Ptolemaic king Ptolemy IV planned to enslave the Jews unless they converted to worshipping Dionysus, the god of wine, and also that he wanted to enter Holy of Holies. Then the book's theme of royal arrogance and divine retribution comes alive when God punishes Ptolemy IV following a prayer by the high priest Simon.

The second part of 3 Maccabees (chaps. 3–7) is a series of re-worked legends originally set in the reign of Ptolemy VII. The theme here is the persecution and vindication of the righteous and the faithful, including one peculiar attempt at the public extermination of the Jews involving a herd of drunk, stampeding elephants (3 Macc. 5–6). Fortunately, God sent two angels—visible to everyone but the Jews—to stand in front of the stampeding drunken herd. The angels threw the elephants into confusion, and they turned back upon their armed Greek zookeepers, trampling and destroying them.

One significant difference between 3 Maccabees and the *Letter of Aristeas,* discussed earlier, is the response to hellenization by the Jews. While the Letter of Aristeas attempts to demonstrate how Greek culture and Judaism have much in common and can (and should) coexist, 3 Maccabees portrays how exclusivist Jewish attitudes about the worship of one God made them the object of derision and persecution. Thus the *Letter of Aristeas* was written in an effort to convince Jews to trust the Greeks, and 3 Maccabees was written to show Jews that God will protect them when they resist the Greeks.

4 MACCABEES

Fourth Maccabees is another text likely written in Alexandria somewhere around the late first or early second century CE. Eusebius of Caesarea and Jerome, who gave it the title "On the Sovereignty of Reason," both wrongly attribute it to Flavius Josephus. It is set as a beautifully written Greek eulogy for the martyred priest Eleazar, his seven brothers, and their mother, praising the "noble bravery of those who died for the sake of virtue" (1:8). A wisdom text that argues "whether reason is sovereign over the emotions" (1:13), 4 Maccabees then attempts to argue that true wisdom is obedience to the Jewish law, even unto death as exemplified by Eleazar. And in good Hellenistic fashion, the author writes of the immortality of the soul, but never mentions the resurrection of the dead.

1–2 ESDRAS

First Esdras is also known as Greek Ezra, because it is an old version of the canonical book of Ezra, only written in Greek and with a sizable addition to the text of chapter 4. It was used by both ancient Jews and Christians and is considered canonical among Eastern churches (like the Eastern Orthodox Church), but considered deuterocanonical among Western churches (like the Roman Catholic Church).

Second Esdras is an apocalyptic text that claims as its author the biblical prophet Ezra, but was composed in parts between the first and third centuries CE. But throughout the years, different parts of the text have been preserved separately using different names. The first two chapters of 2 Esdras are referred to as 5 Ezra by scholars and are found only in the Latin version of 2 Esdras. They are thought to have been composed by Christians who depicted Ezra as a prophet predicting God's rejection of the Jews and their replacement by the church. Second Esdras 3–14 is known as 4 Ezra by scholars and offers a discussion about the significance of Israel's past sufferings followed by a series of seven apocalyptic visions that offer a hope for the redemption of Israel. Second Esdras 15–16 is known as 6 Ezra and consists of a series of oracles pronouncing doom upon the enemies of the church and instructions to those suffering persecutions.[33] Also of note, 2 Esdras was composed far too late to have been included in the Septuagint, but since it was preserved as an appendix in the Latin Vulgate, it wound up in the Apocrypha section of the King James Version.

———

Scholars are not certain why the texts of the Apocrypha were ultimately rejected from the Hebrew canon. It may be because they were written later than most of the canonical books or because many of them were *composed* in Greek and not in Hebrew, which many rabbis considered the holy tongue (*leshon ha-qodesh*). Still, the Apocrypha provided Second Temple–period Jews with examples of faithfulness to God during times of foreign occupation and distress and prayers that could be used in their daily lives.

———

Alexandria is a city that helped build the Bible because, whether the *Letter of Aristeas* is historical or wholly contrived, Alexandria served as the setting for the translation of the Hebrew Bible into Greek. The resulting Septuagint became not only the de facto Bible for Palestinian Jews, but the version used most by the Christian authors of the New Testament, who wrote in Greek. At the very least, inclusion of the Hebrew Scriptures in the Library of Alexandria was the rationale for the creation of the Septuagint.

Alexandria also gave us the Apocrypha via the Septuagint. Although ultimately not canonized in the Hebrew Scriptures, these popular Jewish writings inspired Jews and, later, Christians to faithfulness and righteous behavior in times of persecution. Thus, although it is never mentioned in the Hebrew Bible and is only mentioned in passing in the New Testament, Alexandria played no small role in building our modern Bible.

CHAPTER 8

Jerusalem

Pray for the peace of Jerusalem: "May they prosper who love you. Peace be within your walls, and security within your towers." For the sake of my relatives and friends I will say, "Peace be within you."

—Psalm 122:6–8

It is the city I love: Jerusalem. The very mention of this one name brings to mind a stairway to heaven and horrific images of terror. It is holy to three religions: Judaism, Christianity, and Islam. And it is home to over eight hundred thousand people representing hundreds of ethnicities and nationalities and religious traditions, all crammed together in the hills and valleys of this legendary center of the world.

Of all the cities on earth to be associated with the Bible, Jerusalem stands alone at the top. This is not necessarily because any significant part of the Bible was written here; in fact, it is difficult to claim that *any* part of the Bible was written in Jerusalem, given the lack of evidence for anything other than administrative writing in Jerusalem.

No, Jerusalem is not significant for the composition of the Bible because of what was composed here, but because it was the ideological, political, and theological center of the world for both Judaism and Christianity. David was king here; so was Solomon. Hezekiah rebelled against Assyria from Jerusalem (2 Kings 18:7). Josiah reformed and "found" the Book of the Law here, which many scholars associate with the book of Deuteronomy (2 Kings 22:8). Jerusalem is the city that survived Sennacherib and that

Nebuchadnezzar II destroyed. It was the city rebuilt by Persian Jewish repatriates, annexed by Alexander the Great, retaken by the Maccabees, and then ceded to Rome with the rise of the Roman Empire. It is the place of Herod the Great, and of course it is the place of the death, burial, and resurrection of Jesus of Nazareth. It was the launching point for Christianity, which both admirers and detractors will concede changed the face of the Western world. For these reasons, Jerusalem is the city that *literally* built the Bible.

VISITING JERUSALEM

Jerusalem has a long archaeological history. Much of the archaeological attention paid to Jerusalem revolves around the Temple Mount, which Herod the Great built to support and expand the precinct of the Jerusalem Temple. Today the golden-topped Dome of the Rock crowns the Temple Mount, the Western Wall of which is the holiest place in Judaism. It is this holiest of holy places that has drawn people by the millions to the Old City of Jerusalem for over two millennia.

As I walk through the winding streets of Jerusalem today, I see a beautiful mix of Jewish, Christian, and Islamic traditions—an often confusing amalgam of incense, chants, and barbecued lamb that makes me simultaneously nostalgic and hungry. (Man, I could go for some hummus and roasted lamb right about now. Be right back.)

(Okay, I'm back.)

Wandering through the Old City from the Church of the Holy Sepulchre, the traditional site of Jesus's burial and resurrection, through the endless shops of the Muslim Quarter to the Western Wall, I am reminded of the thousands of years of history and personal investment that people of all ethnicities and faiths have brought to this great city. It is this continued shared heritage that makes, and must continue to make, Jerusalem the special place that it is.

Today, the holiest site in Judaism is the Western Wall, previously referred to as the Wailing Wall, where Jews went to lament the destruction of Jerusalem and its Temple. However, following the annexation of East Jerusalem during the 1967 Six-Day War, the wall came to be called the Western Wall by Israelis, as there was no longer any reason to "wail" over the loss of the city. Instead, the name Western Wall accurately describes the location of the Jewish holy place in relation to the lost Temple.

The Western Wall is the western retaining wall of Herod the Great's elevated Temple precinct, known today as the Temple Mount. The Western Wall is *not* the western wall of the Jewish Temple, as the Temple was *on top* of the Temple Mount and was completely destroyed in 70 CE. Following the destruction of the Temple, Jews wanted to come and worship at the place where the Temple once stood. The Roman emperor Hadrian (r. 117–38 CE) had banned Jews from Jerusalem, and centuries later, following the Islamic conquest of Jerusalem (637), Caliph

The Dome of the Rock in Jerusalem stands where the Jewish Temple likely once stood. The present shrine was built in 691 CE and commemorates the Muslim Prophet Muḥammad's traditional Isrā' and Miʿrāj, or Night Journey into the heavens.

'Abd al-Malik built the Dome of the Rock where the Jewish Temple once stood.

However, once Jews began to resettle in Jerusalem in the fourteenth century, they tended to gravitate toward the Moroccan Quarter, the area closest to the southwestern corner of Herod's Temple Mount. This coincidentally happened to be the area of Herod's retaining wall that is closest to where the Temple's Holy of Holies is believed to have been. Jews had been coming to this western area of Herod's retaining wall (today's Western Wall) for centuries to worship, and in the mid-sixteenth century the Ottoman sultan Suleiman I the Magnificent (1494–1566) allowed Jews the right to worship at the wall legally. Over time, Jews came to believe that the Shekinah, the presence of God, moved to the Western Wall. Today, the Western Wall receives over a million visitors each year.

I remember the first time I tried to take a photo of the Western Wall. As an oblivious tourist, I felt I could do whatever I wanted because this was my first and potentially *only* trip to Jerusalem. I took out my camera at the top of the steps just past the security checkpoint facing the Western Wall and was greeted by a woman wearing a scarf, yelling in broken English, "NO PHOTO! NO PHOTO! SHABBAT!"

At first I thought "Shabbat" was a curse word, and she was letting me have it. I lowered my camera and took a few steps, pretending to walk away. Waiting for the cover of a throng of tourists making their way past me, I sneakily raised my camera in another attempt to get a picture of the wall, when I this time heard the voice of a disgruntled elderly man again yelling, "NO PHOTO! SHABBAT! NO PHOTO!"

I thought to myself, "Again with the swearing!"

I made my way to the bottom step of the staircase in front of the wall, and without ever raising my camera above my chest and comically wrenching my neck and looking up into the sky as if to signal that I am doing *anything* but taking a photo of the massive wall in front of me, I began another attempt, this time to get a completely blind photo of the Western Wall.

The Western Wall, with the Western Wall Plaza in the foreground. The Mughrabi Ramp leading up to the top of the Temple Mount can be seen to the right, and the dome of the Al-Aqṣā Mosque can be seen to the far right.

And that is when I spotted an Orthodox Jewish man dressed in all black walking rapidly toward me. He did not introduce himself; he just began speaking in an assertive, yet polite voice.

"Let me tell you why we do not allow photographs on the Jewish holy day of Shabbat, or Saturday," he began.

I stood there surprised at the forwardness of this zealous font of unrequested information and yet simultaneously relieved at the realization that I hadn't been sworn at twice this morning.

"Okay," I replied, as if I had any choice.

He continued, speaking as quickly as I could listen: "To us, the Jewish people, Shabbat is a holy day of rest and worship. We do not work, and we do not operate machinery, including cameras. So cameras are not allowed here on Shabbat. Besides, it's rude. It's the equivalent of a tourist walking into your church building or synagogue back home and taking a photo of you while you and your family are praying. You wouldn't want me to take a picture of you while you worship, so don't do it to us. Okay?"

I nodded and scurried away down the stairs. From that day forward, I committed myself to learning the rules of courtesy governing religious-tourist photography. As I visited Jerusalem year after year, I came to understand that it really is common courtesy to refrain from taking photos on Shabbat, *even if* (and I've heard all the reasons) this is your *only* day in Jerusalem and your *only* opportunity to get a picture of the Western Wall. As Exodus 23:12 clearly says, "Six days you shall take your pictures, but on the seventh day you shall rest."

The Dome of the Rock shown in relation to the Western Wall in Jerusalem.

One popular tradition at the Western Wall is to write a prayer on a piece of paper and stick it in the wall. I have done this for every one of my children. I write their names and a simple blessing on the paper, fold it up into a toothpick-shaped missile, and attempt to jam it in any remaining open crack in the wall. Those of you who have attempted this know how difficult it is, as every possible crack in the wall is occupied with the hopeful prayers of others, which I am afraid to dislodge and replace with my own blessing for fear of incurring the wrath of the wall and counteracting the entire benefit of the whole blessing-in-the-wall tradition.

*The author at the Western Wall. Note the pieces of paper wedged into the cracks,
which contain the prayers and blessings of visitors to the Wall.*

A couple of times a year, a custodian of the wall collects the
prayers and respectfully buries them on the Mount of Olives. And
don't worry, if you can't make the trip to Jerusalem to place a
prayer in the wall, you can text, e-mail, use the Send a Prayer
iPhone app, and now even tweet your prayers to the wall elec-
tronically. I kid you not. Tweet a prayer to @TheKotel, and the
service prints out the prayer, folds it up, and sticks it in the wall for
you.[1] In fact, Bezeq, the Israeli telephone company, has a fax line
providing the same service. And if you're technophobic, worry
not, because letters addressed to "God, Jerusalem" are sorted by
the Letters to God Department of the Israeli postal service (this
really exists!) and are squeezed into the wall on the days after the
cracks are emptied.[2]

Visiting the Muslim shrines on the top of the Temple Mount
is more difficult. Unless you are a Muslim (and *look* Muslim, as
there are no apologies on either the Palestinian or Israeli side for
the open, rank racial profiling that goes on in a security-obsessed
place like Jerusalem), you can enter neither the Al-Aqṣā Mosque
nor the Dome of the Rock. This policy was established in response to the new U.S. and European regulations following the
attacks of 9/11. Essentially, non-Muslims are not allowed to enter

either building, as they are now purely religious venues for prayer (read: no tourists). I was fortunate enough to enter and visit both structures in 1999 and 2000, prior to 9/11. The Dome of the Rock, which is where most scholars believe the Jewish Temple once stood, is truly amazing, not only because it is a beautiful example of Islamic art and architecture,[3] but because this space was the epicenter of Judaism for over a millennium.

THE EARLY HISTORY OF JERUSALEM

The archaeological evidence we have to date suggests that there was a settlement near the Giḥon Spring by around 3500 BCE. Both the archaeological and the biblical accounts agree that there were Canaʻanites living in Jerusalem long before any Hebrews appeared there. The name of the city first appears in Egyptian execration texts from Luxor during the reign of Pharaoh Senusret III (r. 1878–1839 BCE). The names of nineteen Canaʻanite cities (whom the Egyptians considered to be enemies) appear on the broken shards of multiple ceramic vessels, including the name of Jerusalem, which is written as *Rushalimum* in hieratic (or cursive Egyptian) script.[4]

Execration texts are a form of sympathetic magic in which the names of enemies or persons to be harmed are written on a surface, in this case pottery, that is then broken or otherwise destroyed; the destruction is thought to cause a similar effect on the named parties.[5] An alternate form is creating an effigy of a person to be harmed (think voodoo dolls) and then smashing it, cutting it, poking it, peeing on it (yes, that's one of the things), and ultimately disposing of it by burning it, throwing it in the trash, or burying it.

This form of magical religious writing appears in the Hebrew Bible (e.g., Num. 5:11–31)[6] and the New Testament as well. In Philippians 4:3 and multiple times in the book of Revelation,[7] the names of the saved are said to be *written down* in the "Book of Life."

This is likely echoing the same motif in Daniel 12:1, "But at that time your people shall be delivered, *everyone who is found written in the book*," which in turn echoes Exodus 32:33, "Whoever has sinned against me I will *blot out of my book*." Again, the idea that having your name written in a divine book determines that you are "saved" is very much rooted in the well-established tradition of ancient Near Eastern sympathetic magic and the numinous power of writing.[8]

In addition to the Egyptian execration texts, there are other extrabiblical references to Jerusalem. The name *U-ru-sha-lim* is used to describe Jerusalem in the Amarna Letters dating to around 1400 BCE.[9] Thus, Jerusalem was a known, inhabited, and attested city with a name that resembles the lengthy name of Jerusalem long before any Hebrews or Israelites came to the city. It is this question of how, in fact, the Israelites came to be in the city of Jerusalem that has puzzled scholars for some time. Most important, the question of how David came to be so intimately connected to Jerusalem—so that it came to be called the "City of David"—is what we'll explore next.

DAVID'S CONQUEST OF JERUSALEM

So how exactly did the Israelites come to inhabit Jerusalem? We read in 2 Samuel 5 and its parallel in 1 Chronicles 11 of David's conquest of the Jebusite city (what the Bible calls Jerusalem before David conquered it). Thus, the easy answer appears to be that David conquered Jerusalem and set up his capital there.

But scholars have long acknowledged the problems with the Bible's contradicting claims about early Israelite interactions with Jerusalem. For example, look at the discrepancy between 2 Samuel 5:6–9 and its parallel in 1 Chronicles 11:4–8, which offer varying accounts regarding *who* actually conquered Jerusalem. Second Samuel 5:7 says that *David* took the stronghold of Zion, while 1 Chronicles 11:6 maintains that it was Yo'av (Joab) who took Zion and that David rewarded his bravery and success by making him chief of his army. But this discrepancy is easy to explain: David was the leader, and Joab was the soldier who actually conquered Jerusalem upon David's command. This isn't the *real* problem with the conquest of Jerusalem.

The much larger problem regarding the conquest of early Jerusalem arises from the multiple contradictory literary accounts in the Bible, namely, the question of who conquered Jerusalem, Yehoshu'a (Joshua) or David. The Bible presents conflicting accounts, and there is a dearth of archaeological evidence about early *Israelite* Jerusalem that makes the truth about Jerusalem's early history a mystery. These conflicting texts have caused scholars to suggest that many of the stories surrounding Jerusalem's founding as the capital of ancient Israel were the products of later editors' attempts to demonstrate Jerusalem's significance prior to the conquest of Samaria in 722 BCE. These biblical accounts of the so-called conquest of Jerusalem are difficult, if not impossible, to reconcile. Let's outline them.

A FOUNDATIONAL STORY FOR JERUSALEM

Jerusalem is never mentioned in the Pentateuch (the first five books of the Bible), which is surprising for a faith that ultimately centered on Jerusalem. Furthermore, in much of Israel's patriarchal history Abraham, Isaac, and Jacob interact with sites in Samaria, Shechem, and Shiloh—areas that would later become the center of Judah's rival, Israel—and to the south of Jerusalem in Hebron. Therefore, it was important for those editing the Bible during the exilic and postexilic periods to provide a foundational story for Jerusalem, so that it could compete in historical significance with other storied centers of Israelite worship, especially Samaria.

One tactic used by biblical redactors was to claim that the city of Shalem referred to in Genesis 14:18 was a reference to Jerusalem, despite the fact that at no time was Jerusalem's name ever shortened—it was always some lengthy version of *Ru-sha-li-mum* or *U-ru-sha-lim*. However, by insisting that Melki-ṣedeq's (Melchizedek's) city of Shalem was actually Jerusalem, the editors of the Bible could argue that ancient Jerusalem had patriarchal sanction by none other than Abram himself.[10]

A second tactic to provide this foundational story for Jerusalem was to tell the story of how it became the city of David, God's chosen leader. Let's look for a moment at the conflicting claims about Jerusalem's conquest.

BIBLICAL CONTRADICTIONS REGARDING THE CONQUEST OF JERUSALEM

Jerusalem is first mentioned in Joshua 10:1, when its pre-Israelite king 'Adoni-ṣedeq (Adoni-zedek) joins a coalition of cities warring against Joshua and the Hebrews, who had just invaded Cana'an. It is mentioned again in Joshua 15:8, when we are told that Jerusalem was called the Jebusite city before it was conquered by King David.

Joshua killed the king of Jerusalem, Adoni-zedek, according to Joshua 10:23–27. Joshua 10:40 offers a definitive summary statement that Joshua "defeated the *whole land*" and "left *no one* remaining, but *utterly destroyed all* that breathed, as the LORD God of Israel commanded." Joshua 21:44 underscores this claim stating, "The LORD gave them rest on every side just as he had sworn to their forefathers; *not one of all their enemies had withstood them.*" Joshua 12:10 clearly lists the king of Jerusalem as having been killed, and Joshua 24:11 explicitly states that Joshua and the Israelites defeated the Jebusites. So Joshua and the Israelites clearly conquered Jerusalem.

And yet the Bible *also* says that the Israelites did *not* conquer Jerusalem. Joshua 15:63 makes this explicitly clear when, at the end of a comprehensive list of the cities and lands that the Israelites would inherit, the text reads, "But the people of Judah could not drive out the Jebusites, the inhabitants of Jerusalem;

so the Jebusites live with the people of Judah in Jerusalem to this day." So even though the Bible says Joshua and the Israelite army destroyed all of the surrounding lands and killed all of their kings, and despite the fact that multiple earlier passages say the Israelites defeated the Jebusites, Joshua 15:63 says they did *not* conquer Jerusalem. The question then becomes: Why would the Bible preserve conflicting traditions that the Israelites both conquered and did not conquer Jerusalem?

Judges 1:8 exacerbates the problem with Jerusalem's early history, as it quite clearly says, "Then the people of Judah fought against Jerusalem and took it. They put it to the sword and set the city on fire." And despite the fact that the king's name in this account (1:7) is 'Adoni-bezeq (likely a scribal error or a variant tradition of 'Adoni-ṣedeq, mentioned in Josh. 10:1), the result is the same: the Judahites sacked the city and burned it to the ground. That is, except for the fact that only a few verses later, Judges 1:21 says that the Benjaminites could *not* drive the Jebusites from the very city they just burned to the ground. So now we have *two* claims of the destruction of the city and *two* counterclaims that Jerusalem still remained full of Jebusites!

And then there's the problem with the story of David and Goliath. First Samuel 17:54 claims that after killing Goliath for King Saul, the boy "David took the head of the Philistine and brought it to Jerusalem." The problem quickly becomes obvious: Saul is still king; Saul is still ruling from Givʻah (Gibeah), *not* Jerusalem; and the soon-to-be King David hadn't yet conquered Jerusalem, which doesn't happen until 2 Samuel 5! Why would the text say that David took Goliath's head back to Jerusalem? Some scholars, like James Hoffmeier, have argued that David took Goliath's head to Jerusalem to serve notice that it was "next,"[11] but most scholars see this as an anachronistic error, in which the author mistakenly assumed that David would have returned with Goliath's head as a trophy (as was done through the ancient Near East following battles) to his capital, *Jerusalem*. This story's editor forgot that David had not yet conquered Jerusalem.

We can therefore see from the accounts in Joshua, Judges, and 1 and 2 Samuel that there are internal biblical contradictions regarding the conquest of Jerusalem. The question for scholars is not, "Are there contradictions?" but rather, "Why are these contradicting accounts preserved in the text?" Either the text is wrong in Joshua 10:40 when it claims that "Joshua defeated the *whole land*" and that "he left *no one* remaining" and "*utterly destroyed all* that breathed" because Joshua had not actually taken the Jebusite city (Jerusalem), or Joshua *had* done those things to Jerusalem, but for some reason the editors of the Bible wanted Jerusalem to remain unconquered.

Given the story of David still to come, I suggest that the conquest of Jerusalem in 2 Samuel 5 (and again in 1 Chron. 11) is Jerusalem's foundation myth, just as Virgil's story of Romulus and Remus was the foundation myth for Rome (see Chapter 11). The later redactors of the Bible had in their possession the Joshua and Judges tradition of the conquest of Jerusalem, but may have wanted to reserve credit for Jerusalem's conquest for *David,* which they tell in 2 Samuel 5, so that the "City of David" could become God's chosen city in the same way that David—the "man after God's own heart" (1 Sam. 13:14; cf. Acts 13:22)—became God's chosen king.

Now let's turn to how the newly conquered Jerusalem became the city of God.

HOW JERUSALEM BECAME THE HOLY CITY FOR THE ISRAELITES

THE ARK OF THE COVENANT

The Bible states that once David was happily ensconced in his new capital of Jerusalem, he wanted to bring the ark of the covenant to Jerusalem (see 2 Sam. 6). The ark had been parked safely in Shiloh, which had been the worship center of Israel up until this point. So in one of the more odd scenes in the Bible, David embarks on the task of bringing the ark to Jerusalem.

From the outset, things do not go as smoothly as planned. First, in 2 Samuel 6, while they were transporting the ark and "David and all the house of Israel were dancing before the Lord with all their might" (6:5), the oxen pulling the cart carrying the ark stumbled and shook the ark, which appeared as if it were going to fall over. 'Uzza' (Uzzah), one of the drivers of the ox cart, reached out his hand to steady the ark, and for his efforts God struck him dead on the spot (6:7) for violating the command not to touch the ark (Num. 4:15). David became angry and terrified that the ark would damage him as well, so he detoured it to the house of 'Obed 'Edom the Gittite for three months (6:11).

Seeing that the presence of the ark at 'Obed 'Edom's house caused him to prosper, David once again formed a processional and took the ark to Jerusalem, making sure to stop every six paces to sacrifice an ox and a calf to God just to assuage any potential anger (2 Sam. 6:13). Once the ark reached the tent that David had pitched for it in Jerusalem, David offered sacrifices and threw a party for everyone in attendance (6:18–19).

Bringing the ark to Jerusalem was important because it symbolizes the moment that Jerusalem became *the* city of God. It is from this point forward that Jerusalem would be touted above all other Israelite cities, especially Shiloh, Shechem, and Samaria, which were the chief rivals of the Jerusalem priesthood when many of these biblical materials were being edited and collected. That is to say, the placement of the ark in Jerusalem during the reign of David symbolized to the readers of the Bible that it was *Jerusalem,* and not Samaria and its alternative Samaritan Temple atop Mt. Gerizim (cf. John 4:20), that was the *true* place of worship, the *true* city of God.

The Temple

The ark would ultimately be housed within and replaced by the Temple in Jerusalem. The tale of the building of the Temple was discussed in Chapter 1. There is some debate about whether a temple already existed in Jerusalem prior to David's arrival. Given the references to the Jebusite city and given that most cities had functioning temples, this is highly likely. So we must ask whether David, following his conquest of Jerusalem, took control of an *established* temple and Solomon perhaps refurbished and rededicated it,[12] or whether Solomon did in fact construct the "house of the LORD" in Jerusalem (1 Kings 6).

Either way, we know that the floor plan of the Temple described in 1 Kings 6–7 closely resembles the floor plans of other regional temples, such as the tenth-century BCE temple in 'Ain Dāra in the northwest corner of modern Syria, the nearby ninth-century BCE temple in Tel Ta'yinat in southernmost modern Turkey, and the mid-seventh-century BCE "House of YHWH" at Tel 'Arad south of Jerusalem in southern Judah. This suggests that regardless of who built the Temple, it was built according to plans that characterized many of the temples of Iron Age Cana'an.

And once the ark of the covenant was placed in the Holy of Holies inside the Jerusalem Temple (cf. 1 Kings 8:21), all of the power that was once attributed to the portable ark of the covenant while the Hebrews were nomads in the desert was transferred to the stationary Temple, now that Israel was a people with a land. From this point on, the ark of the covenant is rarely mentioned in the Bible. In fact, Jeremiah 3:16–17 states:

They shall no longer say, "The ark of the covenant of the LORD." It shall not come to mind, or be remembered, or missed; nor shall another one be made. At that time Jerusalem shall be called the throne of the LORD, and all nations shall gather to it, to the presence of the LORD in Jerusalem, and they shall no longer stubbornly follow their own evil will.

The author of this portion of Jeremiah implies that the ark is no longer the representation of God to his people; rather, the city of Jerusalem itself has become the seat of God and the hope of the dispossessed peoples of the earth. And it is this ideal—this symbol of Jerusalem as the city of God and the hope of humankind—that persisted long beyond the ark and the Temple.

EZRA, NEHEMIAH, AND THE REBUILDING OF THE TEMPLE

We have already discussed the destruction of Jerusalem and the Temple at the hands of the Babylonian king Nebuchadnezzar II's army in 587 BCE (see Chapter 4). One of the lowest points in Jewish history, it also resulted in the exile of the nobility to Babylon. Given what the Temple meant to the people of Jerusalem, we can understand just how catastrophic this event was; both the people and their faith would be fundamentally altered forever.

But the rise of the Achaemenid Persians and their conquest of the Babylonians in 540 BCE provided new hope for the members of the exiled Jewish community, who may have seen the shift in overlords as an opportunity to return to Jerusalem and rebuild it. In fact, they would do so with the endorsement and sponsorship of the Persian Empire.

The books of 'Ezra' (Ezra) and Nehemiah record the rebuilding of Jerusalem, at least in literary form. You should know that Ezra and Nehemiah are considered *one* book in the Hebrew Bible, not two, as we see in the Christian Bible. They were typically written on the same scroll, as they deal with the same subject: the rebuilding of the Temple in Jerusalem and the Persian administration of the newly established province of Yehud (later Judea).

Following the so-called Edict of Cyrus as recorded in Ezra 1:2 ("Thus says King Cyrus of Persia: The LORD, the God of heaven, . . . has charged me to build him a house at Jerusalem in Judah"), Ezra recounts the animosity encountered by the returning Jewish exiles from those Jewish residents who had been left behind in Jerusalem. Those left behind had hoped to assist in the rebuilding of the Temple (4:1–2), but the leader of the coalition of Persian repatriates stated, "You shall have no part with us in building a house to our God; but we alone will build to the LORD, the God of Israel, as King Cyrus of Persia has commanded us" (4:3).

This led to constant hostilities between the Persian-sponsored Jews and those who had remained in Jerusalem. In fact, the locals' resistance to the rebuilding of the Temple became so obstinate that they wrote to the king of Persia *in Aramaic,* asking him to stop funding the process, which he did for a time. This is why Ezra 4:8–6:18 and 7:12–26 are written in Aramaic: they preserve the claimed correspondence between Jerusalem and Persia.

Nehemiah, cupbearer to the Persian king Artaxerxes, petitions the king to be allowed to return to Jerusalem (Neh. 2:5) and receives permission. Once there, he tells everyone, "Come, let us rebuild the wall of Jerusalem, so that we may no longer suffer disgrace" (2:17). Of course, the Jews who had been left behind in Judah resisted this request, as they did not want to see the walls of Jerusalem rebuilt, lest the Persian-sponsored Jewish returnees gain control over the city.

Interestingly, there is very little archaeological evidence of Jerusalem from the Persian period. Only now are archaeological excavations in Israel beginning to reveal something about this little-known period in Jerusalem's history. However, one incredible archaeological discovery demonstrates that Jerusalem's residents were already placing their faith and hope in God, and specifically through blessings invoking YHWH that would later be included as a central text of the Bible: the Ketef Hinnom Inscriptions.

THE OLDEST KNOWN
WRITTEN TEXT FROM THE BIBLE

The Ketef Hinnom Inscriptions, presently on display in the Israel Museum in Jerusalem, were discovered by the Hungarian-born veteran Israeli archaeologist Gabriel Barkay in a tomb in 1979. Ketef Hinnom (Heb., "shoulder of Hinnom") is an archaeological site to the southwest of Jerusalem's Old City at the junction of the Hinnom Valley ("Gehenna") and the Valley of Repha'im (see Josh. 15:8; 18:16).

Inscribed on the two tiny silver scrolls are early versions of the famous priestly blessing from Numbers 6:24–26 (a blessing I pronounced over my daughter, Talitha, each night as I put her to bed when she was a child). The biblical blessing reads, "The LORD bless you and keep you; the LORD make his face to shine upon you, and be gracious to you; the LORD lift up his countenance upon you, and give you peace."

Lines 12–18 of the first Ketef Hinnom inscription read:

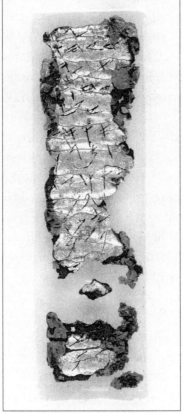

For YHWH
is our restorer [and]
rock. May YHWH bles[s]
you and
[may he] keep you.
[May] YHWH make
[his face] shine.[13]

Like the first inscription, the second Ketef Hinnom inscription preserves the well-known portion of the Aaronic blessing toward the end of the inscription:

-h/hu. May be blessed h/sh-
[e] by YHW[H,]
the warrior/helper and
the rebuker of
[E]vil: May bless you,
YHWH,
keep you.
Make shine, YH
[W]H, His face
[upon] you and g-
rant you p-
[ea]ce.[14]

The tiny silver Ketef Hinnom Inscriptions, which date from between the mid-seventh to the early sixth centuries BCE, were worn as amulets and contain an inscribed blessing that is similar to the Aaronic blessing in Num. 6:24–26. Image courtesy Israel Museum.

In his book *The Priestly Blessing in Inscription and Scripture,*[15] Jeremy Smoak argues that the tiny silver scrolls date from between the mid-seventh and the early sixth centuries BCE, just prior to the destruction of Jerusalem, and were worn as amulets to help ward off evil. One of the scrolls (KH2, lines 4–5) even refers to YHWH as the "Rebuker of Evil," suggesting that the scrolls were worn as jewelry and had a protective function.[16]

We should also be careful not to see the Ketef Hinnom Inscriptions as proof that the Bible had already been written by the sixth century BCE. In fact, the opposite is likely true; Smoak and others argue that many of the words and phrases present in the blessing on the Ketef Hinnom Inscriptions were incorporated into the text of the biblical book of Numbers by its editors. This means that the Bible is a collection of the thoughts and practices of worshippers of YHWH from an earlier time, which were later assembled, edited, and preserved for generations of believers to come. The evidence from the Ketef Hinnom Inscriptions indicates that what became the Bible began as the very real faith and practices of Israelites and Judeans, who quite literally *wore* these verses around their necks.

Thus, it was during this Persian period that the texts that would become the Hebrew Bible were collected, written down, and edited into the earliest versions of it. We can trace the roots of modern Judaism to this Persian period, when the reconstituted Jerusalem Temple and priesthood thrived as the sole religious authority under Persian sponsorship. The Davidic king had been replaced with Persian-appointed governors, but still, the memory of ancient kings—David, Solomon, Ḥezekiah, and Josiah—and the glory of Israel and Judah led by an anointed king, a true Jewish messiah, lingered in the minds of the Jews. And the continued absence of an anointed Davidic king caused Jews to begin looking to the heavens for a *new* kind of messiah, one who would restore the glory of Israel.

THE MAKING OF THE MESSIAH(S)

After King David is said to have established Jerusalem, the Bible makes it clear that Solomon and every subsequent king of Judah were to be anointed king at the Giḥon Spring in the Qidron (Kidron) Valley, which forms the eastern boundary of the City of David. Thus, Jerusalem plays an important role as the place where all new kings of Judah were anointed as God's chosen king.

First Kings 1:32–39 establishes the practice:

> King David said, "Summon to me the priest Zadok, the prophet Nathan, and Benaiah son of Jehoiada." When they came before the king, the king said to them, "Take with you the servants of your lord, and have my son Solomon ride on my own mule, and bring him down to Gihon. There let the priest Zadok and the prophet Nathan anoint him king over Israel; then blow the trumpet, and say, 'Long live King Solomon!'" . . . So the priest Zadok, the prophet Nathan, and Benaiah son of Jehoiada, and the Cherethites and the Pelethites, went down and had Solomon ride on King David's mule, and led him to Gihon. There the priest Zadok took the horn of oil from the tent and anointed Solomon. Then they blew the trumpet, and all the people said, "Long live King Solomon!"

Note here that in the inauguration ceremony Solomon rides the royal mule down to the Giḥon Spring in the Kidron Valley east of Jerusalem and is anointed king. Then there is a blowing of trumpets and a cheer that literally reads, "Let live King Solomon!" (which the NRSV translates colloquially as "Long live King Solomon" and the KJV translates quite Britishly as "God save King Solomon!").

This same custom is mentioned in Zechariah 9:9, which says, "Rejoice greatly, O daughter Zion! Shout aloud, O daughter of Jerusalem! Lo, your king comes to you, *triumphant and victorious* (lit., *having been saved*) is he, humble and riding on a donkey, on a colt, the foal of a donkey." Thus, the coronation of the kings of

Israel and later Judah appear to have followed this same pattern, where the king rides on the royal mule from the Giḥon Spring uphill and westward into Jerusalem, while the *shofar* is blown and the people yell, "Save the king" and "Long live the king."

Of course, we know of one additional example of this very coronation ceremony; it is the staged reenactment of it by none other than Jesus of Nazareth, commonly called the "triumphal entry" into Jerusalem. Mark 11:1–11 and its Gospel parallels[17] tell the story of a prearranged attempt to act out the coronation scene of Israel's kings on the part of Jesus. I say "staged" and "prearranged," because the first parts of each of the Synoptic accounts (Mark, Matthew, and Luke) describe Jesus instructing two of the disciples to go into the city and retrieve a young colt that has never been ridden (11:2); if anyone asks, they are to say, "The Lord needs it," and the owner of the colt will let them have it (11:3).[18]

Mark 11:7–10 then goes on to say:

Then they brought the colt to Jesus and threw their cloaks on it; and he sat on it. Many people spread their cloaks on the road, and others spread leafy branches that they had cut in the fields. Then those who went ahead and those who followed were shouting, "Hosanna! Blessed is the one who comes in the name of the Lord! Blessed is the coming kingdom of our ancestor David! Hosanna in the highest heaven!"

In order to understand the significance of this passage, we must know something about the geography of Jerusalem. Note that the story begins with Jesus and his disciples approaching Jerusalem from the Mount of Olives. Remember that the Kidron Valley and the Giḥon Spring lie between the Mount of Olives to the east and the Jerusalem Temple to the west. This means that in order for Jesus and his disciples to get from the Mount of Olives to Jerusalem, Jesus must ride his donkey down past the Giḥon and up into Jerusalem—roughly the same route as the ancient kings of Israel.

Jesus's triumphal entry into Jerusalem was not an instance of "humble" donkey-powered transportation into Jerusalem. Far from it! Jesus was choreographing a Jewish coronation ceremony, complete with a prearranged ride from the Mount of Olives, through the Kidron Valley, past the Giḥon Spring, and up into Jerusalem on the back of a representative royal donkey in the midst of people shouting the royal praise, "*Hosanna, Son of David!*" Jesus was portraying himself as the new king of the Jews!

JESUS AND JERUSALEM
IN THE NEW TESTAMENT

Many people forget that Jesus was *not* from Jerusalem. He was from Nazareth (or Bethleḥem, depending on which Gospel you read. We'll get to that in Chapter 10). But all of the Gospels unanimously record Jesus as having been tried and crucified in Jerusalem. In the Gospel of Luke, the adult Jesus never enters Jerusalem until the final week of his life.[19] This is different from the way Jesus is depicted in the Gospel of John, which has Jesus entering and departing from Jerusalem on multiple occasions.

One other difference between the Synoptic Gospels and the Gospel of John is that John depicts Jesus as being crucified on the day of preparation for the Passover, which is the day *before* Passover, as John was focused on portraying Jesus as the sacrificial lamb slain for the sins of humankind (see 19:31). However, the Synoptic Gospels depict Jesus as eating the evening Passover meal with his disciples (Luke 22:15) and then being crucified the morning after the Passover meal was eaten (Mark 15:25). Thus although the Gospels do not agree on the day on which Jesus was crucified, they all agree that he was tried and crucified in Jerusalem.

And of course for Christians it is the miracle of Jesus's resurrection from the dead that solidifies Jerusalem as the center of the world around which the fate of humankind revolves. The resurrection and ascension of Jesus in Jerusalem make the city the epicenter of the Christian movement. The church in Jerusalem was led by the disciples-turned-apostles who were with Jesus during his ministry until the apostle Paul (who was *not* with Jesus during his ministry) took over the spreading of the religion to Gentiles throughout the Roman Empire. This, some argue, transformed the Jesus movement from a largely Jewish phenomenon into one that could attract and incorporate Gentile members.

THE JEWISH REVOLT AND THE DESTRUCTION OF JERUSALEM IN 70 CE

The Roman general Titus destroyed the Jerusalem Temple in 70 CE during the Roman effort to suppress the Jewish Revolt, which had begun four years earlier. The Jewish historian Josephus chronicles the events of this conflict in his book *The Jewish War*. The destruction of the Jerusalem Temple is commemorated in a panel on the triumphal Arch of Titus erected in the Roman Forum. The panel depicts the menorah and other objects from the Temple being carted off to Rome.

As Roslyn and I stood beneath the Arch of Titus and gazed upon its depiction of the destruction of Jerusalem, my mind wandered to the southern end of the Temple Mount in Jerusalem, which is now a park serving as an archaeological memorial to the Roman destruction of Jerusalem. As I stared at the menorah on the arch, I recalled standing on the massive stones that once stood atop the Temple platform in Jerusalem. I felt I was in two places at once—Rome and Jerusalem—attempting to reconcile the catastrophic event from these two very different points of view. Rome celebrates. Jerusalem wails. And in that singular moment in history—the second destruction of the Jerusalem Temple—everything changed.

The Arch of Titus on the Via Sacra (the main road in ancient Rome) just southeast of the Roman Forum. Constructed around 82 CE by the Roman Emperor Domitian, it commemorates Titus's victories.

The destruction of the Temple in Jerusalem in 70 CE fundamentally altered Judaism and Christianity; it brought to an end all of the Jewish sectarian groups that were centered on sacrifice at the Temple. For instance, we hear very little of the Jerusalem priesthood and the Sadducees after 70 CE. However, those Jewish groups who had already begun the transition from worship involving ritual sacrifice at the Temple to other forms, like prayer and study of the Hebrew Scriptures, and who congregated in smaller local meetings in synagogues and house churches were able to survive the destruction of the Temple. Most notable among these survivors were the Pharisees, who became the tradition we know today as Rabbinic Judaism, and another Jewish sect who believed that a prophet from Nazareth was the promised Jewish messiah: the Christians.

The sects of the Pharisees and the Christians were able to survive the destruction of the Temple, because they were not tied to Jerusalem and were popular religious movements among the lower classes of the Jewish people. Thus, when Jerusalem was destroyed, many Jews and Christians fled to other cities and countries, inadvertently spreading Rabbinic Judaism and Christianity throughout the region. There, just as the exiled Judahites had done six centuries earlier, both groups began to write down the experiences and the teachings of their respective leaders, and both Rabbinic Judaism and Christianity began to look to their *new* writings for authority and inspiration in addition to the Hebrew Scriptures.

Thus, like the destruction of the Solomon's Temple, the destruction of the Second Temple directly led to the writing down, compilation, and editing of each group's religious traditions, eventually leading to the Mishnah and the Talmud for Rabbinic Judaism and the New Testament for Christians. In this way, the destruction of the Second Temple in 70 CE was the literal impetus for the building of the Bible.

THE EMPRESS HELENA'S
QUEST FOR EVIDENCE OF JESUS

Jerusalem is best known to Christians as the place where Jesus was tried, crucified, buried, and resurrected from the dead. This is the central tenet of the Christian faith. All four of the Gospels place Jesus's death on the cross and his resurrection from the dead as the climax of their accounts of Jesus's life. But despite being arguably the most referenced and written about event in human history, there is absolutely no archaeological evidence that supports the life, death, or resurrection of Jesus. None. To be sure, there is *written* evidence that his followers *believed* that Jesus lived, died, and overcame death, and later on we find some non-Christian literary references to Christians and Jesus, but there is no archaeological evidence of his life, death, and resurrection beyond the physical remains of certain places in Jerusalem that provide the *context* for the literary accounts of Jesus's life.

The lack of evidence for Jesus is not just a problem for modern Christians and scholars; it was an evident problem in antiquity as well. The early church needed *evidence* of Jesus's life, death, and resurrection, and who better than Helena (250–330), the mother of the Roman emperor Constantine the Great (272–337), to find that evidence.

Roman Christianity and the (Supposed) Evidence of Jesus

Empress Helena traveled to Jerusalem in 324 in order to identify the locations of the events that took place in Jesus's life and memorialize them by constructing monuments there. She believed that doing so would provide hard evidence that the biblical claims made about Jesus were true. While in Roman Palestine, Helena dedicated the Church of Nativity in Bethlehem and the Church of the Ascension on the Mount of Olives and oversaw construction of the Church of the Holy Sepulchre. It was also claimed that she discovered the "True Cross" on which Jesus was crucified at the site where the Church of the Holy Sepulchre had been uncovered. The legends told about *how* Helena came to identify many of these places range from straining credibility to comic gold, particularly the story of the discovery of the True Cross.

According to Eusebius of Caesarea,[20] a temple to the Roman goddess Venus had been built over the site of Jesus's crucifixion following Emperor Hadrian's suppression of the Bar-Kokhba Revolt in 135 CE, after which he banned all Jews from Jerusalem and renamed the city Aelia Capitolina in an effort to transform Jerusalem into a more standardized Roman city. Eusebius says that the now Christian emperor Constantine ordered the temple destroyed, the tomb of Jesus uncovered, and a church (today known as the Church of the Holy Sepulchre) to be built in 325 to commemorate the site of Jesus's death and burial.

Socrates of Constantinople added in his account that Helena actually discovered *three* crosses—one for Jesus and the other two for the thieves crucified with him—as well as the *titulus,* or the wooden plaque affixed above Jesus's head that read "King of the Jews,"[21]

The entrance to the Church of the Holy Sepulchre, the church built atop the tomb complex in Jerusalem commemorating the traditional site of the crucifixion and burial of Jesus.

The Edicule (Shrine) of the Tomb inside the Church of the Holy Sepulchre houses the stone remains of the tomb traditionally believed to be the burial place of Jesus of Nazareth (cf. Matt. 27:59–60).

all beneath the destroyed temple to Venus.[22] According to Socrates of Constantinople, Helena ran an experiment, which is hilariously satirized by Mark Twain in his epic Holy Land travel guide, *Innocents Abroad,* to determine which of the three crosses actually belonged to Jesus. Rather than give you Socrates of Constantinople's account, I thought you'd enjoy Mark Twain's version of this early "scientific" experiment:

A noble lady lay very ill in Jerusalem. The wise priests ordered that the three crosses be taken to her bedside one at a time. It was done. When her eyes fell upon the first one, she uttered a scream that was heard beyond the Damascus Gate, and even upon the Mount of Olives, it was said, and then fell back in a deadly swoon. They recovered her and brought the second cross. Instantly she went into fearful convulsions, and it was with the greatest difficulty that six strong men could hold her. They were afraid, now, to bring in the third cross. They began to fear that possibly they had fallen upon the wrong crosses, and that the true cross was not with this number at all. However, as the woman seemed likely to die with the convulsions that were tearing her, they concluded that the third could do no more than put her out of her misery with a happy dispatch. So they brought it, and behold, a miracle! The woman sprang from her bed, smiling and joyful, and perfectly restored to health. When we listen to evidence like this, we cannot but believe. We would be ashamed to doubt, and properly, too. Even the very part of Jerusalem where this all occurred is there yet. So there is really no room for doubt.[23]

Twain's humorous account mirrors the skepticism felt by many scholars about Helena's so-called evidence. Socrates of Constantinople also claims that Helena discovered the "holy nails" used to fasten Jesus to the cross. Helena reportedly sent the holy relics to her son, Constantine, who had the magical talismans fashioned into bridle bits for his horses and a helmet, which kept him safe during battle. Today, the twelfth-century Armenian

Chapel of St. Helena, in the basement of the Church of the Holy Sepulchre, stands over the place where Crusaders claimed Helena discovered the True Cross.

Thus, because of the "verification" of the power still contained within the holy relics of Jesus and the endorsement of Constantine the Great's mother (and be honest, who's going to mess with the emperor's mother?), evidence of Jesus and the claims about him were "authenticated" by Rome, and Jerusalem became a place of pilgrimage for Christians throughout the empire. Galerius's Edict of Toleration (311) may have ended the state-sponsored persecution of Christians and legalized Christianity, and the Edict of Milan (313) may have returned property confiscated by the state to churches, but it was not until well after Helena's visit to Jerusalem in 324 that Rome issued the Edict of Thessalonica (380), which made Christianity the official state religion of the Roman Empire. All Roman subjects were to espouse the Nicene confessions of faith professed by Pope Damasus I (who we'll discuss in Chapter 11) and Peter II, the bishop of Alexandria.

THE LEGACY OF JERUSALEM TODAY

Jerusalem lies at the heart of the Bible. It is the focal point of much of the Hebrew Bible, serving as the capital of Israel and later of Judah. It was home to the ark of the covenant and to the First and Second Jewish Temples, all of which represented the presence of God among his people. For Jews, Jerusalem was, and is, the city of God, and the tale of Jerusalem's rise to glory and its destruction inspired the formation of the Bible.

For Christians, although Jesus spent most of his ministry in the Galilee, Jerusalem became inextricably associated with Jesus and Christianity. The fact that his crucifixion and resurrection took place in Jerusalem and that the early church was centered around the apostles Peter and James in Jerusalem made it the city of God for Christians as well.

Today, Jerusalem is home to Reform, Conservative, Orthodox, and Hasidic Jews; Roman Catholic, Orthodox, Armenian, and all flavors of Protestant Christians; and Shi'a, Sunni, and other Muslim groups. It is a beautiful mess of an eternal city that will always have a place in my heart, not only because it is the home to so many of my friends and colleagues, but because it is *the* place that truly built the Bible. It is not enough simply to pray for Jerusalem; we must continue to work hard for the peace of Jerusalem.

CHAPTER 9

Qumran

The Dead Sea Scrolls are the greatest archaeological discovery of the twentieth century. They were discovered in caves near the ancient settlement of Qumran, and despite never being mentioned in the Bible, Qumran and the scrolls changed the way we read and understand the Bible. The discovery of the first scrolls in 1947 signaled the beginning of the end for the long since debunked, yet lingering concept of what many called "biblical inerrancy," which is the notion that the Bible is the perfect, verbatim, inerrant, noncontradictory Word of God. The scrolls provided us with tangible handwritten evidence that the text of the Hebrew Bible has, in fact, changed throughout the years and that there were different, some say "competing," versions of the biblical books early on in history.

The scrolls provided modern Bible translators and publishers access to versions of the books of the Hebrew Bible that were a thousand years older than any previously known copies of these books. The fact that the text of the books of the Bible discovered among the Dead Sea Scrolls is *different* from that in many of our modern Bibles is evidence itself that the text of the Bible—the Word of God—has changed over the past two thousand years. Thus, we can say that Qumran has become a key city in the development of the *modern* Bible we know today, as many versions of the Bible published since the 1950s have taken into account what we've learned from the scrolls; newer versions of the Bible often side with the text of the Dead Sea Scrolls when traditional versions of biblical books preserve variant textual traditions.

THE DEAD SEA SCROLLS
UP CLOSE AND PERSONAL

In 2010, I was fortunate enough to host a National Geographic Channel documentary entitled *Writing the Dead Sea Scrolls*. In the show, I explored the question of who *really* wrote the Dead Sea Scrolls. While filming *Writing the Dead Sea Scrolls,* I met Adolfo Roitman, the curator of the Shrine of the Book on the campus of the Israel Museum, where the Dead Sea Scrolls are housed and displayed. I had been in the shrine before, but Dr. Roitman led me to a place that few people have ever been: the underground vault where the Dead Sea Scrolls are kept.

Behind a nondescript door inside the Shrine of the Book lies a highly secure hallway protected by multiple secured gates and doors, including a thick blast-proof door that protects these national treasures from a bomb attack. The high-tech hallway leads to the archaeological Holy of Holies: the Dead Sea Scrolls vault. Following Dr. Roitman through door after door reminded me of the title sequence of the classic TV show *Get Smart,* only the doors in the Dead Sea Scrolls vault required any number of keys, passwords, and codes from Dr. Roitman in order to open them. And each door locked behind us as we passed through, just to ensure that no one gets out without proper authorization.

I got the shivers as I followed Dr. Roitman into the vault— and not only because of the temperature-controlled climate. For an archaeologist, this was an exhilarating experience. These were the *actual* Dead Sea Scrolls. Fascination turned to veiled giddiness when Dr. Roitman asked me to help him remove the Great Isaiah Scroll (1QIsaᵃ) from the vault and place it on the examination table. I did so, careful to touch only the foam board on which the priceless scroll was mounted. It might as well have been the ark of the covenant, such was the feeling of nearly overwhelming enthrallment I was experiencing in that vault. And the ark is an apt comparison in that the same penalty—death—awaits anyone who touches the scrolls with their hands (or so I learned with a wink from Adolfo).

The author in the underground scroll vault with Dr. Adolfo Roitman, the curator of the Shrine of the Book in Jerusalem, where the Dead Sea Scrolls are housed.

Just then, to complete my fantasy experience, Dr. Roitman invited me to read from the Great Isaiah Scroll with him while the camera crew filmed us. He asked me if I could make out some letters toward the beginning of the scroll. As I worked through the ancient script and read the words he was pointing to aloud, I found myself reading Isaiah 2:4: "They shall beat their swords into plowshares, and their spears into pruning hooks; and nation shall not lift up sword against nation, neither shall they learn war any more."

I had chills. I had just read in the original Hebrew from the oldest copy of any biblical manuscript known to humankind.

As we cut and our cameraman, Lawrence, lowered his camera, I exhaled. I fought off tears, stunned at what I had just experienced.

Dr. Roitman looked at me and said, "Not bad."

I replied, "That is an important verse. Do you think we'll ever experience this?"

He looked me in the eye and replied hopefully, "Pray for the peace of Jerusalem."

The author reading the Great Isaiah Scroll (1QIsaᵃ) in the underground scroll vault with Dr. Adolfo Roitman, the curator of the Shrine of the Book in Jerusalem, where the Dead Sea Scrolls are housed.

As we exited the vault, I didn't notice the gauntlet of doors. I had just been behind the proverbial curtain with the "high priest" of the Dead Sea Scrolls, and I had just read from a twenty-two-hundred-year-old copy of the book of Isaiah. There are no words.

These Dead Sea Scrolls help us better understand the origin of our Bible. But before we examine how the discovery of the scrolls affects how we read our modern Bibles (and what our modern Bibles *actually say*), let us first look at the (often comical) story of the discovery of the scrolls as well as the controversies that have surrounded the archaeological interpretation of Qumran.

THE DISCOVERY OF THE SCROLLS

The tale of Qumran goes back to a legend about a Bedouin sheepherder named Muḥammad Aḥmed el-Ḥāmed, who was nicknamed edh-Dhib, or "the Wolf." The Bedouin are nomadic and seminomadic tribes of ethnic Arabs who typically occupy the Arabian Peninsula. In my interactions with them, I've found them to be suspicious of city life, warmly hospitable, and possessing a deep, proud sense of tradition and tribal customs.

There are several Bedouin families of various tribes located east of Jerusalem whose tents are visible as you descend down the Ma'ale 'Adumim, the section of Highway 1 leading east of Jerusalem down toward the Dead Sea. There are also several Bedouin families who operate tours in Wadi Rum on the way from 'Aqaba to Petra in Jordan. I took a Bedouin tour of Wadi Rum with my Iowa students one summer following a season excavating at Tel 'Azeqah. We spent the day hiking the Jordanian desert, climbing on mind-blowing rock formations and through deep desert canyons, and in

A Bedouin cook at Rum Stars Camp in Wadi Rum cooks dinner in a zarb, *which uses the warmth of the desert sand to barbecue food.*

the evening we danced the night away in a Bedouin camp. We fell asleep under a blanket of stars in a traditional Bedouin enclosure on the warm desert floor with bellies full of lamb and roasted vegetables that had been cooked in an underground barbecue called a *zarb*. I kid you not; you must do this at least once in your life.

Returning to the discovery of the Dead Sea Scrolls, the story goes that some time in the winter of 1946 or early in 1947, Muḥammad the Wolf and some pals were out grazing his sheep on the lands just below the marl cliffs (the lime-rich mudstone that indicates the cliffs' underwater history) that contain what is now Cave 1. On that fateful day, one adventuring member of Muḥammad the Wolf's flock wandered up into the cave. Climbing the precipitous scarp leading up to the cave, Muḥammad the Wolf threw a rock into the cave in an attempt to scare the wayward sheep out of the cave. He heard something shatter! Curious as to what he'd broken, Muḥammad the Wolf climbed up into the cave and discovered that he had accidentally shattered a ceramic jar, which had apparently been exposed, but yet (suspiciously) not been shattered (or even noticed) for two millennia—until now.

For this reason, some argue that parts of the story of the discovery of the scrolls were invented to cover up the fact that Bedouin regularly seek out (read: loot) caves, ancient settlements, and excavation sites in order to find archaeological artifacts that can be sold to antiquities dealers (both licensed and on the black market) for a profit. This still happens today, and perhaps more so now than in decades past.

At Tel 'Azeqah, where I excavate with my Iowa students, we hire a guard to watch the site at night so that looters don't steal the exposed in situ objects that are in the process of being excavated. One night, our guard never showed up, and that very evening looters came to our site and wrested from it a number of exposed vessels from a productive archaeological square. In the morning, we discovered small holes that pockmarked the square, the result of looters with metal detectors and hand spades looking for coins that can be harvested and sold on eBay or on the black market.

This happens to every archaeological site every year. So the tale about a shepherd "accidentally" discovering a jar and scrolls in caves may have been concocted to disguise the fact that the first of the Dead Sea Scrolls were, to be blunt, looted.[1]

Subsequent rummaging led the Bedouin herdsmen to discover ten jars, several of which contained rolled-up pieces of leather. Muḥammad the Wolf took the scrolls to a Bethleḥem antiquities dealer named Ibrahim 'Ijha, who returned them, fearing they were stolen from a synagogue.

Muḥammad the Wolf then took the scrolls to a Bethleḥem cobbler named Khalil Eskander Shahin, nicknamed "Kando," who also dealt in antiquities on the side. Kando saw the Semitic writing on the scrolls and immediately purchased the scrolls from Muḥammad the Wolf.

Because of the prospective danger of possessing potentially illicit antiquities originating from desert Bedouin, Kando had a colleague sell the scrolls on his behalf, and soon four scrolls were purchased by the local leader of the Syrian Orthodox Church, Metropolitan Athanasius Yeshue Samuel, also referred to as "Mar Samuel," for £24 ($97 U.S. at the time). This buyer, Mar Samuel, could not read all the ancient characters, and so in November of 1947 he invited Hebrew University professor of archaeology Eleazar Sukenik to Jerusalem to examine and, he hoped, decipher the scrolls and confirm their authenticity and value, so that Mar Samuel could sell them, with the proceeds going to his church.

Sukenik was so taken with the scrolls and their significance that he purchased two of the remaining three scrolls (1QH, or *Hodayot,* also called the *Hymns Scroll,* and 1QM, or *Milḥamah,* the *War Scroll*) being shopped around by dealers on behalf of the newly formed State of Israel. Many Jews saw tremendous symbolism in the timing of the purchase of these newly discovered scrolls, as they were acquired on November 29, 1947—the very day that the United Nations voted in favor of UN Resolution 181(II), the Partition Plan for Palestine, which created the modern Jewish State of Israel.[2]

This is why, in addition to their scholarly value, the Dead Sea Scrolls have such national value to Israel; they are understood as symbolic refounding documents of the Jewish state. In the same way that the earliest Dead Sea Scrolls were composed during the last time an independent state of Israel existed (i.e., the Hasmonean period beginning in 141 BCE), so too does the discovery and reacquisition of the Dead Sea Scrolls represent to many the refounding of an independent Jewish state.

About a month after the UN voted to partition Palestine, Sukenik purchased the third remaining scroll, which was a second copy of the biblical book of Isaiah (1QIsa^b). Meanwhile, Mar Samuel feared that the war in Palestine would deter the highest bidders from Europe and America from purchasing his scrolls, so to maximize his profits he smuggled the scrolls to Beirut, Lebanon.[3] Unsatisfied with the bids that were coming in for his scrolls in Beirut, Mar Samuel then smuggled the scrolls to the safety of Worcester, Massachusetts, and later to Washington D.C., where he put them on display in the Library of Congress to attract buyers.

Still unsatisfied with the offers, Mar Samuel did what you do when you wanted to sell something in the 1950s: he placed an ad in the paper. On June 1, 1954, an ad in the *Wall Street Journal* read:

MISCELLANEOUS FOR SALE

"The Four Dead Sea Scrolls"

Biblical Manuscripts dating back to at least 200 BC, are for sale. This would be an ideal gift to an educational or religious institution by an individual or group.
Box F 206, The Wall Street Journal.

The ad placed in the Wall Street Journal by Mar Samuel attempting to sell the Dead Sea Scrolls.

It is still debated today whether this ad in the paper was an act of lunacy or genius. As it turned out, Mar Samuel did end up attracting some attention for his scrolls. Eleazar Sukenik's son, Yigael Yadin, a recently retired Israel Defense Forces general, had used his keen knowledge of the land of Israel to start a second career as an archaeologist. Yadin wanted Mar Samuel's scrolls, but couldn't simply make a bid on them, as once Mar Samuel realized that the newly formed Israeli government was in the market for his scrolls, the price would skyrocket.

Yadin used intermediaries who posed as representatives for a private collector to negotiate the purchase. He also employed his friend, Harry Orlinsky, who, under the name "Mr. Green," authenticated the scrolls as worthy of the asking price. When the charade was complete, Yadin had purchased Mar Samuel's four scrolls: 1QIsa^a, or the *Great Isaiah Scroll,* a copy of the book of the prophet Isaiah; 1QpHab, or the *Commentary on Habakkuk;* 1QS, the *Manual of Discipline,* which is also known as the *Community Rule;* and what is today known as 1QapGen, or the *Genesis Apocryphon,* an Aramaic and highly elaborative rewrite of the primordial and patriarchal stories from Genesis. Yadin paid $250,000 for the scrolls, the lion's share of which was proudly contributed by David Samuel Gottesman, a Jewish philanthropist, who would later be appointed as one of the trustees of the Shrine of the Book.

And that was just the beginning. It wasn't long before everyone's attention turned toward the ancient settlement of Khirbet Qumran, buried atop a plateau next to a cluster of the scroll caves. It is this small settlement of Qumran to which we turn next.

THE EXCAVATION OF QUMRAN

It didn't take long before official excavations were begun at Khirbet Qumran to determine if anything could be learned from the site sitting in the midst of the caves that had preserved the scrolls. It is here, with the archaeology of Qumran, which sits atop

The famous Cave 4 at Qumran, as seen from the visitor's viewpoint south of the Khirbet Qumran settlement.

a plateau on the northwest shore of the Dead Sea, that some of the nastiest battles in the history of biblical scholarship have taken place. These battles are shaped by one central question: Who wrote the Dead Sea Scrolls?

The leaders of the first excavation of Qumran—Gerald Lankester Harding, a British archaeologist and director of the Department of Antiquities of Jordan from 1936 to 1956, and Father Roland de Vaux, director of the French Dominican École Biblique et Archéologique Française in Jerusalem—began excavating Qumran in December 1951 and excavated the site for five seasons. It didn't take long for Harding and de Vaux to form an opinion about the remains of Qumran.

In 1956, following a theory advanced by Eleazar Sukenik prior to the excavations, de Vaux endorsed what has come to be known as the Qumran-Essene Hypothesis, which postulates that a little-known group of Jewish sectarians living between Jerusalem and the Dead Sea called the Essenes built the settlement at Qumran and wrote the scrolls that had been hidden in the caves surrounding the site. De Vaux argued that the residents of Qumran were responsible for the scrolls following his discovery of two inkwells in a room he dubbed the "Scriptorium" and another inkwell in

an adjacent room. Thus, de Vaux concluded that the settlement
at Qumran was a sectarian Jewish settlement built by highly ob-
servant religious Jews in the second century BCE who practiced
communal living and self-subsistence and wrote and copied scrolls
for their own personal study and governance. He maintained that
members of the sect hid the scrolls in the nearby caves when the
Romans invaded in 66 CE. The Romans attacked Qumran and the
residents never returned to collect their hidden scrolls, which lay
dormant until their auspicious discovery in 1947 by Muḥammad
the Wolf (and the hordes of archaeologists, spelunkers, searchers,
and scavengers who followed).

A view of the Qumran plateau visitor's lookout from inside Cave 4.

Other scholars since de Vaux, including myself, disagree with the Qumran-Essene Hypothesis. Some scholars argue that, although sectarian Jews may have lived at Qumran, they may not have been as "monastic" as the Dominican Father de Vaux may have believed them to be. Other scholars and I believe that the site was initially built for an entirely different purpose, namely, as a Hasmonean military fort or lookout post, which was abandoned and later reoccupied by a Jewish sectarian group who may or may not have been the Essenes and who did not necessarily write all of the scrolls, but were perhaps responsible for writing or copying a few of them.

Another group of scholars argues that Qumran had nothing whatsoever to do with the Dead Sea Scrolls, and because of this the site should be interpreted secularly, without any sectarian understandings tainting its interpretation. They argue various Jewish refugees fleeing the destruction of Jerusalem placed the scrolls in caves along the shore of the Dead Sea, and that whatever was going on at Qumran had no connection to the scrolls.

So essentially the question—and the academic squabble—comes down to this: Were the Dead Sea Scrolls composed, copied, or collected at Qumran? Or did Jews who had nothing to do with Qumran hide them in the various caves? This question has been debated so vociferously that one participant in the debate actually crossed the line into cybercriminal activity.

THE CURSE OF THE DEAD SEA SCROLLS

The blood sport that is Qumran scholarship and what many dub the "curse of the Dead Sea Scrolls" continue. The scrolls were at the center of a recent criminal court case that landed the son of one scholar who has written about the scrolls in prison!

I was personally involved in the case of Dr. Raphael Golb, a lawyer and the son of a University of Chicago specialist in medieval Judaism, Norman Golb, who was the author of a book entitled *Who Wrote the Dead Sea Scrolls?* In the book, Norman

Golb, like many scholars before him, made arguments that contested the prevailing Qumran-Essene Hypothesis.[4] The book was dismissed by most Qumran and scrolls scholars at the time—a fact that Norman Golb, and later his son, did not appreciate.

With the rise of the Internet, Norman Golb's son began using the alias "Charles Gadda" and a number of other aliases in an attempt to advocate anonymously on his father's behalf. Using these aliases, Raphael Golb created blog sites that criticized scholars working with a traveling exhibition of the Dead Sea Scrolls making its way through U.S. museums. Each new blog would be accompanied by a massive anonymous e-mail campaign targeting museums hosting scrolls exhibitions and universities where faculty affiliated with the exhibitions taught. The e-mails, addressed to any number of administrators at these institutions, criticized the scholars for essentially being wrong about Qumran (because they did not accept Norman Golb's theories) and chastised the museums for not inviting Norman Golb to speak at them.

E-mails obtained from Raphael Golb's computer during the police investigation included messages from his father, Norman Golb, and his mother offering advice and instructions about what to say and how to avoid getting caught. One e-mail from Raphael Golb to his mother read, "By the way, if Dad has some comment on the latest Charles Gadda exchange, he can send it through your email, that way there would be no trace of it in his account."[5] A response from his mother read, "We can't send via Dad's email so we'll send via mine."[6] And however trollish this behavior may seem, his lack of success in promoting his father's theory led him to cross the line into criminal activity.[7]

During the anonymous e-mail campaign, Raphael Golb used an alias to target one of his father's old academic rivals, NYU's Lawrence Schiffman, and accused him (anonymously, of course) of plagiarizing Norman Golb. Raphael Golb then engaged in activities that the State of New York determined to be criminal and for which he was charged, arrested, and found guilty.[8]

Raphael Golb was arrested by the NYPD on the morning of March 5, 2009, and charged with fifty-one felony and misdemeanor counts of identity theft, forgery, criminal impersonation, aggravated harassment, and the unauthorized use of a computer in his campaign against a number of Dead Sea Scrolls scholars, including Dr. Schiffman and me.[9] Having been in the process of creating a 3-D virtual reality reconstruction of Qumran as part of my UCLA dissertation (with which Dr. Golb and his son disagreed), I was asked to provide reconstructions and movies to a number of museums hosting scrolls exhibitions.

When Raphael Golb began targeting me personally in his Internet campaign, I used my tech skills to track the massive list of aliases, e-mail addresses, and IP addresses he had used in his campaign against scroll scholars. I handed my findings over to the NYPD, and on September 24, 2010, I was asked to testify against Raphael Golb during his trial, in which I was cross-examined (and yelled at a lot) by none other than civil rights defense attorney Ron Kuby (of *The Big Lebowski* fame).

On September 30, 2010, Raphael Golb was found guilty of two felony and twenty-eight misdemeanor counts. He was later sentenced to six months in prison and automatically disbarred from the New York State Bar Association. Some of these charges were later overturned on appeal and Golb's prison sentence was reduced to two months in prison and three years probation for being found guilty on nineteen counts of identity theft and criminal impersonation. As of the publication of this book, Raphael Golb is still out of prison pending multiple additional appeals.

Raphael Golb was sentenced to prison for criminal acts he committed against another scholar, which stemmed from a debate over who wrote the Dead Sea Scrolls. *That* is how crazy Dead Sea Scrolls scholarship got at its ugly apex. It also shows that the scrolls are a topic of great importance to a number of people, not just because of the implications of the archaeological debate, but because of how the discovery of the Dead Sea Scrolls fundamentally altered our perception of the creation of the Bible, which we'll explore next.

HOW THE DEAD SEA SCROLLS
AFFECT THE BIBLE

The discovery of the Dead Sea Scrolls caused shock waves throughout the world of biblical studies because they not only changed the
way we read the Bible; they quite literally changed what the Bible
says! The Dead Sea Scrolls are both powerful and controversial,
because they provide hard evidence that the text of the Bible was
changed early and often. Although many people touted the discovery of the scrolls as evidence of the reliability of the text of the Bible,
because well over 90 percent of the text from the copies of biblical
books discovered among the scrolls is similar to the text of the Bibles
we have today, the fact that they are not 100 percent identical proves
the point that the text of the Bible has changed over time.

The Dead Sea Scrolls demonstrate to us that the texts that became the Bible were literary attempts to convey ideas about God
and his activity in history, and the words used to convey these
ideas could (and did) vary from manuscript to manuscript. And
this is okay!

The important thing to remember is that these corrections and
changes were not made by skeptics and those who hated Scripture,
but by those who gave their lives to preserve it. These copyists
were faithful Jews. Copyists and editors changed the text based on
a variety of factors from personal preference to the correction of
perceived errors, but ultimately all changes were made in order to
make the Bible align with what the authors of the scrolls believed.
The Dead Sea Scrolls' revelation about the changing nature of
early biblical texts does not challenge the faith of Jews and Christians who read the Bible as a record of God's activity in history.
The scrolls do, however, destroy any lingering fundamentalist
notion that the text of the Bible we have today is "inerrant" or
"unchanged" over time, as I'll demonstrate shortly.

The science of identifying changes to copied and translated
texts and then attempting to identify a reason for these changes
is part of a discipline within biblical studies called "redaction

criticism." Below I offer a few of many examples of how the text of the Dead Sea Scrolls differs from the text of the Bible we had before their discovery.

There are lots of places where the Dead Sea Scrolls help us decide which biblical manuscript tradition is better when there is a disagreement between manuscripts. An example of this is the differing accounts of the Philistine champion Goliath's height. First Samuel 17:4 in the Masoretic Text of the Hebrew Bible says, "And there came out from the camp of the Philistines a champion named Goliath, of Gath, whose height was *six cubits and a span*."

A cubit is about 18 inches, or 1½ feet, and a span is half of a cubit. So six cubits and a span is about 9¾ feet tall, which means the head of a person this tall would almost touch a regulation NBA basketball rim. *That's* a giant—bigger than Shaq, bigger than Andre! So the Hebrew Bible says that Goliath was six cubits and a span, or 9 feet 9 inches tall.

However, the Septuagint's translation of that same verse (1 Sam. 17:4) says that Goliath's height was *four* (Gk. *tessarōn,* τεσ-σάρων) cubits and a span, or 6 feet 9 inches tall. Granted, this is still very tall—certainly tall enough to play center in the Philistine Basketball Association—but it isn't the inhuman 9 feet 9 inches that Goliath is said to be in the Hebrew text. And before you dismiss the Septuagint's version as a mistake, remember that the Septuagint is the Bible of the New Testament authors, which they quote far more often than the Hebrew Bible. Furthermore, Josephus supports the Septuagint's reading in *Antiquities* 6.9.1 (6:171) when he says, "Goliath, of the city of Gath, a man of vast bulk, for he was of *four* (Gk. *tessarōn,* τεσσάρων) cubits and a span in tallness." Josephus supports the Septuagint's reading, and the Hebrew tradition appears to be the outlier.

So which is it? Is Goliath six cubits and a span (9 feet 9) or *four* cubits and a span (6 feet 9)?

The Dead Sea Scrolls provide another source against which to compare biblical accounts. In a copy of 1 Samuel discovered in Qumran Cave 4 (4QSamᵃ), the verse reads, "His height was *four*

(Heb. *'arba'*, ארבע) cubits and a span." So the Dead Sea Scrolls help us solve the mystery of just how tall Goliath actually was; he was a big 6-foot-9 man. Given that the average height of players in the NBA is a little over 6 feet 7, Goliath would have been truly considered a *giant* among men—just not a 10-footer as the Hebrew Bible says.

Another discrepancy between versions is in Deuteronomy 32:8, where the Masoretic Text says that God divided the nations according to the "children of Israel," the Septuagint says according to the "angels of God," and 4Q37 of the Dead Sea Scrolls says according to the "children of God." Or consider that the Dead Sea Scrolls (11QPs^a, the *Psalms Scroll*) and the Septuagint supply an entire extra verse in between vv. 13 and 14 in Psalm 145; this verse is missing in the Masoretic Text of the Hebrew Bible. Once again, this serves as evidence that there were multiple manuscript traditions in the first centuries BCE and CE and that the version in your Bible may be the minority and, dare I say, erroneous version.

Thus, we learn from the Dead Sea Scrolls that those who copied them either had different manuscript traditions of the biblical texts or felt free to substitute and change certain words as they pleased. Either way, it is evidence that the *words* that make up the "Word of God" were actually somewhat fluid and not as fixed in the first centuries BCE and CE as some would like to believe.

———

Although the Dead Sea Scrolls are significant because they are the oldest known copies of the books of the Hebrew Bible by over a thousand years, they are also politically important because their discovery and acquisition are intertwined with the very formation of the modern state of Israel.[10] They also have caused great controversy in scholarly circles, which has even led one person to criminal activity!

The scrolls give us an abundance of evidence that the text of the Bible was changed frequently as it was copied and that these variant copies often became manuscript traditions of their own.

Thus, although Qumran is never mentioned in the Bible, the scrolls discovered in the caves surrounding the site have directly helped build the Bible we read today, often because the Dead Sea Scrolls provide variant traditions or expansions that are as informative to us today as they were to the Jewish sectarians who wrote them two millennia ago.

CHAPTER 10

Bethleḥem and Nazareth

The cities of Bethleḥem and Nazareth are often associated with
Jesus. Even most nonreligious people can usually sing "O
Little Town of Bethlehem" around Christmastime, yet many are
often surprised to learn that neither city was ever a hub of early
Christian intellectual activity. In many ways, both cities function
today as symbols of Jesus for Christians more than they ever func-
tioned as historically significant locations. Although both cities
later came to be revered as pilgrimage sites for those wanting to
visit the places that Jesus was said to have been, as far as the Christian tradition and the composition of the Bible are concerned,
other cities we've explored here were far more significant. Still,
we should take a look at the history of these two cities, as both
possess a surprising past.

DISCOVERING BEAUTY IN
MODERN BETHLEḤEM

In 2006, as the towering border fence between Israel and the West
Bank was being constructed, I was headed to Israel to dig at Tel
Ḥaṣor (Hazor or Hatzor) and would be spending a few days in
Jerusalem prior to the excavation. When a Palestinian friend of
mine learned of my plans, he arranged a dinner for me with his
mother and family in Bethleḥem. I invited my colleague Kyle
Keimer to join me. My friend even arranged for our transportation, which I would soon learn was a bit more complicated than
simply taking a cab to their house due to the politically charged

climate. On the night of the dinner, we were picked up by a cab and dropped off at a large pile of boulders in between sections of the unfinished border fence. We were instructed to walk over the rocks and that there would be another car waiting for us, as the driver could not drive his car into the West Bank.

Kyle and I looked at each other and slowly got out of the car. We clambered over the boulders to the other side, where, sure enough, another car was waiting for us. Kyle and I got into that car, which then drove to a residential home. The garage door of the home began to open, and we drove into a garage. Then, immediately, the garage door began to close behind us, *while we were still in the car.*

We sat in silence.

I spoke up: "Um, hi. Salaam. What are we doing?" I asked.

The driver chuckled and said, "No worry. I'm not kidnapping you. We need to change cars," he said typing something into his cell phone.

"Why?" I asked.

"*They* are watching us," he responded without looking up from his phone.

We were then told to get out of the car and to get into the Mercedes parked next to us in the garage. We did as we were told.

When we were all settled, the driver opened the garage door and said, "Okay, now we go."

We backed out and began driving to my friend's mother's house. I later learned that when you don't go through the Israel–West Bank Barrier Fence checkpoint, the Israelis can still see you from the lookout towers (and the cameras, and the satellites, and the men stationed as lookouts, etc.). So Palestinians often take to switching cars under the cover of a closed garage in an effort to confuse anyone who might be looking at the car picking up the people scrambling over the rubble hole in the border fence. I'm not sure how effective it is, but I know that no one bothered us that night.

We proceeded to drive to my friend's mother's house, where they had quite literally killed the fatted calf for us. Well, actually, it was a lamb, but there it was, roasting on the spit. Nearby were an impressive array of pita bread, hummus, roasted tomatoes, cucumbers, and onions, a plate full of *kibbeh* (which I describe as meat hand grenades), and endless dishes of salads.

The driver led us into the house, where my friend's mother was waiting for us, flanked by two other Palestinian men. The face of the short, elderly woman betrayed a lifetime of both happiness and the difficulties of raising a Palestinian family in Bethlehem in the twentieth century.

She leaned toward Kyle and me, smiled, and said in her best English possible, "Thank you. Welcome."

Kyle and I nodded in gratitude, and I replied, "Thank you for your kind hospitality."

"We're glad you made it," one of the men said in perfect English.

He then lifted the phone he was holding in his left hand and handed it to me saying, "He wants to speak to you."

I took the phone hesitantly. I looked at Kyle, then at the phone, and said, "Hello?" not knowing to whom I was speaking.

"Bob, you made it!" came booming through the phone. I immediately recognized the voice of my friend, who had been on the phone the entire time to make sure we didn't run into any "problems" during our trip to his mother's house.

And it was at that dinner with Kyle, my friend's mother, her sons, and their children—a house full of twenty people in all—that I first experienced the sheer joy that Palestinian families share with one another, despite all of the ongoing militant chaos around them. We talked politics, but mostly made jokes. Kyle and I talked of our travels in Israel and Palestine, and they spoke of their travels to the United States. We made all the stereotypical jokes you tell when meeting someone from another country for the first time.

I then realized something profound: contrary to everything I had heard in the news about Palestinians, this Palestinian family was exactly like *my* family. We weren't rich, we worked hard, we took pride in our family, we tried to stay away from hostile people and keep our kids out of gangs, we believed what we believed, we liked to eat, tell jokes, laugh, criticize the government, and enjoy the beauty we found around us.

It was in Bethlehem that I discovered the beauty of the Palestinian people. And it wasn't in the Church of the Nativity or Manger Square, but over a wonderful dinner of roasted lamb and vegetables in the home of a woman I'd never met, whose son, seventy-five hundred miles away, had befriended me. It made me appreciate the struggles of honest, proud, hardworking Palestinians and completely forget about the three cars and closed-door garage swap needed to get there.

THE ARCHAEOLOGY THAT NEVER WAS

The site in Bethlehem that attracts all of the attention is the Church of the Nativity, which is built over the traditional place of Jesus's birth. As you approach the Church of the Nativity, you walk through the Door of Humility, a passageway entrance into the basilica in which visitors have to bow low to the ground, forcing a humbling prostration before entering the birthplace of Jesus.

And as you walk underneath the ornamental lamps and censers hanging above, you are directed around to the right of the altar, which leads to a staircase descending to a point directly beneath the altar. It is here that pilgrims find the grotto, the well-worn tapestry-covered remains of a cave that possesses at its center a hole in the now marble floor, the edge of which is preserved by a fourteen-point silver star and ringed by an assortment of hanging oil lamps and paintings of religious icons that keep watch over the traditional birthplace of baby Jesus. I have seen my own students sigh, weep, and become both enraptured and emotionally overwhelmed at the experience of visiting the traditional place of Jesus's birth.

The problem with the grotto for historians, however, is that there is no archaeological evidence telling us that this is, in fact, the

The Door of Humility, the entrance to the Church of the Nativity in Bethlehem, West Bank, built to commemorate the traditional birthplace of Jesus of Nazareth.

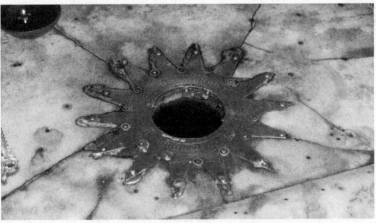

The fourteen-point silver star in the Holy Cave, the Grotto of the Nativity, marking the traditional spot where Jesus was born. The Latin inscription reads: "HIC DE VIRGINE MARIA IESUS CHRISTUS NATUS EST," meaning "Here Jesus Christ was born of the Virgin Mary."

place of Jesus's birth. I should note that there is an important difference between a traditional pilgrimage site and an archaeological site (though some archaeological sites can also be pilgrimage sites). Some sites traditionally associated with certain biblical characters or events produce no archaeological evidence to support any claim of historical association with the person or event.

But just because a site does not possess an archaeological record does not mean that the site cannot evoke emotions in the hearts and minds of believers. Traditional sites can inspire just as much faith and hope and sense of identity in religious individuals as archaeological and historical sites do in archaeologists, scientists, and historians. That is to say, pointing out that a religious site has no archaeological support for its association with a biblical figure does not mean that believers cannot have a spiritual experience at the site. Rather, when it comes to religious experiences, even a simple wall can have tremendous religious significance if a certain group believes it does.

Like I said, the Grotto of the Nativity—the cave in which Jesus was said to have been born in Bethlehem commemorated by the Church of the Nativity—has no archaeological evidence to support the claim that Jesus was born here. In addition, there is no clear biblical reference that points to this particular location as the birthplace of Jesus. So where did the story of this cave come from?

By examining secondary texts, we learn that the legend of the cave was first documented by the Christian apologist Justin Martyr (100–165), who claimed that when there was "no room at the inn," Joseph and Mary took refuge in a cave, which contained the manger in which Jesus was said to have been born. Justin first wrote about Jesus's birth in a cave in *Dialogue with Trypho* as part of his harmonization of Matthew's and Luke's birth narratives. In chapter 78, Justin states:

> *But when the Child was born in Bethlehem, since Joseph could not find a lodging in that village, he took up his quarters in a certain cave near the village; and while they were there Mary brought forth the Christ.*[1]

So where did Justin get the idea that Jesus was born in a cave? The answer lies in a mistranslation.

In chapter 70 of *Dialogue with Trypho,* Justin quotes at length from Isaiah 33:13–19, specifically v. 16, saying, "he shall dwell in the lofty cave of the strong rock." The problem is that the Hebrew text of Isaiah 33:16 reads that for the one who is righteous, *meṣadot sela'im miśgabo* (מצדות סלעים משגבו), or "fortresses of rocks (are) his refuge." Note that the Hebrew text says *nothing* about a cave; rather, the word *meṣadot* (here in the plural) is actually from the same Hebrew root that gives us the name of Masada, the nearly impenetrable desert fortress in the southern desert of Israel. It's not a cave; it's a high place. Likewise, the word *sela'* (here in the plural) is the standard Hebrew word for "rock," and *miśgav* (here in the possessive) is the Hebrew word for "refuge." So if the Hebrew prophecy of Isaiah 33:16 says nothing about a cave, but instead mentions living "on the heights" in "fortresses of rocks," how did Justin Martyr get a reference to a cave from Isaiah 33:16?

The answer comes once again from the Septuagint, which translates this passage, "he shall dwell in a *high cave* (σπήλαιον) *of a strong rock.*"[2] Note that the Septuagint translates the Hebrew word *meṣadot* (מצדות), or "fortress," with the Greek word *spēlaion* (σπήλαιον), meaning "cave" or "grotto," resulting in a "cave of strong rock" in place of the Hebrew "fortresses of rocks (are) his refuge."

Justin Martyr was obviously reading from the Septuagint's translation of Isaiah 33:16, not the Hebrew version, which was common for this time. But in doing so, Justin claims that the "cave" mentioned in the Septuagint of Isaiah 33:16 refers *not* to the cave revered by the Mithraic Mysteries (which is the context of his comments in *Dialogue with Trypho* 70), but to the cave in which *Jesus* was born, because he was reading Isaiah's reference to the "king" in the next verse (33:17) as a prophetic reference to Jesus. So although the Gospel writers *never* allude to this particular prophecy of Isaiah in reference to Jesus, Justin Martyr clearly saw a connection and, in his critique against the Mithraic Mysteries, inadvertently began the tradition of the birthplace of

Jesus being in a cave in Bethleḥem. This is how legends are made, and this is why when you visit the birthplace of Jesus, you visit a (highly adorned) cave over which a church was built, despite the fact that there is absolutely *no* archaeological evidence to support this claim; the tradition is rooted in a mistranslation.

Of course, a single highly creative exegesis of Justin Martyr does not prove that the grotto beneath the Church of the Nativity in Bethleḥem was the birthplace of Jesus. Others point to the second-century Protoevangelium of James (18–21), or to the third-century Greek Christian theologian Origen of Alexandria (184/5–253/4), who wrote in *Against Celsus* regarding the grotto:

> *There is shown at Bethlehem the cave where He was born, and the manger in the cave where He was wrapped in swaddling-clothes. And this sight is greatly talked of in surrounding places, even among the enemies of the faith, it being said that in this cave was born that Jesus who is worshipped and reverenced by the Christians.*[3]

But although Origen repeats the legend of the cave of Jesus's birth, he does so in the early third century, over two hundred years *after* Jesus was born. Likewise, his repetition of Justin's invention of the cave tradition suggests that Origen was simply repeating that tradition that had been passed down to him.

Nonetheless, the tradition grew, and the cave became the place associated with the birth of Jesus. In 327, Helena, the mother of the emperor Constantine the Great (whom we'll read more about in Chapter 11), began construction on the first basilica in Bethleḥem, the Church of the Nativity, as part of her larger campaign to commemorate sites traditionally associated with Jesus. These shrines formally signified the empire's (and therefore the church's) endorsement of these places throughout the Holy Land as *the* places where the events in the Bible *actually* took place. The basilica was dedicated in 339 and stood until the middle of the sixth century, when it was burned to the ground during the

Samaritan Revolt of 529.[4] A larger basilica replaced it during the reign of Emperor Justinian I, which incorporated many elements present in the original basilica, including the location of the grotto.[5]

And it is this sixth-century basilica, the Church of the Nativity, that has stood throughout the ages, although it has experienced extended periods of disrepair, especially under Ottoman control in the mid-nineteenth century. Despite extensive earthquake damage to the buildings, feuding between the Crusaders and the Greek Orthodox Church over control of the basilica, and even the theft of the silver star covering the grotto, the Church of the Nativity still stands as a symbol commemorating Jesus's birth.

OLD TESTAMENT BETHLEHEM

Many readers may not be aware that Bethlehem (Heb. *Beit Lehem,* בית לחם) has a long checkered history prior to the birth of Jesus. The name *Beit Lehem* in Hebrew means "house of bread," which is due to its reputation as fertile agricultural land.[6] When I lived in California, I used to refer to Bethlehem as "the Fresno of ancient Israel," as my hometown is known worldwide for its agricultural productivity, especially California raisins. Now, as a proud Hawkeye, I have altered my analogy of Bethlehem to "the Iowa of ancient Israel."

It was this agricultural village just to the south of Jerusalem that became famous for its affiliation with Jesus of Nazareth. But how did a town south of Jerusalem come to be associated with the birth of a man from Galilee far to the north? Scholars argue that Bethlehem was highlighted in the Gospels as the birthplace of Jesus because of its history, especially its association with the kings of ancient Israel and Judah. So before we look at the texts narrating the birth of Jesus, let's look at a few references to Bethlehem from the Hebrew Bible that contributed to the expectation of a Davidic messiah coming forth from Bethlehem.

RUTH

The story of Ruth introduces the city of Bethleḥem's role in the creation of the Israelite monarchy. 'Elimelek, his wife Na'omi, and their sons Maḥlon and Kilyon, a family from Bethleḥem, were on their way to the country of Mo'ab. In Mo'ab 'Elimelek died, and the two sons married Ruth and 'Orpah. Upon the deaths of the sons, their mother Na'omi decided to return to Bethleḥem, and Ruth chose to join her.

Back in Bethleḥem, while gleaning grain Ruth learns that the man in whose field she had been working, Bo'az, is actually a relative of her dead husband, making him eligible to marry and "redeem" her according to Jewish levirate marriage laws, which instruct a brother or the next of kin to produce a child with a dead relative's widow in order to provide protection for the widow and a legacy for her dead husband.[7] And after a nearly disastrous encounter with a more closely related next of kin, the humorously nameless *peloni almoni* (literally "Mr. So-and-So" in English), Bo'az legally acquires Ruth, and they live happily ever after.

The role of Bethleḥem as a birthplace of the house of Israel comes full circle in the story of Ruth when the people pronounce a blessing upon Ruth:

> *"May the LORD make the woman who is coming into your house like Rachel and Leah, who together built up the house of Israel. May you produce children in Ephrathah and bestow a name [i.e., become famous] in Bethlehem." (4:11)*

Furthermore, the child born to Ruth and Bo'az was named 'Obed, who was the father of Yishai (Jesse; 4:17), who was, of course, the father of King David (4:18–22). Thus, because Bethleḥem was known as David's hometown and the place where the prophet Shmu'el (Samuel) anointed him king (see 1 Sam. 16:1–13), it came to be the place associated with the kings of the Davidic line. And any *true* descendant of David, heir to the throne of Israel, and king of the Jews would be expected to hail from Bethleḥem.

THE BENJAMINITES

Although the inspiring tale of Ruth is associated with the beginning of King David's family tree, a story in Judges 19–21 offers a more revealing glimpse at the tribal and political rivalries that plagued Israel in the early years leading up to the establishment of the Israelite monarchy. This horrific event took place in the town of Gibeah, in the territory of Benjamin, and is significant not only because of the gruesome details of this deadly attack against a sexual slave and what it tells us about the significance of hospitality in the ancient world, but because it sets in motion a series of events that would lead to the near annihilation of the tribe of Benjamin.

Judges 19 tells the story of the gang rape and murder of a runaway concubine from Bethlehem who was turned over to an angry mob in order to save her Levite owner's neck. Careful readers of the Bible will notice a similarity between the details of this story and the story Lot just prior to the destruction of Sedom and 'Amorah (Sodom and Gomorrah) in Genesis 19.[8] Ironically, in disgust over the mob's actions, the concubine's owner cut her dead body into twelve pieces and sent them to the twelve tribes of Israel to protest the inhospitality against *him*. This ignited the Battle of Gibeah, in which members of the other eleven tribes of Israel attacked the Benjamites, who had rushed to defend the perpetrators of the crime at Gibeah. The tribe of Benjamin was nearly annihilated as part of a mass honor killing to avenge the mistreatment of the Levite (and his concubine).

That is the story of the Benjaminites. That's how the tribe of Benjamin was nearly wiped out and was (forcibly) reconstituted according to the Bible. And this was the fate of the town of Gibeah following its involvement in the murder of a Levite's concubine. For those of you asking what the story of Judges 19–21 has to do with Bethlehem (other than the fact that the murdered concubine was from there), allow me to explain how this is relevant.

Yes, the murdered concubine was from Bethlehem. But this grisly story was included in the Bible because 1 Samuel 9:1–2 tells us that the first king of Israel, Saul, was from the tribe of Benjamin. Thus, we can begin to see why the Bible's editors might have wanted to retain the macabre tale of the hometown of an early rival of King David. Saul was from Gibeah of Benjamin, while David was from Bethlehem of Judah. The Bible tells the story of the struggle between Saul and David, because it favors the transition of power in ancient Israel from the tribe of Benjamin (and King Saul) to the tribe of Judah (and King David). This may explain why the editors of the Bible chose to include the horrific story of the murdered concubine in Judges 19 and the subsequent story of the near annihilation of the tribe of Benjamin in Judges 20–21; the Bible's editors wanted to offer an *additional* reason why God dismissed Saul in favor of David as king. Although the two tribes for all intents and purposes came to be understood as a single state following the rebellion of Jeroboam, the inclusion of Judges 19–21 helps to sway the opinions of the readers of the story against Benjamin and toward Judah. Understanding the rivalry between Saul and David helps explain why such a morally reprehensible set of stories would have been included in the Bible.

Once again, this shift from Saul to David and from Gibeah of Benjamin to Bethlehem of Judah helps us understand how the tradition that the promised messiah of Israel was to come from Bethlehem was established. Simply put, because David was the first messiah from Bethlehem, the prophets argued that *all* of Israel's subsequent *messiahs,* or anointed kings (from the Hebrew *mashaḥ,* משח, meaning "to smear" and in the context of the monarchy "to anoint" with oil) must be born in David's hometown of Bethlehem. The famous prophecy of Micah reflects this expectation: "But you, O Bethlehem of Ephrathah, who are one of the little clans of Judah, from you shall come forth for me one who is to rule in Israel, whose origin is from of old, from ancient days" (5:2; 5:1 HB).

And thus Bethlehem became the city that built the monarchy of Israel; at least that was the *expectation* as long as Israel and (later) Judah retained independent control over their relative kingdoms. But after Judah's defeat and Jerusalem's destruction at the hands of King Nebuchadnezzar II of Babylon (2 Kings 25), the Davidic line came to an end. However, David's association with Bethlehem continued and later influenced the authors of the Gospels to believe that the promised messiah of Israel would be born in the little town of Bethlehem. And that most famous of Bethlehemites was none other than Jesus . . . of *Nazareth*.

BETHLEHEM, NAZARETH, AND JESUS

We've all been taught that Bethlehem was the birthplace of Jesus. However, two of the canonical Gospels (Mark and John) never associate Jesus with Bethlehem, and the apostle Paul makes no mention of Bethlehem in any of his writings (or of Nazareth, for that matter).[9] When referring to Jesus, Paul always calls him some combination of "Jesus," "Christ," and "Lord," but never includes Bethlehem or Nazareth. So with no mention of Bethlehem in connection with Jesus in fully one-half of the canonical Gospels and in the writings of Paul or, for that matter, in *any* of the remainder of the New Testament books, we come to the Gospels of Matthew and Luke. It is while reading Matthew and Luke that we first realize that Bethlehem is only referred to in the birth narratives of Jesus. In all other references, when a location is used in relation to Jesus, he is consistently referred to as "Jesus of Nazareth," *never* "Jesus of Bethlehem."

So Jesus's relationship to Bethlehem in the New Testament is limited to the birth narratives of Matthew and Luke. Although this might seem to be the end of the peculiarities surrounding Jesus's association with Bethlehem, when we actually read the two birth narratives alongside one another, we immediately notice another problem—one with which biblical scholars for centuries have been struggling: Where did Jesus live at the time of his birth?

And there is one other issue we must examine, and this is where Nazareth collides with Bethlehem. Simply put, Jesus has a Nazareth problem, and his Nazareth problem is this: *Jesus was from Nazareth*. The reason the question of where Jesus lived at the time of his birth has perplexed scholars for so long is because Matthew and Luke give two different answers to this question. Let us first look at Matthew's account of Jesus's birth to see if we can identify the problem and find a solution.

MATTHEW'S ACCOUNT

After the opening lines of Matthew's Gospel, which consist solely of a genealogy designed to show that Jesus is of the line of David and therefore eligible to be the anointed king and promised Messiah of Israel, Matthew 2:1 reads, "In the time of King Herod, *after Jesus was born in Bethlehem of Judea,* wise men from the East came to Jerusalem." Notice that at no time prior to this in Matthew's Gospel does the author say anything about Nazareth. The first location that is given in Matthew comes in 2:1, where it reads, "*after* Jesus was born in Bethlehem of Judea." In Matthew's Gospel, it is simply implied that Jesus and his family *lived* in Bethlehem and that Jesus was born at home! There is no prior mention of Nazareth, no story of a pilgrimage to Jerusalem, no manger, no barn, no cave or grotto, nothing! Matthew simply relates that Jesus had been born in Bethlehem of Judea.

And the farther we read in Matthew, the more we see that Jesus and his family simply lived in Bethlehem. Note the response to King Herod after he asked the chief priests and the scribes where the Messiah was to be born:

> *They told him, "In Bethlehem of Judea; for so it has been written by the prophet: 'And you, Bethlehem, in the land of Judah, are by no means least among the rulers of Judah; for from you shall come a ruler who is to shepherd my people Israel.'" (2:5–6)*

Because the prophecy of Micah 5:2 was interpreted as a prediction that the messianic king of Israel would come from Bethlehem, the author of Matthew was sure to include the prophecy in his narrative, as this advanced Matthew's agenda of portraying Jesus as the promised messianic son of David. But anyone who reads Matthew 2:6 will quickly notice that the prophecy quoted to King Herod is actually a *combination* of biblical texts. The first part comes from Micah 5:2, which predicts that the Messiah will come from Bethlehem, and the second part comes from 2 Samuel 5:2, which recalls when the tribes of Israel came to David at Hebron to pledge their allegiance to him and anoint him king over Israel. These two texts are combined because they share the theme that the leader of Israel will come from line of David and from his hometown of Bethlehem.[10]

The second bit of evidence that suggests that Jesus and his family had been living in a home in Bethlehem at the time of his birth comes from the story of the Magi, who had come to worship Jesus. Matthew 2:11 clearly states, "On entering the *house* (οἰκίαν, *oikian*), they saw the child." Matthew's Gospel again suggests that Jesus was *not* born in a manger in a barn, but in a *house*. Because there is no story of a pilgrimage to Jerusalem, this was likely the home in which Jesus and his family resided in Bethlehem.

According to Matthew, Joseph is then warned in a dream to take Mary and Jesus and flee to Egypt, as Herod the Great was coming to kill Jesus. This flight to Egypt, which is not mentioned in the Gospel of Luke, gives Matthew the additional opportunity to cast Jesus as the "new Moses," a new Jewish lawgiver like Moses. Matthew 2:15 further underscores the connection to Moses by citing Hosea 11:1: "Out of Egypt I called my son."

Matthew 2:16 provides a final piece of evidence suggesting that in Matthew's Gospel Joseph, Mary, and Jesus lived in a house in Bethlehem. According to the text, when Herod the Great heard that the Magi had tricked him, he "killed all the children in and around Bethlehem *who were two years old or under*, according to the time that he had learned from the wise men." In addition to being yet another episode that is not mentioned in Luke's birth narrative, this text states that Herod didn't just kill all the newborns, but all of the children two years old and younger, "according to the time that he had learned from the wise men," suggesting that the elapsed time between Jesus's birth and Herod's "slaughter of the innocents" was at least a year, if not two. Herod wanted to make sure that he killed the child Jesus, so he slaughtered all of the children who could have possibly been born in the two-year period since Jesus's birth. Since pilgrims traveling to Jerusalem from Nazareth to register for a census (Luke 2:4) didn't typically stay for *a year or two,* this suggests that according to Matthew Jesus was born at his family's home in Bethlehem.[11]

Thus, the trek to Egypt provided Matthew with a mechanism to harmonize his tradition that Jesus was born at home in Bethlehem, *as should all of the Davidic kings of Israel,* with the tradition that Jesus was raised in Nazareth.

LUKE'S ACCOUNT

The Gospel of Luke, however, goes about solving these conflicting Bethlehem and Nazareth traditions differently. After providing the lengthy backstory of the birth of Jesus's cousin, John the Baptist, Luke 1:26–27 states that the angel Gabri'el was sent to "a town in Galilee called Nazareth" to inform Mary of her impending pregnancy. And other than Mary's trip to an unspecified Judean town in the hill country (1:39) to stay with Elizabeth for three months, Luke makes no mention of any town in the remainder of chapter 1.

Luke then employs a highly problematic census in order to provide a mechanism by which Jesus could be born in Bethlehem, since according to Luke's Gospel Jesus's family lived in Nazareth:

In those days a decree went out from Emperor Augustus that all the world should be registered. This was the first registration and was taken while Quirinius was governor of Syria. All went to their own towns to be registered. Joseph also went from the town of Nazareth in Galilee to Judea, to the city of David called

With its tall green cupola, the Basilica of the Annunciation in Nazareth is built over the traditional spot where the angel Gabri'el announced to Mary that she would give birth to Jesus.

The altar of the Basilica of the Annunciation in Nazareth sits in a cave traditionally thought to be the home of the Virgin Mary.

Bethlehem, because he was descended from the house and family of David. He went to be registered with Mary, to whom he was engaged and who was expecting a child. (2:1–5)

Luke's census is problematic for a number of reasons. First, censuses were taken for the purpose of taxation. Although there are certainly literary records of censuses taking place throughout the Roman Empire at this time,[12] there is no evidence that those who were being counted were required to travel to their *ancestral* hometowns in order to be counted. Indeed, an Egyptian census edict of Gaius Vibius Maximus, the Roman prefect of Egypt from 103 to 107, did require that "all persons who for any reason whatsoever are absent from their home districts be alerted to return to their own hearths, so that they may complete the customary formalities of registration and apply themselves to the farming for which they are responsible."[13]

Although this edict of Gaius Vibius Maximus does mention a return home for the purposes of taxation, residents were not required to return to their *ancestral* homes, but to their *present* homes, so that both people and assets could be assessed for purposes of taxation. Essentially you couldn't be "out of town" when the government came to take the census and collect taxes. Indeed, traveling to one's ancestral home would not allow pilgrims to "apply themselves to the farming for which they are responsible." Rather, residents under Roman rule were to go to their *present* homes so that they and their possessions could be counted and taxed. Luke further strains credulity by arguing that the nine-months-pregnant Mary would have made the arduous three-day journey from Nazareth to Bethlehem. Thus, any registration would have required Joseph and his family to return to their *present* homes to be counted, and Jesus's present home was in Nazareth, not Bethlehem.

So why does Luke 2:4 state that Mary and Joseph returned to their *ancestral* home instead of being counted in "their *own* town of Nazareth" (2:39)? Because Luke depicts Jesus and his family as living in Nazareth (not in Bethlehem, as in Matthew), Luke likely employed the census as a device to bring Mary to Bethlehem *temporarily* to satisfy the tradition that Jesus was born in Bethlehem, while still allowing him to remain Jesus "of Nazareth."

Second, and even more problematic, is the timing of the census of Publius Sulpicius Quirinius according to Luke's Gospel. Indeed, the legate governor of Syria, Quirinius, did hold a census in order to get a count of the population of the Roman provinces of Syria and Judea for tax purposes, but according to Josephus this census took place in 6 or 7 CE,[14] *after* the exile of Herod the Great's inept son, Archelaus, who had been appointed ethnarch of Judea following the death of Herod. The problem with the timing of Luke's description of Quirinius's census is that Luke depicts it as taking place during the reign of King Herod the Great (1:5) who died in 4 BCE,[15] making Luke's chronology out of sync by over a decade and therefore impossible.[16]

Of course, once Mary and Joseph get to Bethlehem, Mary gives birth: "And she gave birth to her firstborn son and wrapped him in bands of cloth, and laid him in a manger (Gk. φάτνῃ, *phatnē*), because there was no place for them in the inn" (2:7).[17] Once baby Jesus had been visited by *shepherds* (as opposed to the Magi mentioned in Matt. 2:1), had been circumcised to fulfill the requirements of the Jewish law, and received blessings from Simeon (2:25–35) and Anna (2:36–38), Luke says that Jesus and his family "returned to Galilee, to their own town of Nazareth" (2:39).

The differences between Matthew's and Luke's birth narratives are therefore striking. According to Matthew, Jesus was born in a house in Bethlehem where Joseph and Mary lived; according to Luke, Jesus was laid in a manger while temporarily in Bethlehem. Matthew depicts Jesus as being visited by Magi, while Luke says lowly shepherds visited Jesus. Furthermore, Luke makes no mention of Herod's infanticide or of the angel's warning to flee with Jesus and Mary to Egypt in order to avoid it (Matt. 2:13). Instead, Luke has Mary and Joseph remain in Bethlehem for forty days and then return directly to Nazareth, mentioning nothing of Matthew's lengthy flight to Egypt.[18]

So what do we do with these two separate traditions? For one, we must recognize that there were, in fact, many traditions about Jesus's birth.[19] Although the details of the two accounts that we have in the Bible may not match, it's important to know why both Gospels wanted to include Jesus's link to Bethlehem. The Davidic kings of Israel were from David's hometown of Bethlehem, and if Jesus was the Messiah and king of the Jews, the story of his birth in Bethlehem needed to be told—*even if* he was Jesus of Nazareth.

———

Bethlehem is a fascinating city, full of history, culture, and beauty. Though it doesn't hold the early historical significance that many faithful people think it does, it is still very much worth visiting.

The different accounts of Jesus's birth in Bethlehem are designed to appeal to different audiences. The author of Matthew wants his readers to see Jesus as the fulfillment of Jewish prophecy, as the promised son of David, and as the new royal king and lawgiver, who came out of Egypt like Moses and who entertains wealthy Magi from the east. The author of Luke, on the other hand, wants his readers to view Jesus as a poor child from Nazareth, born in a manger in a temporary residence and visited by lowly shepherds, who would then go on to preach a message of hope to the poor.

The Gospels are not meant to be harmonized! Bethlehem demonstrates as much. Rather, the Gospels are different perspectives from different authors for different audiences that reflect different traditions concerning Jesus's life. Luke's depiction of lowly shepherds visiting Jesus as a child resonated with the poor and marginalized, while Matthew's account of wise men from far away coming to pay tribute to the new king of the Jews resonated with those steeped in Jewish tradition. Bethlehem of Judea tied Jesus to the line of David and fulfilled what many believed to be a prophecy (or a combination of prophecies) that claimed the "anointed ones" were to be from Bethlehem. And this is how a small Judean agricultural city with no archaeological evidence to support any claim to Jesus's birth came to play such an important role in building the Bible.

CHAPTER 11

Rome

Rome may very well be the most important city in the history of the world. The Roman Empire's conquest of the eastern Mediterranean made Roman Palestine the setting of the birth of Christianity, which in turn influenced the entire Western world. Rome obviously plays an important role in the crucifixion of Jesus. But Rome also gave us Paul's Letter to the Romans—arguably Paul's most important summary of the gospel—and helped decide which books would ultimately comprise the Bible we know today. Thus, Rome is perhaps, more than any other city, responsible for building the Bible.

ALL ROADS LEAD TO ROME

"All roads lead to Rome." Nowhere is this truer than with the creation of the Bible. This is why every summer, when I take students to Israel to dig, we stop over in Rome. Rome not only destroyed Jerusalem and the Jewish Temple, but it also adopted Christianity as its state religion and is responsible for the actual formation of the Christian Bible. The history of Rome is intimately entangled with the history of Judaism, Christianity, and the Bible. This is because all roads truly lead to Rome.

I once led Roslyn on a scavenger hunt, of sorts, through the Roman Forum to prove this very point.

"It's over here somewhere," I yelled to Roslyn through the bone-chilling Roman winter wind.

The Foro Romano, *or Roman Forum, was the center of Roman public life, hosting several monuments and temples honoring Roman emperors and deities.*

"What is? There are a million different things in here, and they're all old and broken . . . *like you,*" Roslyn rightly observed. She was very cold, wearing two jackets, and wondering why I was dragging her through the mud in the Roman Forum on New Year's Eve. We had a party to prep for, food to eat, wine to drink, Iron & Wine to listen to, and friends to meet, yet I was hauling her through ancient buildings to look at old carved pieces of rock.

"It's over here somewhere, but no one is sure exactly where," I replied, confidently waving her over to me.

"What are you looking for?" Roslyn asked curiously.

"All roads lead to Rome," I replied, "but *where* in Rome?"

"The Grom gelato shop?" Roslyn responded hopefully.

I shook my head.

"Dolce and Gabbana?" she tried again, this time with a smile.

"No," I replied. "All roads led to the Milliarium Aureum— the Golden Milestone—the huge golden pillar that served as the reference point for all Roman milestones throughout the Roman Empire. It was the physical point at which all roads leading to Rome intersected. It probably once stood over here by the Temple of Saturn."[1]

"Where is it?" Roslyn asked. "I wouldn't expect a huge golden pillar to still be lying around in the open . . . in Rome . . . in the *cold,*" she continued. "I'd expect someone would have taken it, melted it down, and spent it . . . on a nice bottle of New Year's Eve wine," she quipped. Hard to miss that hint.

Roslyn was right (as she usually is, as she constantly reminds me). The Golden Milestone is lost to time. But like so many other lost objects in Rome, the Golden Milestone symbolizes what the Arch of Titus also commemorates: that the history of Rome is inextricably intertwined with the history of Judaism, Christianity, and the formation of the Bible. So in order to complete our journey, we must explore Rome's impact on the building of the Bible.

Latin inscription on a milestone near the Temple Mount in Jerusalem dating from 72–79 CE in the Roman period. The inscription mentions both the Roman emperor Vespasian and his son Titus, who destroyed the Temple. Image courtesy Israel Museum.

ROMULUS AND REMUS

Like many cities and nations, Rome has two early histories: one historical and one mythological. The historical reality of early Rome is a topic for another book. However, the foundation myth of Rome has many points of contact with various stories in the Bible.

The mythological story of the founding of Rome centers on the story of Romulus and Remus, the twin sons of the god Mars (the Roman god of war), who were (and tell me if you've heard this story before) saved by being placed in a basket in the Tiber River and allowed to float downstream. When the flooded Tiber receded, a wolf whose pups had recently died discovered the abandoned twins. Instead of eating them, the wolf nursed them as her own offspring, and a woodpecker assisted in feeding the twins. Both animals are sacred to the god Mars.[2]

A shepherd named Faustulus discovered the twins and brought them to his wife, Acca Larentia, and they raised them as their own. When they became adults, they discovered the truth about how they wound up in a basket in the Tiber to be raised by wolves. The twins had been condemned to death by their grandfather's brother, Amulius, who stole the throne from their grandfather, Numitor, king of Alba Longa and descendant of the Trojan hero Aeneas (the focus of Virgil's *Aeneid*), and murdered all of Numitor's male descendants.

Their mother, Rhea Silvia, had been forced to become one of the Vestal Virgins, the priestesses of the Roman goddess Vesta, goddess of family, hearth, and home. However, Rhea Silvia became pregnant—a conception that the Roman poet Livy says was the result of being raped by an unknown man,[3] but that (and again, tell me if you've heard this before) Rhea Silvia attributed to miraculous conception by a deity (in this case, the Roman god Mars). When Amulius heard of it, he ordered the twins to be killed and their mother imprisoned, but a servant instead set them adrift, allowing the river to decide their fate.

Upon learning about the crimes committed against their family, Romulus and Remus avenged Amulius's usurpation of their grandfather's throne by confronting Amulius, killing him, and reinstating their grandfather Numitor as king. They then chose to found a city of their own on the site on the banks of the Tiber where the wolf had nursed them. However, they could not agree where to build the city. They engaged in augury (the ancient practice of watching birds and interpreting their actions as a divine omen), and after a disputed result Romulus built the walls of his city, *Roma,* on the Palatine Hill (which overlooks the Roman Forum), while Remus began building on the more easily defensible Aventine Hill farther south. Anxious to prove his brother *and* his chosen site to be militarily inferior, Remus mockingly jumped over Romulus's walls. Embarrassed by his brother's exposure of his vulnerable city walls, Romulus killed the invading Remus in a fit of rage, vowing, "So too will perish every one hereafter who shall leap over my walls."[4]

The first citizens of Rome were said to be outlaws and fugitives to whom Romulus gave residence (so, like Australia). But since most of the new settlers were men and there were not enough women to form families and grow the city, Romulus decided (once again, tell me if you've heard this before—hint: read Judges 21) to steal women from the nearby tribe of the Sabines while the Sabine men were distracted at a festival of Cronus in the Circus Maximus. The abduction and "rape of the Sabine women" resulted in war between the Sabines and Romulus, which ended only when, according to the myth, the Sabine women expressed total affection for their Roman husbands, and the two parties agreed to end their fighting and live together in peace.[5] Romulus is believed never to have died, but rather (yet again, tell me if you've heard this one) to have been taken up to heaven in a violent storm (cf. Elijah in 2 Kings 2:1–11).

My colleague Sarah Bond made an observation concerning Romulus and Remus and the Bible. She compared them to Peter and Paul, and I believe the comparison is apt. Peter and Paul are the patron saints of Rome and are credited as the founders of *Christian* Rome in the same way that Romulus and Remus are considered the founders of ancient Rome.[6] Furthermore, in the same way that Romulus ultimately overtook Remus and later became the primary representative of Rome, so too did the apostle Paul ultimately eclipse the apostle Peter (the "rock" upon whom Jesus built his church) to become the primary representative of the gospel of Jesus Christ. Paul is credited with thirteen letters in the New Testament canon, while Peter is credited with only two letters (and scholars think later forgers wrote those).

The book of Acts supports this theory. The first chapters of Acts begin with the eleven disciples (minus Judas) and focus upon Peter and his preaching in and around Jerusalem. But from the story of Paul's conversion in Acts 9 onward, we see that Paul begins to displace Peter as the principal preacher of the gospel. In fact, Peter's and Paul's messages so conflicted with one another— Acts 15:2 says there was "no small dissension and debate"—that a conference was convened in Jerusalem to reconcile the differences between the messages concerning circumcision and the consumption of meat sacrificed to idols (Acts 15; cf. Gal. 2). But from that point on, the book of Acts follows Paul (*not* Peter) on his missionary journeys, demonstrating that it was Paul who ultimately triumphed over Peter and that it was Paul's gospel to the Gentiles that would become the normative message of Christianity.

THE FORMATION OF THE ROMAN EMPIRE

Whether you follow the mythological or the archaeological founding of Rome, the founding of the Roman Republic in 509 BCE marks the end of the early Roman Kingdom. The Roman Republic was characterized by the establishment of the Roman Senate, in which elected representatives made decisions on behalf of the Roman populace. As Rome increased in political, economic, and military strength, it expanded its control over the Italian peninsula through military conquests and political alliances.

By the third century BCE, Rome's control had spread west along the Mediterranean coast to Spain and south across the Mediterranean to northern Africa. By the end of the first century BCE, Rome had taken control of what is now France to the northwest, spread east along the Mediterranean coast into mainland Greece and the Greek islands, and continued east into the western part of what is today Turkey and south along the eastern Mediterranean coast into modern Syria and Lebanon.

In many ways, the Romans are to the Greeks what the Persians were to the Babylonians. The Romans essentially took over all of the lands that had previously belonged to Greece. In doing so, the Romans also incorporated many aspects of the Greek culture, including their pantheon, most of whom they simply rebranded with Roman names. This is how Zeus became Jupiter, Aphrodite became Venus, Hermes became Mercury, Poseidon became Neptune, and Ares became Mars. (The Romans essentially turned the Greek gods into planets.) It is this Roman adoption of Greek culture and the blending of it into their own Roman culture that causes scholars today to speak of a combined Greco-Roman culture.

The Roman Republic stood until the assassination of Gaius Julius Caesar (100–44 BCE) on the Ides of March (March 15) 44 BCE and the victory of Caesar's adopted son, Octavian (63 BCE–14 CE), over Mark Antony (83–30 BCE) and Cleopatra (69–30 BCE) in the final war of the Roman Republic, the Battle of Actium, in 31 BCE. The Roman Senate voted to give Octavian supreme autocratic military and civil authority for life along with the honorific title Augustus in 27 BCE, marking the end of the Roman Republic and the establishment of the Roman Empire. The ascension of Octavian to the new role of Roman emperor instituted a period of relative peace called the *Pax Romana* ("Roman Peace"), which lasted over two hundred years, from 27 BCE until 180 CE. Ironically, it was during the *Pax Romana* that the ministry and crucifixion of Jesus as well as the destruction of Jerusalem (twice) took place.

POMPEY AND ROMAN PALESTINE

Rome greatly impacted the lives of Jews in the Holy Land when the Roman general Gnaeus Pompeius Magnus, commonly called Pompey the Great (106–48 BCE), annexed Jerusalem, Syria, Phoenicia, and Coelesyria for Rome in 63 BCE. Pompey was a successful military commander—so much so that in 60 BCE he joined arguably the wealthiest man in history, Marcus Licinius Crassus, a general, politician, and real-estate speculator (talk about an economic "triumvirate"), and the general and politician Gaius Julius Caesar in a military-political alliance known as the First Triumvirate, which was essentially (and stop me if you've heard of this before) three individuals ruling together as a single (yet triune), unassailable, ultimate authority. The Holy Trinity, er, triumvirate of Crassus, Caesar, and Pompey dominated Roman politics until 53 BCE, when Crassus was killed by the Parthians during truce negotiations following the Roman defeat at the Battle of Carrhae.

When General Pompey conquered Jerusalem, he walked into the Jerusalem Temple and then into the Holy of Holies and back out again without any reprisal from the local religious authorities, political authorities, or God himself. Pompey transgressed the sacred precinct of the Jewish Temple to make a point: he wanted to demonstrate to all that *he* was now in charge. Pompey's transgression of the Jerusalem Temple echoed a similar act by the Seleucid king Antiochus IV Epiphanes, who a little over a century earlier had also desecrated the Temple, which led to the Maccabean Revolt.[7] Pompey's transgression is commonly referred to as the "abomination of desolation" or "desolating sacrilege," and the New Testament authors also allude to it as a symbolic act that takes place when chaos and destruction are about to befall Jerusalem.[8]

Of course, one cannot help but see echoes of this act—of walking in and around the Temple precinct as a demonstration of authority—in Ariel Sharon's ironically comparable walk atop the Temple Mount in September 2000. It was an act that many credit with instigating the Second Palestinian Intifada in Jerusalem, as it was essentially a demonstration that Sharon was in control of *all* of Jerusalem (not just west Jerusalem) and could go where he chose within the city.

Following Caesar's crossing of the Rubicon in 49 BCE and subsequent victory over Pompey in the Battle of Pharsalus (48 BCE), an Idumean Roman client governor to the south of Jerusalem named Antipater pragmatically shifted allegiances from Pompey to Caesar and even arranged to rescue Caesar from the Siege of Alexandria following the battle. This further ingratiated Antipater with Caesar, who in 47 BCE granted Antipater Roman citizenship, relieved him of all taxes, and installed him as the first Roman procurator of Judea. Antipater's sons were also appointed as local rulers, including one son named Herod (74–4 BCE), who ruled Galilee.

HEROD THE GREAT

Following the murder of Antipater in 43 BCE, his son Herod the Great rose to prominence in Judea. Having served as governor and then as tetrarch of Galilee from 47 to 40 BCE, Herod was declared king of Judea by the Roman Senate in 39 BCE. After taking his sweet time returning to Jerusalem, Herod began actively ruling Judea in 37 BCE.[9]

There is some debate about whether Herod the Great was a good king for the Jews. In many ways, his rule was a very accommodating, positive time for the Jews, as he implemented many policies and construction projects that benefited the Jewish people.[10] Although Herod is rightly called a megalomaniac and a self-aggrandizing tyrant who built colossal monuments so that he might be remembered, those building projects were essentially government-funded economic stimulus projects that employed hundreds if not thousands of Jewish workers, which they appreciated.

But regardless of the good Herod the Great may have done for the Jews in the late first century BCE, the Jews always hated him. For one, he was paranoid and impulsive. He killed a number of his own sons and wives as well as his political opponents. In this sense, although the Gospel of Matthew's inclusion of the "slaughter of the innocents" (2:16–18) is considered historically spurious by scholars because it is nowhere mentioned by Josephus (who mentions everything else Herod was even *rumored* to have done), scholars do not dismiss the story outright, because it is consistent with other murderous acts that Herod commonly ordered, especially in his later years.

I once held a coin of Herod the Great in my hand. It was the archaeological equivalent of a religious moment; I felt the pickax, the brush, and the holy trowel flowing through me. I remember feeling a connection to Herod the Great, not in any spiritual or metaphysical sense, but in the sense that I was *touching* history. I was holding the *same* bronze coin that perhaps a Roman soldier used to buy dinner or a Jewish shop owner received as payment for new pair of sandals.

I stared at the Greek letters inscribed around the edge of the coin, ΗΡΩΔΟΥ ΒΑΣΙΛΕΩΣ, *Ērōdou Basileōs,* "Of King Herod," and at the symbolic propaganda that was present in the center of the coin, the sacrificial tripod holding a large *lebes* bowl, a ceremonial vessel used for mixing items during pagan rituals. I imagined how the Jewish shopkeeper might feel receiving this coin, reminded even on the money he used that Jews were subjects of Rome and that their own king was Rome's client, who went so far as to parade symbols of pagan religion on his coinage.

Carefully flipping the coin over, I noticed the image of a soldier's helmet—a constant reminder of Rome's military presence in Judea.

A coin of Herod the Great dating to 40 BCE. Obverse: ΗΡΩΔΟΥ ΒΑΣΙΛΕΩΣ, ('Ērōdou Basileōs) "Of King Herod," surrounding a sacrificial tripod holding a large lebes *bowl. Reverse: Military helmet with cheek pieces surrounded by a wreath with a star at the top. Photo courtesy John F. Wilson.*

It wasn't enough to tacitly support pagan religion; Herod needed to remind his people who was *really* in charge, and a soldier's helmet on a coin was the simplest, most ubiquitous way to do so. My thoughts raced back to Jerusalem as I clenched the coin in my fist, and I was reminded that, regardless of the good Herod the Great may have done for his Jewish subjects, the Jews of Jerusalem felt their so-called king was a sellout to Rome. Instead of being a *real* messiah and king of the Jews and rising up against Rome to lead the reestablishment of the kingdom of Israel for the Jewish people, he worked for Rome to *suppress* Jewish cries for independence. And *that* is why they hated him.

JUDEA AFTER HEROD

Following Herod's death, Rome divided his kingdom up and placed it under the authority of three of Herod's sons (the ones he hadn't murdered) and Herod's sister, none of whom received the title of king. The division of the kingdom had a huge impact on the daily lives of Jews under Roman rule. This is the period in Jewish and Roman history—the first and early second centuries CE—that contributed the entirety of the New Testament to the Bible. From the Gospels, which describe Jesus's birth under Herod the Great (Matt. 1–2) and/or Quirinius (Luke 1–2) and his trial and execution before the prefect Pontius Pilate and Herod Antipas "the Tetrarch"; to the letters of Paul, which were written to newly established churches in Roman territories; to the pseudonymous Pastoral Letters written to instruct the young churches throughout the empire; to the "Little Apocalypse" in Mark 13, which appears to be describing the fall of the Jerusalem Temple in 70 CE; to the (much larger) Apocalypse of John (the book of Revelation) encouraging Christians to keep the faith in the face of Roman persecution—*all* of these letters and books were composed within the context of the Roman occupation of Judea. That is, the New Testament is a wholly Roman phenomenon and is inseparable from the Roman context in which the story of Jesus and the early church is set.

Roman prefects, procurators, and legates were appointed to rule over Judea in place of Herod's heirs throughout the first century CE. They were largely insensitive to Jewish religious, political, and general cultural practices, which caused conflict between the Roman authorities and the Jewish people. Both sides suffered greatly, as the Jews were regularly imprisoned and killed in response to their protests against Rome, and Roman governors were regularly recalled for not keeping the peace.

One of these largely ineffective, yet well-known Roman prefects was Pontius Pilate, who the Bible says presided over the trial and crucifixion of Jesus. There is archaeological evidence that confirms Pilate's tenure as prefect in Judea in the form of coins he minted and the famous Pilate Stone, an inscription discovered in secondary use as a stepping stone in the Roman theater of Caesarea Maritima, which reads in part, "[Po]ntius Pilate . . . [Pref]ect of Juda[ea]." The Pilate Stone is presently on display in the Israel Museum in Jerusalem. (There is a replica on display outdoors in Caesarea at the location the inscription was uncovered.)

The "Pilate Stone" on display in the Israel Museum in Jerusalem. Discovered at Caesarea Maritima, the Latin inscription preserves the lines, "[PO]NTIVS PILATVS . . . [PRAEF]ECTVS IVDA[EA]E," or "Pontius Pilate . . . Prefect of Judea." Image courtesy Israel Museum.

The inscription was discovered in Caesarea because, following its institution of prefects, Rome moved the administrative center of *Iudaea* from Jerusalem to Caesarea. Pilate likely lived in Caesarea, overlooking the Mediterranean, and traveled to Jerusalem only for significant matters requiring his personal oversight.[11] And he will forever be remembered for one of those significant matters: lending Roman approval to the crucifixion of Jesus of Nazareth.

The political tension between the Jews, early Christians, and their largely inept Roman governors became such a powder keg in Jerusalem that militant conservative Jews rebelled against Rome in 66 CE, which today is called the Great Jewish Revolt. This war changed the course of both Judaism and Christianity, as it resulted in the destruction of the Second Temple in Jerusalem in 70 CE and the dispersion of Jewish groups (including the Christians) who subsequently adapted their practices to those that could survive without needing the Temple. And it was the loss of the Jewish Temple that served as a watershed moment between Judaism and Christianity, as both Jews and Christians physically fled their separate ways and began to write down the stories and histories of their respective faiths. Thus we can say that in the same way that the destruction of the First Temple largely produced the Hebrew Bible, so too did the destruction of the Second Temple produce the bulk of the New Testament and the Mishnah, the first written redaction of Jewish oral tradition.

PAUL'S LETTER TO THE ROMANS

Another example of the role that Rome and its empire played in the creation of the Bible is the apostle Paul's Letter to the Romans, which is arguably his magnum opus. The letter not only presents Paul's apologetic masterpiece for the supremacy of Christ; it also represents the relationship between early Christians and Rome. Given the fact that Paul wrote his letters *before* the destruction of the Temple, Paul's letters hold the distinction of being the earliest

Christian writings known to us today. And no letter of Paul is more important than Romans.

According to Brendan Byrne, professor of New Testament at Jesuit Theological College, the apostle Paul wrote Romans for several reasons.[12] First, Paul wanted to introduce himself to the church in Rome—a church that, unlike the recipients of so many of his other letters, was a church that he did not found. Paul was going to visit Rome on his way to Spain and needed a home base for his operations there. Therefore, Paul does not condescend to the Romans in the same manner as he does with the churches he founded in Galatia (Gal. 1) and Thessaloniki (1 Thess. 4), but lays out the gospel to the Romans in much broader, more inviting strokes.

Second, Paul is laying out what is essentially a systematic account of his theology of the Jewish Messiah, Jesus of Nazareth, for an audience made up largely of Gentile Roman converts to Christianity. That is, one of the true strengths of the book of Romans is that it explains this essentially Jewish religious tradition and messianic expectation in terms that Jews *and* non-Jews can understand. It also appears to encourage Roman Gentile and Jewish converts to Christianity not to denigrate Jews or the Jewish heritage upon which Christianity is inextricably based. Paul regularly reminds the Roman Christians that Jesus is thoroughly Jewish, making direct quotations and appeals to Jewish Scripture on at least fifty-seven occasions in Romans.[13] Thus, in much the same way that Josephus chronicled Jewish history for Romans fifty years later, Paul presented the Jewish faith in a manner that would be understood and accepted by Roman Christians.

One key difference between Paul's Letter to the Romans and the writings of Josephus is that, while Josephus was attempting to cast the Jewish faith in terms of Hellenistic philosophy so that it would be palatable to the Roman establishment, thereby offering an apology for the Jews whose rebellion the Romans had recently suppressed, Paul does not write Romans simply to *inform* his readers about Jesus; he writes for the purpose of *converting* them to the faith and *compelling* them to do the things Jesus instructed his disciples to do. Paul is not writing history for the sake of chronicling the story of Jesus; he wants Romans to *believe* what he's saying and to join the movement. Josephus wanted Romans to understand the importance of Jewish contributions to society; Paul wants the Romans to recognize Jesus as the savior of the world and become his disciples—a desire that coincidentally would be fulfilled three centuries later.

Finally, Paul wrote Romans for the purpose of raising money and support for his missionary activity. The entire final chapter of Romans is a lesson in name-dropping and the power of public praise of those who have already contributed to a campaign.[14]

Thus, Rome helped build the Bible not only because of its cultural significance as the setting in which the New Testament was written, but because Paul's Letter to the Romans serves as the single greatest summary of the gospel of Jesus to Gentiles in the Bible. Furthermore, it was this letter to the Romans that so encapsulated Paul's message of Jesus's grace that it later served as the centerpiece of Martin Luther's theology during the Protestant Reformation.

ROME'S ROLE IN THE CANON

Rome had one final role in building the Bible we have today, and it involves canonization, or the process of choosing the books that would become included in what we call the Bible. "Canon" is from the Greek κανών (*kanōn*) meaning "rule" or "measuring stick." Thus, a canon is something by which other things are measured, namely, the authority of a particular Christian writing. Those books included in the canon are thought to be "divinely inspired," "God's Word," "Scripture," "God-breathed," and therefore authoritative. Indeed, the Bible is the record of God's message to humanity for many Jews and Christians around the world.

But the process of canonization is much messier than most people realize (or want to know). Indeed, the Bible is a product of a very political process. For those interested in delving deeper, I recommend Professor Michael Barber's excellent three-part summary of the process of canonization for both the Old and New Testaments.[15]

HOW THE HEBREW BIBLE CAME TO BE

Let's look at the Hebrew Bible first. Once upon a time, scholars thought that the books that came to be officially included in the Hebrew Bible were decided in three stages: the Torah was determined around 400 BCE, the Nevi'im (Prophets) by around 200 BCE, and the Ketuvim (Writings) by 100 CE. Scholars believed that, following the destruction of the Temple by the Romans in 70 CE, all of the Jewish sages and scholars fled and convened at a theoretical Council of Jamnia in modern Yavne, Israel, on the Mediterranean coast, in order to decide which books were to be included in the Hebrew Bible. Many scholars insisted that such a council took place to settle debates similar to the one found in Mishnah *Yadayim* 3:5, which preserves a debate between Jewish rabbis about which books "made the hands impure" due to their holiness, meaning which books would be included in the official Jewish canon.[16]

This theory was largely dismissed after the discovery of the Dead Sea Scrolls at Qumran (see Chapter 9), when scholars found that the Jewish sectarian books in caves surrounding Qumran included references to books that were not limited to the Hebrew canon we know today, including *Enoch, Jubilees,* and liturgical works like extra psalms and *Songs for Sabbath Sacrifices.* The scrolls discovered at Qumran also included copies of Greek books and targums (Aramaic translations of Hebrew biblical books), some of which were included in the Septuagint (see Chapter 7) and some of which were previously unknown.

Furthermore, multiple copies of the same biblical books were discovered at Qumran. These copies often did not match each other word for word, and some of the copies more closely matched the Septuagint's versions of the books than the Masoretic Hebrew texts we have today. Thus, scholars quickly realized that multiple versions of the biblical books were circulating in antiquity, meaning that Jews in the first century CE weren't sure not only which *books* were canonical, but which *versions* of the books were "authoritative."

There is also evidence from the Talmud that the Hebrew canon had not yet been settled. For instance, the book of Sirach is quoted as Scripture in the Talmud and preserves the introductory formula "for so it is written in the Book of Ben Sira."[17] In fact, Sirach 13:15 appears to be quoted in the Talmud as representative of the Ketuvim (the Writings section of the Hebrew Bible): "Every fowl dwells near its kind and man near his equal."[18]

So scholars realized that the biblical canon was not as "fixed" as we originally thought. Different Jewish groups venerated different Jewish writings, and there were sometimes multiple copies of certain biblical books that differed from one another. As we learned in Chapter 7, the Septuagint is significantly different from the Masoretic Text in that it includes over a dozen more books than were canonized in the Hebrew Bible. Today, the twenty-four books of the Hebrew Bible are:

The five books of the Torah: Genesis, Exodus, Leviticus, Numbers, and Deuteronomy.

The eight books of the Prophets (Nevi'im): Joshua, Judges, Samuel, Kings,[19] Isaiah, Jeremiah, Ezekiel, and the "Book of the Twelve" minor prophets: Hosea, Joel, Amos, Obadiah, Jonah, Micah, Naḥum, Habakkuk, Zephaniah, Ḥaggai, Zechariah, and Malachi.

The eleven books of the Writings (Ketuvim): Psalms, Proverbs, Job, Song of Songs, Ruth, Lamentations, Qohelet (Ecclesiastes), Esther, Daniel, Ezra-Neḥemiah (which is a single book in Judaism), and Chronicles.

Many Christians have been taught that there are thirty-nine books of the Old Testament, while Jews have been taught to count twenty-four books. The way I was taught to remember this was that there are three letters in the word "Old" and nine letters in the word "Testament," so thirty-nine books in the Old Testament. (And then multiply three times nine to get twenty-seven, the number of books in the New Testament.) The discrepancy between thirty-nine and twenty-four can be explained by noting that Jews count the Book of the Twelve (minor prophets) as one book, not as twelve, so that takes us from twenty-four to thirty-five. The books of Ezra and Neḥemiah are counted as one book in the Hebrew Bible, but as two books in the Old Testament, taking us to thirty-six. The books of Samuel, Kings, and Chronicles are also each counted as a single book, while Christians count them as two books each (i.e., 1–2 Samuel, 1–2 Kings, and 1–2 Chronicles), which brings us to thirty-nine books. This is how the twenty-four books of the Jewish Hebrew Bible are counted as thirty-nine books in the Christian Old Testament.

Thus, the Hebrew Bible was decided over a much longer and much less understood period of time, meaning that what Jews and Christians today consider to be the Hebrew Bible was not boomed forth from the top of a mountain and did not float down from the heavens in completed fashion. Rather, the process of canonizing the Hebrew Bible had a lot more to do with what different groups *believed* to be true and chose to include.

And if you thought determining which books would be in the Hebrew Bible was confusing, just wait until you see how the New Testament came into being.

How the New Testament Came to Be

When we look at how both Old and New Testaments of the Christian Bible were canonized, we know that by the end of the first century CE there had been several Christian works composed by a number of authors. The letters of Paul, the Gospels, and some of the non-Pauline letters like Hebrews had been written. But so too had a number of documents that were incredibly popular at the time, but that are unknown to many people today.[20] Thus, the church had to decide which of these books would be canonized as the "Word of God."

Many Christian readers would be surprised to discover that the word "canon" originally had nothing to do with the books that were considered authoritative and therefore included in the Bible. Rather, the idea of canon originally had to do with the agreed-upon doctrinal and liturgical decrees issued by the church fathers and councils. The church decided what it believed and how it should worship long before any official biblical canon was ever authorized. Now to be sure, many of those beliefs that were debated and decided upon by the early church fathers were rooted in *specific* writings of those early Christian authors they believed to have been eyewitnesses of Jesus and his ministry. But the church decided much of what it believed *before* there was a biblical canon. This means we can say that the early church *first* decided what it believed and *then* selected Christian writings that largely supported those beliefs.

All of the evidence we have from the early Christian authors and councils supports these facts. We know of several lists of biblical books that were made throughout the first centuries of Christianity. Surprisingly, the lists vary, often dramatically, regarding the books that are to be considered canonical. And these differences of opinion do not reach a general consensus until the end of the fourth century!

Marcion of Sinope (85–160), the bishop of Asia Minor, compiled a canon list between 130 and 140. His list included ten of the Pauline letters, *excluded* the Pastoral Letters and the book of Hebrews, and possessed a modified version of what was later known to be the Gospel of Luke. However, Marcion excised from his version of Luke the passages pertaining to Jesus's birth and childhood as well as some of the passages that linked Jesus with the Old Testament, because Marcion believed that many of Jesus's teachings were incompatible with the deeds of the God described in the Old Testament. He developed a system of beliefs that argued that there were actually *two* distinct deities—a heavenly father who created the earth, the God of the Old Testament; and Jesus, the Lord of the New Testament. His belief in two deities and in the incompatibility of the Old Testament and the Jewish faith with Christianity were later condemned as heresy, and he was excommunicated from the church.

The Muratorian Fragment is a copy of what might be the oldest known list of the books of the New Testament. It was discovered bound with a seventh-century Latin manuscript discovered at the Columban monastery library in Bobbio, Italy. Scholars date the fragment to somewhere between the late second and the early fourth centuries. The Muratorian Fragment's New Testament includes four Gospels (Matthew, Mark, Luke, and John), Acts, thirteen letters of Paul (not including Hebrews), Jude, 1 Peter (but not 2 Peter), 1 and 2 John (but not 3 John), and the book of Revelation *as well as* the Wisdom of Solomon and the Apocalypse of Peter, adding that "some of us will not allow the latter to be read in church." The Muratorian Fragment also mentions the Shepherd of Hermas, stating that "it ought indeed to be read," but warned that "it cannot be read publicly to the people in church either among the Prophets, whose number is complete, or among the apostles, for it is after their time,"[21] meaning that there appeared to be a time limit to inclusion in the canon and that books written after the time of the apostles could not be included.

Around 180, Irenaeus (130–202), the bishop of Lugdunum in Gaul (present-day Lyon, France) developed a canon containing the four Gospels. In his work *Against Heresies,* he also made over a thousand citations from books that would become the canonical New Testament, including citations of every canonical book except Philemon, 3 John, and Jude.[22]

Sometime in the early fourth century, Eusebius (260–340), the bishop of Caesarea, gave a detailed breakdown in *Ecclesiastical History* regarding the books he believed should be included in the canon as well as the books that Origen (185–254) and others accepted as authoritative.[23] Origen's list includes the Old Testament plus the books of Maccabees as well as the four Gospels, but then betrays some of the debate surrounding the other books that should be understood as authoritative for Christians. Eusebius recounts the books considered universally accepted by all Christians (the *homologoumenoi*), the ones universally rejected (heretical), and the ones in between (the *antilegoumenoi*)—those books that are in dispute due to their content, a question over who actually wrote them (i.e., whether they were actually written by the author claimed in the text), or their date of composition.

Universally accepted (homologoumenoi): In *Ecclesiastical History* 3.25, Eusebius states that the canon should definitely include the four Gospels (Matthew, Mark, Luke, John), Acts of the Apostles, the Letters of Paul, the Letter of John (1 John), the Letter of Peter (1 Peter), and the Apocalypse of John (Revelation), but notes that Revelation's inclusion is disputed by others. In *Ecclesiastical History* 6.25, Eusebius states that Origen called for the twenty-two books of the Hebrews,[24] the books of Maccabees, the four Gospels, Acts, fourteen letters of Paul (Romans, 1 and 2 Corinthians, Galatians, Ephesians, Philippians, Colossians, 1 and 2 Thessalonians, 1 and 2 Timothy, Titus, Philemon, and Hebrews; Eusebius includes a lengthy discussion on whether Paul actually wrote Hebrews), 1 John, and 1 Peter. Origen elsewhere refers to the story of Susanna, among other canonical works,[25] and refers to Sirach as "Scripture."[26]

Disputed genuineness and/or authority (antilegoumenoi): In *Ecclesiastical History* Eusebius says that the letters of James, Jude, 2 Peter, 2 John, and 3 John are all disputed (3.25; in 3.3 he states explicitly, "[Peter's] extant second Letter does not belong to the canon"). Elsewhere in *Ecclesiastical History* (6.14), Eusebius refers to the Epistle of Barnabas and the Apocalypse of Peter as disputed. Eusebius states that Clement of Alexandria (150–215) makes use of "disputed" books including the so-called Wisdom of Solomon, the Book of Sirach, the Letter to the Hebrews, the Epistle of Barnabas, the First Letter of Clement of Rome, and Jude (6.13). Eusebius also lists the Gospel of Peter and the Apocalypse of Peter as disputed, but only because "no ecclesiastical writer, ancient or modern, has made use of testimonies drawn from them" (3.3). He also states that the Shepherd of Hermas is considered disputed by some, but "quite indispensable" by others.

Heretical (firmly rejected): In *Ecclesiastical History,* Eusebius rejects by name the Acts of Paul, the so-called Shepherd (of Hermas), the Apocalypse of Peter (which he lists as "disputed" in 3.3), the Epistle of Barnabas, and the so-called Teachings of the Apostles (the Didache), followed by a note that many place the Apocalypse of John (i.e., book of Revelation) in this category (3.25). Eusebius also rejects the Gospel of the Hebrews (which should not be confused with the Letter to the Hebrews) and by name the Gospel of Peter, Gospel of Thomas, Gospel of Matthias, "or of any others besides them," as well as the Acts of Andrew and the Acts of John.

I know it's confusing, but that's the point. As late as the middle of the third century—over *two hundred years after* Jesus was crucified—the church was *still* debating which books were actually considered authoritative. And many of the church fathers gave different opinions about the same books in different writings of their own!

We should note that a number of the books, like the four Gospels and some undisputed letters of Paul, were *never* really in dispute. But others were. This is important because it shows that early Christian doctrines came from *men*—the early church fathers—*not* from any biblical canon. *The canon of the Bible came after the church fathers had debated and decided what Christians were supposed to believe.* Thus, the notion that the "Word of God" (i.e., the Bible) instructs Christians regarding what they are to believe and do is *not* consistent with history and reality. In fact, the reverse is true; prominent men of the early church decided what the "Word of God" would consist of. They determined the rules of the church for Christians based on *some* of the writings from the first and early second centuries and then filled out the canonical books of the Bible by selecting those books that were consistent with what they had already decreed.

So not only were the books that became the Bible still in question two hundred years after Jesus came and went, but the literary evidence we have from the early church shows us that the biblical canon did not become fixed for at least another century. One important artifact that illustrates the volatility of the Bible during this time is the Codex Sinaiticus, which dates to about 350 and was discovered in 1844 by Constantin von Tischendorf in St. Catherine's Monastery on the Sinai Peninsula in modern Egypt (hence the name "Sinaiticus"). It is one of the earliest complete copies of the Bible (Old and New Testaments) we have. Sinaiticus is important to our discussion for two reasons. First, the New Testament books in Sinaiticus do not possess many parts of the Bible that scholars have argued were late additions to the NT text, lending support to these claims.[27] But what is truly fascinating about Codex Sinaiticus is that it contains two books that are not in our Bibles today: the Shepherd of Hermas and the Epistle of Barnabas. Think about that: the oldest complete manuscript of the Bible that we have today contains books that are no longer in the Bible! This fact alone reveals just how much human interpretation and debate shaped the Bible in the first four centuries of the church's existence.

And just think, had a few influential church fathers chosen differently, you might be quoting Scripture from the Epistle of Barnabas and asking, "What are the Letter of Jude and the Apocalypse of John? I've never heard of them."

And yet *that* is how we got the New Testament canon: different influential men over four centuries made different lists of books and argued about them. Yet today many see the Bible as the complete and holy "Word of God" written by "inspired men."

So by now you're probably asking where Rome comes into the process of the canonization of the Bible? I'm glad you asked.

ROME'S ROLE IN CREATING THE BIBLE

Rome's role comes into play beginning with Constantine the Great (272–337). Constantine had already legalized Christianity with the Edict of Milan in 313, and as Constantine came to embrace Christianity, he took an interest in Christianity's inner political workings. Specifically, Constantine wanted a politically stable empire, and his empire could be made all the more tranquil by ridding it of religious bickering. Thus, Constantine promoted a religious orthodoxy among Christians. This meant sponsoring ecumenical church councils, like the Council of Nicea in 325, for the purpose of producing orthodox creeds, like the Nicene Creed, that would streamline what Christians "officially" believed.

Constantine also ordered fifty copies of the Bible in Greek in 331 for use by Alexander, the bishop of Constantinople, about a year after moving the capital of his empire from Rome to his newly founded eastern capital of Constantinople (modern Istanbul). The task of creating the Bibles was given to Eusebius of Caesarea.[28] Then around 340, the Archbishop of Alexandria, Athanasius, claimed he created additional "volumes containing the holy Scriptures" in Rome for Constantine's son, the emperor Constans (323–50).[29] The increasingly frequent request for Bibles required that translators actually know (or decide) exactly which books they would translate for their Bibles.

The lack of an official canon list was also an issue for church leaders, who were debating theological issues and issuing decrees announcing what Christians should believe. In attempting to root theological arguments in the teachings of Jesus and the apostles so that Christians would find them authoritative, church leaders cited different Christian writings, some of which other church leaders did not accept as authoritative. The church needed a canon.

In his 39th Festal Letter on Easter of 367 CE, Athanasius authorized a list of twenty-seven canonical New Testament books, *including Revelation,* making it the earliest list to include what would later become the canonical New Testament books. Interestingly, he authorized all of the books of the Hebrew Bible *except* the book of Esther, which he left out, authorizing instead the book of Baruch and the Letter of Jeremiah (which was treated in the Latin Vulgate as the sixth and final chapter of Baruch).[30]

At the end of the fourth century, the bishop of Rome ("the pope"), Damasus I (305–84), sought to reform the church's liturgy. Because the reading of Holy Scripture was a part of the weekly liturgy and because in the third and fourth centuries Latin was slowly replacing Greek as the common language of the eastern Roman Empire, in 382 Pope Damasus I commissioned Jerome (347–420), whom he'd later appoint as his personal secretary, to provide the church with an official Latin translation of the Bible, which has come to be known as the Vulgate.

Of course, producing a Latin translation of the Bible meant translating the books of the Bible from their original languages as well as selecting which books would be included in the church's official Latin Bible. Jerome's Latin Vulgate included the twenty-seven books of the New Testament that we now have, solidifying their status as canonical.

But there was still a fight over which version of the Hebrew Bible, the Hebrew text or the Greek Septuagint, should be used for the official Latin version of the Old Testament. The Septuagint included several additional books and its versions of some books differed at times significantly from the Hebrew versions. Augustine of Hippo (354–430) argued that the Septuagint should be used, as it was the version that was most often used by the authors of the New Testament. However, Jerome wanted to use the Hebrew version of the Old Testament because, as he explained to Augustine in a letter,[31] he considered the Septuagint to be an inferior version largely (and ironically) because he felt it had become the "Hebrew Bible of the Christians." Jerome considered many of the differences between the Septuagint and the Hebrew text to be additions made by Christians, and therefore he felt it was the Hebrew text, which had *not* been translated into

Greek and did *not* include all of the extra books present in the Septuagint, that was the superior version of the Bible.

This answers the question of how the biblical Apocrypha came to be a separate collection of books within the Old Testament; Jerome argued in the preface of the Vulgate that the Apocryphal books of the Hebrew Bible contained in the Septuagint should be set aside as a separate collection.[32] But, as Michael Barber points out, Jerome later changed his mind concerning the Apocrypha![33] Jerome claimed that the book of Judith was considered among the sacred Scriptures at the Council of Nicea[34] and quotes Judith 13 in his *Letter to Eustochium*.[35] Thus even among those making the translations themselves, there was ambiguity about which books were to be considered part of the holy canon.

Meanwhile, the church councils were having their say. A summary of the canons issued by the Synod of Laodicea, which met sometime between 343 and 381, contains a final canon (Canon 60) that states that it is a list of books of the Old and New Testaments that are "appointed to be read." Interestingly, the list of Old Testament books includes all of the canonical books in our modern Bibles today as well as 1–2 Esdras, Baruch, and the Letter of Jeremiah. Although this might be expected, as there was much debate over whether or not the Apocryphal books were considered canonical, the far more interesting detail is that the New Testament list contains every canonical New Testament book *except Revelation*![36]

The exclusion of the book of Revelation was apparently quite common in the late fourth century. In his letter to Letoïus, St. Gregory, who was bishop of Nyssa from 372 to 376, issued a canon (Canon 7) that lists the books of the Bible that ought to be read, lest "other books seduce [the] mind: for many malignant writings have been disseminated."[37] Gregory's list omits "one Esdras and all the Deutero-Canonical books" as well as the book of Esther from its Old Testament and once again omits the book of Revelation from the list, *despite* making an allusion to it by referencing the author of the Gospel of John as the "enterer of heaven."

However, according to a written compilation of decrees issued by various church councils during the fourth and fifth centuries,[38] the Council of Carthage (397) issued Canon 24, which addresses which books are to be definitively considered "Scripture." A portion of it reads:

> It was also determined that besides the Canonical Scriptures nothing be read in the Church under the title of divine Scriptures. The Canonical Scriptures are these: Genesis, Exodus, Leviticus, Numbers, Deuteronomy, Joshua the son of Nun, Judges, Ruth, four books of Kings [i.e., 1–2 Samuel and 1–2 Kings], two books of Paraleipomena [i.e., 1–2 Chronicles], Job, the Psalter [i.e., Psalms], five books of Solomon [i.e., Proverbs, Ecclesiastes, Song of Songs, Wisdom of Solomon, and Ecclesiasticus], the books of the twelve prophets, Isaiah, Jeremiah, Ezechiel, Daniel, Tobit, Judith, Esther, two books of Esdras, two books of the Maccabees. Of the New Testament: four books of the Gospels, one book of the Acts of the Apostles, thirteen Epistles of the Apostle Paul, one epistle of the same [writer] to the Hebrews, two Epistles of the Apostle Peter, three of John, one of James, one of Jude, one book of the Apocalypse of John.[39]

Note that although the above list includes the twenty-seven books of today's canonical New Testament, it also includes many of the Apocryphal books, including the Wisdom of Solomon, Ecclesiasticus (Sirach), Tobit, Judith, 1–2 Esdras, and 1–2 Maccabees. Thus, although the Third Council of Carthage is said to have confirmed the twenty-seven books of the New Testament in the *very* late fourth century, a number of the books of the Apocrypha were considered fully canonical and not separate from the other Old Testament Books, while others were excluded.

And this, *this* is how we got the Bible that we have. The emperor Constantine the Great wanted fifty Bibles, so Eusebius had to decide what books went into these Bibles. The emperor Constans needed Bibles, so Athanasius created more Bibles. And this is also how the Apocrypha came to be separate from the Old and New Testaments. Pope Damasus I wanted an official Latin translation, and Jerome, who favored the Hebrew version over the Septuagint, set the Apocrypha aside in a separate section, which became the deuterocanon accepted by Catholics and dismissed by Protestants. Meanwhile, the church councils continued to debate which books were authoritative well into the late fourth century. Thus, the Roman emperor, the bishop of Rome, and the early church councils contributed to the canonization and proliferation of the Bible that we have today.

———

It is difficult to underestimate Rome's contribution to the Bible. The military history of Rome set the stage for the major events of Christianity, including Jesus's birth under Herod and his trial and crucifixion under Pilate. Rome also fundamentally altered Judaism and Christianity when it destroyed the Temple in Jerusalem. Paul's letter to the church in Rome is the longest letter in the Bible and serves as the best summary of the gospel to a Gentile world, which Rome itself ironically helped spread through its early persecution of Christians as well as by its later adoption of Christianity. Furthermore, Rome played a key role in shaping the canon of the Bible, determining precisely which books would come to be known as the Word of God.

So our journey ends in Rome, as Rome is the city that is responsible for the canonization of both the Old and New Testaments for Christians. And this is fitting, as all roads truly lead to Rome.

Conclusion

As we've seen, building the Bible was a complicated, messy process. It did not float down from the sky as the complete inerrant, infallible, noncontradictory Word of God. It is the product of dozens of authors and hundreds of anonymous editors and redactors. The canonization process took many centuries, not a few years and a single vote, and multiple influential opinions contributed to the Bible we have today. Because of the length of time it took to compose the Bible and because of the many different contributors to the Bible from different time periods and different perspectives, the separate books of the Bible often make contradictory claims that cannot be reconciled, despite two thousand years of attempts by systematic theologians. And this is okay!

It is this process of wrestling with the aggregate books of the Bible that has given rise to many of the Jewish and Christian traditions we have today. For example, we would not have the Trinity without competing claims that there is only one God and that Jesus is also God. We would not have an apocalyptic Jewish messiah, if we did not have claims that Israel's kings will forever come from the line of David despite the reality that the Babylonians ended the Davidic monarchy, causing Jews to look to the sky for a divine messiah.

Most important for our purposes, a number of different cities in and around the Holy Land played significant roles in the construction of the Bible. We have the pages of our Bible because of Byblos and an alphabetic text because of the cities of Phoenicia like Tyre and Sidon. The deities of the Ugaritic pantheon made their way south and came to be worshipped in Israel and Judah (against the Hebrew prophets' many objections). Likewise, some of the stories we have in the Bible, like that of Job, bear uncanny resemblance to earlier stories from Ugarit.

Nineveh and the Assyrians brought destruction to the Northern Kingdom, Israel, and caused those in Judah to interpret Samaria's demise as divine displeasure toward Israel for its rebellion against Judah and Jerusalem, the city of God. And the Babylonians fundamentally altered the history of what would become Judaism, destroying the Temple in Jerusalem and forcing its residents into exile. Out of the ashes of this existential crisis, what would become the Hebrew Bible began to be written down, collected, and edited for future generations.

Megiddo became the symbol of great battles in Israel, and we see how the control of a single geographic location can alter the fate of nations in all directions. The rise of Athens and the philosophy and literature of ancient Greece fundamentally influenced the Bible. The hellenization of the Jewish faith required new perspectives on the events of Israel's past as well as a new Bible that could be read by Greek-speaking Jews.

Moving to Alexandria, we find the concentration of knowledge at the Library of Alexandria provided a motivation for the Septuagint and introduced us to a number of the books of the Bible that many Jews and Christians may not have been familiar with, but that were included in many of the early canonical lists. We also learned why the New Testament was written in Greek, as it became the common written language in first-century Roman Palestine.

Of course, the central city of the Jewish and Christian faiths is Jerusalem, and Jerusalem had a strong influence on the formation of the Bible. We learned that Jesus and other Jews in Jerusalem came to speak Aramaic because of the Persian endorsement of the Jewish return to Jerusalem and of the rebuilding of its Temple. And we saw how the crucifixion and resurrection of Jesus in Jerusalem became the central point of early Christian literature.

The discovery of the Dead Sea Scrolls at Qumran was arguably the most important archaeological discovery of the twentieth century. It changed the way we understand the earliest versions of the

Bible, as the scrolls preserve traditions that are often slightly different from those we have in the Hebrew Bible and the Septuagint.

Bethlehem became what it is today because the father of a shepherd boy (David) happened to live there and because all subsequent kings of Israel were expected to come from Bethlehem. We also learned how Nazareth inspired stories about the birth of a Jewish messiah from the north, who was accepted by some and rejected by others.

Finally, the rise of the Roman Empire shaped and altered first-century Judaism and Christianity by being responsible for the crucifixion of Jesus and the destruction of the Temple in Jerusalem. We also saw Rome's role as both political and theological leader of the early church and how it contributed to determining which books would ultimately be considered the holy Word of God. We have a biblical canon because of the beliefs of a few influential translators (Eusebius, Athanasius, and Jerome, and even *they* disagreed) who were making Bibles for various Roman emperors and because of later Christian councils (like the Third Council of Carthage in 397) that finally issued a canon regarding which books would be considered canonical—and this canon included several of the Apocryphal books!

The Bible as we have it today is the product of three thousand years of believers in a Cana'anite deity attempting to reconcile their socioeconomic, geographical, geological, political, and military realities with their personal ideologies, identities, and philosophies. The Bible is a product of those ancient individuals who dared to struggle with God and who survived to write down their reflections. In this regard, the Bible is not a rule book, a spiritual sword, or a telephone for speaking to God; rather, it is a record of the faithful attempting to make sense of what has happened to them. The Bible is a chronicle that has been augmented and edited, redacted, reshaped, and rewritten over the years for the purpose of presenting an account of the history of a people who believed God had broken into history and was guiding them through their time on earth.

We must also remember that the Bible is not holy of its own accord; rather, people ascribe holiness. The Bible is simply a book, but it is a book built *by* people *for* people. Any holiness attributed to the Bible comes from the fact that it is *venerated by* the faithful and not because its pages are holy on their own.

Thus, the Bible today is not a "living document"; rather, it is quite dead. The Bible is powerful only when it is *translated, interpreted* (in a manner that seeks to discover what the author of the text was trying to communicate and not what it happens to mean to you personally two thousand years later), *considered* and *evaluated* (not only to determine which claims are factual or historical, but to decide which ancient directives are morally defunct and ethically obsolete by our modern civil standards), and if you are a person of faith, *lived*. Without these actions—translating, interpreting, considering and evaluating, and enacting—the Bible is powerless. Thus, it is *you,* the reader, who gives the Bible its authority and its efficacy. Without the *faithful,* the Bible is just another ancient collection of documents.

Furthermore, it is how we choose to enact the claims and directives present in the Bible that will determine the Bible's future worth. If the Bible is read with an insistence that its text is perfect, inerrant, and noncontradictory and that the ethical directives given over two thousand years ago are still irrefutable and unquestionable today, then each subsequent generation will continue to walk away from the Bible, discarding it (with disdain) as a product of a bygone era.

However, if the Bible is read and understood *properly,* not as a blueprint for modern society, but as a historical record of the struggles of people of faith who believed in a God who would rescue them from their present difficulties—a record that serves to inform and encourage people of faith today as they struggle through their daily lives—then the Bible will not only continue to live; it will become all the more relevant, as it not only shows us how far we've grown and developed as humans over the centuries, but also reminds us of the perpetual philosophical questions we will continue to face in our fast-approaching future. Why should I care about my fellow humans? What damage is done by greed, jealousy, hate, lust, and pride? How much of a difference can a cup of cold water really make? A visit to a sick friend? Clothing the naked? Feeding the hungry?

There will always be sectarian divisions among the faithful, who will continue to argue and fight and die over questions that can never be proved. The Bible should give us an appreciation for the history of humanity, not make us loathe those who read it. It should cause us to reflect on the decisions made by those recorded within its pages and inspire us not to make some of the same bad decisions. The Bible should be celebrated as a chronicle of our history, not used as a legal framework for our future. The Bible shows us how human beings adapted to the challenges around them in the past and should provide inspiration for us as we continue to face many of these same challenges.

It is my hope that this book has offered a responsible way in which to view the interaction of the biblical text and archaeological record. I intentionally cited a multitude of biblical passages in a deliberate attempt to show you exactly how much these cities have influenced the text of the Bible. As I said in the Introduction, I don't expect every reader to agree with everything I've said—trust me, I'm used to it. I'm a scholar, and disagreement comes with the territory. But it has been my desire (and my distinct privilege) to present you with a narrative that walks you through some of history's most important cities and shows you how they helped shape the Bible and the beliefs of those who revere it.

It is also my hope that this book has encouraged you to buy a ticket to visit the places that you've only ever read about in the Bible. I hope you get to visit the places I've visited and walk in the steps of those who made the Bible what it is. I hope you get to meet people like those I've met and interact with scholars and chefs and mothers and worshippers and skeptics. In the end, whether you are a Catholic, Protestant, or Orthodox Christian; Reform, Conservative, or Orthodox Jew; deist; secular humanist;

Pastafarian; agnostic; or atheist, we can all agree that it is how we should act—doing justice, loving kindness, and walking humbly—and how we should treat others—feeding the hungry, clothing the naked, welcoming strangers, visiting the sick and imprisoned—that is ultimately the unifying message cultivated from the experiences of those who lived in the cities that built the Bible.

NOTES

Introduction

1. George Rush et al., "Nicole Calls In A Scripture Doctor."
2. For more on this topic, please read my article, "Why Christians Should Adopt the BCE/CE Dating System."
3. This calculation represents the number of pages, not simply the number of books.

Chapter 1: Phoenician Cities

1. See Tzaferis, "Jewish Tombs at and near Giv'at ha-Mivtar, Jerusalem" and "Crucifixion."
2. Not only do we have many signs of wealth in Phoenicia and their colonies; we also have mentions of Phoenicia by the Greek geographer and historian Strabo (*Geography* 3.5.11; 16.2.22–24), who, for example, states that the Phoenicians engaged in a lucrative trade with other nations. For more on Phoenicia, see Moscati, ed., *The Phoenicians*.
3. As in Spanish, the letter *b* often produces an English *v* sound. For example, Be'er She*b*a is pronounced Be'er She*v*a.
4. Bartoloni, "Commerce and Industry."
5. The Phoenician alphabet, which is often referred to as the Proto-Cana'anite alphabet for inscriptions using this alphabet dating earlier than the tenth century BCE, is actually derived from an earlier pictographic alphabet called the Proto-Sinaitic alphabet, named after several rudimentary inscriptions dating to the seventeenth to sixteenth centuries BCE discovered on a mountain called Ṣerabiṭ el-Ḥadim on the Sinai Peninsula. Another example of this earliest of alphabets comes from the Wadi el-Hol inscriptions, also from Egypt, dating to the nineteenth to eighteenth centuries BCE. The Proto-Sinaitic alphabet represents a transitional state between Egyptian hieroglyphics (pictures that represent words) and pictures that came to represent sounds. Thus, the stylized pictures that became the letters (or graphemes) in this consonantal alphabet look like the objects they once represented, and the sound (or phoneme) represented by each grapheme was often the first sound of the name of the object. Scholars call this an acrophonic script. For example, the *'aleph* looks like an ox (West Semitic:

'alph) with horns, the *mem* looks like water (Heb: *mayim*), the *'ayin* looks like an eye (Heb: *'ayin*), the *resh* looks like a human head (Heb: *ro'sh*), etc. These Proto-Sinaitic symbols evolved into the letters of the Proto-Cana'anite and ultimately the Phoenician alphabet. For more on the early history of the Semitic alphabet, see Rollston, *Writing and Literacy in the World of Ancient Israel*, 11–46, and Naveh, *Early History of the Alphabet*, 23–42.

6. According to Herodotus's *Histories* 5:58: "These Phoenicians . . . among many other kinds of learning, brought into Hellas (Greece) the alphabet, which had hitherto been unknown, as I think, to the Greeks; and presently as time went on the sound and the form of the letters were changed. At this time the Greeks . . . having been taught the letters by the Phoenicians, used them with some few changes of form, and in so doing gave to these characters (as indeed was but just, seeing that the Phoenicians had brought them to Hellas) the name of Phoenician" (*Herodotus: The Persian Wars, Volume 3, Books 5–7*, 62–65).

7. In his book *A Social History of Hebrew*, William Schniedewind notes a claim made by the Assyrian king Sargon II (r. 721–705 BCE), recorded on the Dûr-Sharrukîn Cylinder: "People of the four regions of the world, *of foreign tongue and divergent speech*, dwellers of the mountain and lowland, all that were ruled by the light of the gods, the lord of all, I carried off at Ashur, my lord's command, by the might of my scepter. *I made them of one mouth* and settled them therein" (Daniel David Luckenbill, trans., *Ancient Records of Assyria and Babylonia* [Chicago: Univ. of Chicago Press, 1927]). Schniedewind believes this likely refers to the imposition of a single, unified language over the diverse peoples of the lands he conquered; see also Schniedewind, *How the Bible Became a Book*, 65. Whether that language was Akkadian or Aramaic and whether Aramaic was the "official" language of the Neo-Assyrian Empire or merely the lingua franca in Persia is debated. See Rosenthal, *A Grammar of Biblical Aramaic*, 5. For an opposing view, see Frye, "Review of G. R. Driver, *Aramaic Documents of the Fifth Century B.C.*," 457. However, it is noteworthy that by the time of the sixth century BCE in the Persian period, Aramaic had risen from lingua franca to become the official administrative language of the empire.

8. There is some debate over whether the language of the Gezer Calendar is Hebrew, or some form of proto-Hebrew that scholars refer to simply as Cana'anite.

9. Hebrew characters written during the first few centuries BCE that attempted to replicate the Old Hebrew characters are referred to as Palaeo-Hebrew. Some also refer to Old Hebrew characters as Palaeo-Hebrew script, which causes some confusion.

10. Dan. 2–7 are in biblical Aramaic, as are Ezra 4:8–6:18 and 7:12–26, which contain transcripts of letters written in biblical Aramaic. There is also a single verse in Jer. 10:11 that is written in Aramaic as well as an Aramaic place-name in Gen. 31:47.

11. Lipiński, "Hiram of Tyre and Solomon."

12. Additional claims of Solomon's commercial ventures with Phoenicia are preserved in 1 Kings 10: "Moreover, the fleet of Hiram, which carried gold from Ophir, brought from Ophir a great quantity of almug wood and precious stones. From the almug wood the king made supports for the house of the LORD, and for the king's house, lyres also and harps for the singers; no such almug wood has come or been seen to this day" (vv. 11–12); "For the king had a fleet of ships of Tarshish at sea with the fleet of Hiram. Once every three years the fleet of ships of Tarshish used to come bringing gold, silver, ivory, apes, and peacocks" (v. 22).

13. See Katzenstein, "Tyre in the Early Persian Period."

14. In 126 BCE, Tyre regained its independence from the Seleucids, but was soon annexed by Rome in 64 BCE. Rome designated Tyre as a *civitas foederata,* or "federated citizenry," which was a semi-independent client kingdom that had a treaty with Rome exempting it from paying tribute to Rome and from many Roman laws. See Hardy, ed. and trans., *Roman Laws and Charters,* 95.

Chapter 2: Ugarit

1. Yon, *City of Ugarit at Tell Ras Shamra*, 106–10.

2. Yon, *City of Ugarit at Tell Ras Shamra,* 110.

3. Some scholars refer to this temple as the Temple of 'El, arguing that Dagon and 'El were understood to be the same deity at Ugarit. See Fontenrose, "Dagon and El." For more on Dagon, see Healey, "Dagon." *KTU* (from the German title, *Keilalphabetische Texte aus Ugarit*) is used as a catalog for texts from Ugarit.

4. Crowell, "The Development of Dagan."

5. There was a temple honoring Dagon at Ebla. The Ebla Tablets mention him, and the name Dagon is incorporated into many personal names. See Pettinato and Waetzoldt, "Dagan in Ebla und Mesopotamien."

6. Yon, *City of Ugarit at Tell Ras Shamra,* 111.

7. For more on the archaeology of Ugarit, see Yon, *City of Ugarit at Tell Ras Shamra;* and Curtis, *Ugarit (Ras Shamra).*

8. Isa. 14:13 reads: "You said in your heart, 'I will ascend to heaven; I will raise my throne above the stars of God; I will sit on the mount of

assembly on the heights of Zaphon; I will ascend to the tops of the clouds, I will make myself like 'Elyon (the Most High)." See also Ps. 48:2 (48:3 HB), which may contain a reference to "the heights of Mt. Ṣafon."

9. It is worth noting that the other tall mountain in the region, Mt. Hermon, north of the Golan Heights, mentioned on several occasions throughout the Bible, is referred to as Ba'al-Hermon in Judg. 3:3 and 1 Chron. 5:23, preserving some legacy of association with the deity atop the mountain.

10. 'El Berit may be the same god as Ba'al Berit mentioned in Judg. 8:33 and 9:4, the god of the Cana'anite and later Israelite city of Shechem. Interestingly, 'El Berit is also mentioned at Ugarit and in Phoenicia. A deity named *brt* (Berit) is mentioned in the Ugaritic texts in connection with Ba'al (see Mulder, "Baal-Berith"), and 'El Berit is perhaps the deity Beruth in the purported Phoenician historian Sanchuniathon's writings as preserved by Philo of Byblos (809:15). See Baumgarten, *The Phoenician History of Byblos,* 186.

11. This is common with Hebrew and other Semitic languages. For example, the number three in Hebrew is שלש (*shalosh*), but in Aramaic it is תלת (*thalath*).

12. Lit. *rbt 'aṯrt ym*.

13. Judg. 3:7; 1 Kings 15:13; 18:19; 2 Kings 21:7; 23:4–7; 2 Chron. 15:16.

14. See also Job 37:2, 4–5; 40:9; Ps. 29:3.

15. To view an image and Louvre Conservateur Général Honoraire Annie Caubet's description of the Ba'al Stele in the Near Eastern Antiquities Department in the Sully Wing on the ground floor, Room B (item AO 15775), visit the Louvre's website: http://www.louvre.fr/en/node/38663.

16. See, e.g., Num. 25:3–5; Judg. 6:30–32; and 1 Sam. 7:4, where Ba'al is mentioned alongside 'Asherah; also Judg. 8:33; 10:6–10; 1 Kings 16:31–32; 18:18–40; 22:53.

17. The infrequency of 'Anat in the Bible may be due to competing myths about her origin and role, especially as worship of the Ugaritic pantheon spread south into Cana'an. 'Anat was a companion of Ba'al at Ugarit, but 'Asherah came to be associated with Ba'al in Cana'an (see Judg. 3:7; 1 Kings 18:19; 2 Kings 23:4). It may also be the case that since many of the characteristics attributed to 'El were merged into YHWH, 'El's apparent disappearance caused his popular consort 'Asherah to become associated with the other popular "foreign" deity, Ba'al, leaving 'Anat to be remembered only in place-names. Then again, it may be the case that Ba'al was associated with *both* female deities (male gods did this on more than one occasion in ancient literature) or that, given the fluidity of many of these mythical legends from region to region, some

'Anat and 'Asherah legends may have been confused or simply merged into the same deity.

18. Elephantine was known locally then as Yeb.

19. See Berlin Ägyptisches Museum Papyrus 13485, document number B52, in Porten, *The Elephantine Papyri in English,* 266–67.

20. For more on 'Anat-Yahu, see Mondriaan, "Anat-Yahu and the Jews at Elephantine." See also Day, *Yahweh and the Gods and Goddesses,* 143; Smith, *The Early History of God,* 61; and Van der Toorn "Anat-Yahu, Some Other Deities."

21. You read that correctly. The actual name of the body of water that Moses and the Hebrews crossed is the *Reed* Sea, not the *Red* Sea, farther to the south, as the Hebrew word for the body of water crossed in Exod. 13–15 is *yam suf* (יַם־סוּף), and *suf* in Hebrew means "reed" (cf. Exod. 2:3), not "red." The confusion between *yam suf* ("Sea of Reeds") and the "Red Sea" stems from a mistranslation in the LXX, which we shall discuss in Chapter 7.

22. Scholars consider the Mesopotamian Gilgamesh Epic one of the first great works of literature. The story is dated to about 2100 BCE and exists in multiple versions written on several cuneiform tablets. The story follows the travels of its hero, King Gilgamesh, as he searches for the plant that brings immortality, which is stolen from him by a serpent (which parallels the biblical story of the Garden of Eden); survives a great flood by building an ark, loading his family and all of the animals on it, and sending out birds to determine when the flood had ended (which parallels the biblical flood story); and struggles with the idea of death and mortality (which parallels the biblical discourse of Qohelet or Ecclesiastes). Thus, the Gilgamesh Epic, which predates these biblical stories by at least a thousand years, is thought to have influenced the stories of Eden, the flood, and Ecclesiastes.

23. The Atraḫasis Flood Epic is another flood parallel that predates the Bible. From the eighteenth century BCE, this Akkadian myth tells the story of the creation of humans out of the dust of the ground, how the gods regretted having created them, and of their decision to send a flood to destroy humankind. The deity Enki warns Atraḫasis of the coming flood, and Atraḫasis tears down his house and builds an ark, covers it with pitch, loads up his family and animals, and survives the flood. When the flood is over, Atraḫasis sacrifices to the gods. It is easy to see why scholars argue that the Atraḫasis Flood Epic is an ancient parallel that predates and influences the biblical flood stories in Gen. 6–9.

24. Rollston, *Writing and Literacy in the World of Ancient Israel,* 16–17.

25. Lewis, "El's Divine Feast." For an excellent discussion about the "hair of the dog," see Cook, "Hair of the Ugaritic Dog."

26. Ps. 74:13–15 reads almost like the story of Ba'al and Yam: "You divided the sea by your might; you broke the heads of the dragons in the waters. You crushed the heads of Leviathan; you gave him as food for the creatures of the wilderness. You cut openings for springs and torrents; you dried up ever-flowing streams." Interestingly, Isa. 27:1 also appears to reference this same battle: "On that day the LORD with his cruel and great and strong sword will punish Leviathan the fleeing serpent, Leviathan the twisting serpent, and he will kill the dragon that is in the sea." This is notable because the Ba'al Cycle records an almost identical verse centuries before Isaiah lived. *COS* 1.86.265 reads: "When you smite Lôtan (Leviathan), the fleeing serpent, finish off the twisting serpent, the close-coiling one with seven heads." Cf. Pardee, "The Ba'lu Myth," 265.

27. *CTA* 3, 5.19–25.

28. *CTA* 4, 5.120–6.15.

29. *ANET* 129–42; *KTU* 1.1–6. For more, see Smith, *Ugaritic Baal Cycle*. One question to ponder is why two gods of water, namely, Yam (the god of the sea and rivers) and Ba'al (the storm god) would be so opposed to one another in the mythology. It can't be a matter of salt vs. fresh water, as Yam is also referred to as Ruler *Naharu,* or "Ruler of the River," and therefore rules both freshwater and saltwater. (Note that not only is *yam* the Hebrew word for "sea," but the Hebrew cognate *nahar* is also the word for "river.") There is little evidence to support an early dispute between dry farming and irrigation. One could make a case for a debate about the use of water in moderation (represented by Ba'al) vs. the devastating extremes of flooding rivers and the untamable tempests of the sea and its effects on maritime trade and fishing economies. The contest between Yam and Ba'al is most likely a metaphor for the various agricultural economies espoused by the nations surrounding Ugarit. The sea may represent seafaring nations like the Mycenaeans, while the rivers represent river-based agricultural economies like Egypt (which thrives due to the flooding of the Nile) and Mesopotamia (which is dependent upon the Tigris and Euphrates). These other nations are represented by Yam, the god of the sea and rivers, whereas Ugarit and the surrounding Levantine nations are represented by Ba'al, who uses storms and rains to water fertile lands independent of rivers or a dependence on maritime trade. The fact, then, that Ba'al defeats Yam in the Ugaritic myths would represent not only Ugarit's superiority over Egypt, Mycenae, and Mesopotamian cultures, but also that Ugarit had become a successful trade hub in all three of these realms. Thus, in

addition to telling us how Ba'al got to be so popular in Ugarit (and Cana'an, where he was a popular fertility deity throughout the Bible), the Ba'al Cycle says as much about how Ugarit felt about itself as it does in explaining how the gods of the Bible came to be in Cana'an.

30. *Legend of Keret,* Tablet C, col. 6, 25–53.

31. O'Connor, in "The Keret Legend and the Prologue-Epilogue of Job," points out an additional, rather unique parallel between the two: "Job and Keret . . . are now finally blessed with a new family. Job with seven sons and three beautiful daughters (42:13); Keret with a new wife who bears him seven sons and at least six daughters (Keret III, iii, 5–12). An extraordinary parallel emerges in the manner of giving the names of all the daughters, but not of the sons. The names of Job's three daughters are given (42:14). In the epic *Baal and Anat* (also from Ugarit) their three daughters are named, but not the sons. In the Keret poem there is no list of his sons by their names, but when it comes to the birth of the daughters we get six parallel lines, short lines of only three words each, but the final word in each gave the name of the girl. Unfortunately, only in the sixth line can the name of the (favourite) daughter of Keret be reconstructed, the text is damaged in the other five, but the space for the name was there."

32. Note that although the NRSV and other translations refer to "heavenly beings" presenting themselves to YHWH in Job 1:6 (again, remember the assembly of the Ugaritic deities on Mt. Ṣafon), the Hebrew here literally reads "sons of God" (*bnei ha'Elohim*). Furthermore, the *satan* mentioned in Job 1:6 is written with a definite article (*ha-śatan*) and should therefore be read as "*the* satan," which is Hebrew for "the accuser," and not as the proper name "Satan."

33. *ANET* 142–49. For more, see Margalit, "The Legend of Keret." See also Pardee, "The Kirta Epic (1.102)."

34. "Repha'im" can refer either to an ancient race of giants (Gen. 14:5; 15:20; Deut. 2:10–21; 3:11; Josh. 12:4; 13:12; 15:8; 17:15; 18:16; 2 Sam. 5:18–22; 23:13; 1 Chron. 11:15; 14:9; 20:4) or to dead ancestors, commonly referred to in English Bible translations as "shades" (Isa. 14:9; 26:14, 19; Ps. 88:11; Prov. 2:18; 9:18; 21:16; Job 26:5). See Pardee, "The 'Aqhatu Legend (1.103)," 343, n. 1.

35. *ANET* 150, AQHT A, col. 1, lines 31ff.

36. *ANET* 152; AQHT A, col. 6, line 40.

37. *ANET* 153; AQHT B, col. 4, lines 28ff.

38. Dan'el calls upon Ba'al to break the wings of the birds above, so that they might fall to the ground allowing Dan'el to cut them open and retrieve the remains of his son. Ba'al agrees and breaks the birds' wings,

they fall, and Dan'el cuts them open, but he cannot find the remains of 'Aqhat. Not wanting to be blamed for the demise of the now exonerated vultures, Dan'el asks Baʿal to mend their wings (and I'm assuming also their guts) and allow them to fly away. After repeating the whole process with Hargab, the father of the vultures, Dan'el spots Ṣamal, the mother of the vultures, and again asks Baʿal to break her wings, so that he can check her. Dan'el finds his son's remains, takes them from Ṣamal's belly, and gives them a proper burial.

39. Many scholars assume that some sort of compensation is given to Dan'el, in the form of either a resurrected 'Aqhat or a newborn son, which allows the drought to end and the earth to once again become fruitful, but this is speculation.

40. Homer, *Odyssey* 11.60–78.

41. Gen. 23.

42. John 19:38–42.

43. Ezek. 14:14: "and were these three men in it, Noaḥ, Dan'el, and Job, they by their righteousness would only save their (own) lives, declares the lord YHWH" (translation mine). Note that Noaḥ and Job were both understood to be pre-Israelite, non-Jewish characters. Job is said to be from the unknown "land of Uz," while Noaḥ's place of origin is never given. Furthermore, Noaḥ was not considered to be Jewish, otherwise all of his descendants (i.e., all of the earth's population) would be Jewish! Furthermore, the reference to Dan'el in Ezek. 28:3 is made as part of a prophecy to the king of Tyre, claiming that he is "wiser than Dan'el." Tyre (in Phoenicia) and Ugarit are both kingdoms to the north of Israel that share much of the same pantheon. Ezek. 8:14 also demonstrates that the prophet is knowledgeable of non-Israelite mythology, as he references women sitting at the gate of the Temple "weeping for Tammuz," the Sumerian shepherd who legend says was deified as a demigod of death and rebirth and married to the goddess Inanna and who was worshipped at least through the Neo-Assyrian and Neo-Babylonian Empires. Ezekiel's comparison of the king of Tyre to Dan'el in 28:3 certainly predates the composition of any of the biblical Daniel stories and may very well in fact provide the link for the "wise Daniel" tradition in Babylon and postexilic Judea. In fact, *Jubilees* 4:20 attempts to appropriate further the reference to Dan'el by supplying it as the name of Enoch's father-in-law (cf. Gen. 5:21), suggesting that in the second century BCE Jews in fact understood Dan'el to be the wise figure from a primordial legend, not the Daniel of Babylonian exile fame.

44. *ANET* 151, AQHT A, col. 5, lines 6–9 states that Dan'el "is upright, sitting before the (city) gate . . . judging the cause of the widow, adju-

dicating the case of the fatherless." Sitting at the city gate and judging cases is a frequent description of a wise, righteous city elder. Cf. Job 29:7–12: "When I went out to the gate of the city, when I took my seat in the square . . . because *I delivered the poor who cried, and the orphan who had no helper.*" For other examples of righteous judgment being adjudicated at the city gate, see Ruth 4; Prov. 31:23; Jer. 1:15; Lam. 5:14; 2 Sam. 15:2–6.

45. *ANET* 149–55. For more on the Epic of 'Aqhat, see Pardee, "The 'Aqhatu Legend."

46. *COS* 2.47A; *AHI* 8.017; *HAE* 1:59–61. Although P. Kyle McCarter argues that many biblical references to 'Asherah may be to a wooden object of worship instead of the deity herself, he states that in this case the inscription "suggests the pairing of the God of Israel with a consort" ("Kuntillet 'Ajrud [2.47]").

47. *COS* 2.47B; *AHI* 8.018–22; *HAE* 1:59–61.

48. Some translations say, "'Uriyahu the governor." Here I follow McCarter, "Khirbet el-Qom (2.52)."

49. *COS* 2.52; *AHI* 25.003; *HAE* 1:199–211. Cf. Dever, *Did God Have a Wife?*

50. Haupt ("Der Name Jahwe"), Albright ("The Name of Yahweh"), and Driver ("The Original Form of the Name of 'Yahweh'") all argue for the causative (*hif'il*) imperfect (future) form of the verb, rendering the name of YHWH as "I will cause to be what I will cause to be."

51. The deity 'El's name is often translated in the Hebrew Bible as simply "God," as the early compilers and editors of the Bible would have simply understood it as an abbreviation for *'Elohim*, the generic Hebrew word for God (and plural "gods"). Gen. 35:7 reads, "[Jacob] built an altar and called the place 'El Beth-'El" which literally means "'El *of* Beth-'El," with "Beth-'El" meaning "the house of 'El" or, more generically, "the house of God." Thus, when the deity 'El's name is given at the beginning of this place-name, it is likely referring to the *deity* 'El, giving us "'El (the deity) of Beth-'El" and distinguishing this particular deity from deities found elsewhere, as rendering the place-name as "God of the house of God" is redundant. The name only makes sense in a polytheistic context.

52. The Hebrew says, "'Elohim (God) has taken his place in the council of 'El."

53. See LXX Gen. 14:18–20, 22; Num. 24:16; Deut. 32:8; 1 Esd. 9:46; Add. Esth. 16:16; Tob. 1:4, 13; and several times in the Psalms, most interestingly Ps. 82, particularly v. 1, which speaks about God taking his place in the council of 'El, and v. 6, where the speaker refers to other deities specifically as gods ("You are gods")!

Chapter 3: Nineveh

1. For an excellent summary of Nineveh, see O'Brien, "Nineveh."

2. My George Washington University colleague Eric Cline has written a brilliant new book entitled *1177 B.C.: The Year Civilization Collapsed,* which offers an insightful look at the events leading to the end of the Bronze Age.

3. See Judg. 2:13; 10:6; 1 Sam. 7:3; 31:10; 1 Kings 11:5, 33; 2 Kings 23:13.

4. See 2 Kings 19:36–37, which records the death of Sennacherib at the hands of his own sons.

5. For more on the two palaces, visit the University of Pennsylvania's ORACC (Open Richly Annotated Cuneiform Corpus) Ashurbanipal Library Project, http://oracc.museum.upenn.edu/asbp/index.html.

6. For the Lachish Relief Panels, in Room 10b of the British Museum, see http://www.britishmuseum.org/explore/galleries/middle_east/room _10a_assyria_lion_hunts.aspx.

7. For the replica of the Lachish Relief Panels, see http://www.imj.org.il /imagine/collections/item.asp?itemNum=376868.

8. Cf. the *Babylonian Chronicle* for the years 615–609 BCE in the British Museum (BM 21901). See Jenkins, "Nabopolassar, Father of Nebuchadnezzar, Destroyed Nineveh," for an excellent summary and photos of these items.

9. In fact, it is possible that the Hebrew word *qaṭanni* (קטני), which literally means "my little (thing)" and which most Bibles translate as "my little finger," may also be a veiled reference to Reḥoboam's genitals.

10. The Black Obelisk of Shalmaneser III (ME 118885) was excavated by Sir Austen Henry Layard. It is presently located in Room 6 (Assyrian sculpture) of the British Museum.

11. On the Black Obelisk, the inscription misidentifies Jehu' as a "Son of 'Omri." This is technically incorrect because Jehu' was not a descendant of King 'Omri, but rather a usurper who killed 'Omri's royal descendant, King Jehoram of Israel. It is likely that Assyria understood the "house of 'Omri" as epithet for the kingdom of Israel, whose sixth king, 'Omri, established the long-running 'Omride dynasty, which ruled the Northern Kingdom for over four decades. Furthermore, McCarter and others argue that the inscription "Yaw" on the obelisk actually refers to a different king, Jehoram of Israel, but this doesn't change the fact that the Black Obelisk is still the earliest depiction of any character from the Bible. See McCarter, "'Yaw, Son of 'Omri.'"

12. Translation of lines 25–41 from Younger, "Nimrud Prisms D & E" (2.118D). Cf. Gadd, "Inscribed Prisms of Sargon II from Nimrud."

13. Watch it at https://www.youtube.com/watch?v=ey0wvGiAH9g.

14. In order to prevent the Hebrew words for (as my two-year-olds say) "pee" and "poop" from appearing in the Bible, the later Masoretes created a *qere-ketiv,* which is Hebrew for "that which is read (*qere*) vs. that which is written (*ketiv*)," next to each of the words, suggesting that the word "filth" be read in place of "dung" and that the rather creative words "waters (at) their feet" be read in place of "urine."

15. *ANET* 288. For resources concerning the Assyrian campaigns into Judah, see Younger, "Assyrian Involvement in the Southern Levant."

16. Cf. 2 Kings 15:19–20 (Menaḥem of Israel), 2 Kings 16:7–18 and its parallel in 2 Chron. 28:21 ('Aḥaz), 2 Kings 17:3 (Hoshea'), 2 Kings 23:33–35 (Jeho'aḥaz), and this payment of Ḥezekiah to Sennacherib mentioned in 2 Kings 18:13–16.

17. Some speculate that Jonah may be the same Jonah, son of 'Amittai the prophet from Gath-Ḥefer (just north of Nazareth) mentioned in 2 Kings 14:25 as prophesying during the reign of Israelite King Jeroboam II (r. 786–746 BCE), who reigned at a point of relative Assyrian weakness in Cana'an.

18. The Hebrew term *ṣaba'* (צבא) is the term for "army," "war," or some kind of military service. The Hebrew term here is *ṣaba' ha-shamayim* (צבא השמים), meaning "army of the heavens." Thus, the name YHWH Ṣaba'oth, which is usually rendered "LORD of hosts" (284 instances, e.g., 1 Sam. 15:2), is usually used in the context of YHWH or his people going to war or "YHWH the Warrior." It may initially have been a designation distinguishing between different YHWH traditions in the same way that Ba'al was known as Ba'al Hadad (as we saw in Phoenicia), Ba'al Ḥermon (Judg. 3:3), Ba'al Gad (Josh. 13:5), etc. In this manner, we would interpret the name as "YHWH of Ṣaba'oth." Inscriptions bearing the names "YHWH of Teman" and "YHWH of Samaria" support this early belief. See Mettinger, "Yahweh Zebaoth."

19. The identity of the city of 'Elqosh (אלקש) has yet to be determined by scholars.

Chapter 4: Babylon

1. Babylon 3D is available at http://www.kadingirra.com/.

2. John Francis Xavier O'Conor explains, "The name Babylon occurs in many different forms in the Babylonian inscriptions. Commonly it is written KA-dingir-RA = 'the gate of god,' Bab-ili, Bâbîlu; ka, being the Akkadian for 'gate,' and dingir, the ideogram for 'god'" (*Cuneiform Text of a Recently Discovered Cylinder,* 13).

3. In Hebrew, the second letter of the alphabet, ב, or *bet,* can be pronounced either as a hard *b* or as a softer *v.*

4. Do not confuse an *etiology*, which is an explanation of how something came to be, with *etymology*, which is the study of the derivation of a word, how it developed from earlier into later forms. And of course, one should not confuse either of these with *entomology*, which is the study of bugs.

5. Enuma Elish, tablet 6, lines 60–90 (*ANET* 68–69) describes the construction of the Ésagila in Babylon.

6. According to 1 Kings 6:1: "In the four hundred eightieth year after the Israelites came out of the land of Egypt, in the fourth year of Solomon's reign over Israel, in the month of Ziv, which is the second month, he began to build the house of the LORD." This means the exodus would have happened 480 years before the Temple was built (which would have taken place about 970 BCE), that is, around 1450 BCE, some three hundred years *after* the establishment of Hammurabi's law code. But Exod. 1:11 states that the Hebrew slaves "built supply cities, Pithom and Rameses, for Pharaoh," meaning Exod. 1 understands the exodus as having taken place *later*, around 1250 BCE, during the reign of the city's namesake, Pharaoh Ramesses II "the Great" (r. 1279–1213 BCE). This internal discrepancy regarding the date of the exodus is what some biblical scholars refer to as the "early exodus" (ca. 1450 BCE) vs. the "late exodus" (ca. 1250 BCE) debate. Because there is absolutely *no* archaeological evidence to support *any* mass exodus of Hebrews from Egypt, many scholars and archaeologists today, based on the archaeological evidence coming out of Israel over the past few decades, argue that those who became the Israelites were actually Semitic Cana'anites who had always lived in Cana'an, that the exodus narrative was based on tales of escaped slaves and military conquests that were reworked to form a foundation myth for ancient Israel, and that therefore there was no biblical exodus at all.

7. For more, see Wright, *Inventing God's Law*.

8. Translation in Harper, *Code of Hammurabi King of Babylon*.

9. Harper, *Code of Hammurabi King of Babylon*.

10. You can do so at http://oll.libertyfund.org/titles/1276 or https://en .wikisource.org/wiki/The_Code_of_Hammurabi_%28Harper_trans lation%29.

11. See Finkel and Seymour, *Babylon*, 52. There is also no contemporary Babylonian textual reference to the Hanging Gardens. A Babylonian priest named Berossus writing in Greek around 290 BCE is cited as mentioning them. Josephus claims to quote Berossus's account, *History of Ancient Times*, in *Against Apion* 1:19 (1:141). But since Berossus's account wasn't written until almost 250 years *after* the Persians conquered

Babylon and since we know his writings only from secondhand citations, the literary legends must suffice as testimony that the Hanging
Gardens actually existed. We also know that Alexander the Great was
so impressed with the city after he defeated the Persian Achaemenid
Empire at the Battle of Gaugamela in 331 BCE and conquered Babylon
that he sought to make it the capital of his vast empire. See Wiener,
"Hanging Gardens of Babylon . . . in Assyrian Nineveh."

12. Jehoiachin is also called Jeconiah and Coniah in the Bible.

13. Reverse side, lines 11–13. See also the "Cuneiform tablet with part of
the Babylonian Chronicle (605–594 BC)" (item ME 21946) in the British
Museum; Sigrist, Zadok, and Walker, *Catalogue of the Babylonian
Tablets;* Grayson, *Assyrian and Babylonian Chronicle;* and Glassner,
Mesopotamian Chronicles. Read the chronicle at Livius.org, http://
www.livius.org/sources/content/mesopotamian-chronicles-content
/abc–5-jerusalem-chronicle/.

14. Jer. 44:30: "Thus says the LORD, I am going to give Pharaoh Hophra, king
of Egypt, into the hands of his enemies, those who seek his life, just as
I gave King Zedekiah of Judah into the hand of King Nebuchadrezzar
[*sic*] of Babylon, his enemy who sought his life."

15. Second Kings 25:4–7 is paralleled in 2 Chron. 36:11–13. Note that Jer.
52:7–11 preserves an almost identical text. It is in the parallel between
2 Kings 24:18–25:21 and Jer. 52:7–11 that scholars have noted concrete
evidence of redaction in the books of Kings (or in Jeremiah).

16. Babylon 28178, obverse ii 38–40; cf. *ANET* 308.

17. Babylon 28186, reverse ii 13–18; cf. *ANET* 308. For more, see
Schniedewind, *How the Bible Became a Book,* 149–53.

18. The destruction of the Temple in Jerusalem at the hands of the Romans
in 70 CE was said coincidentally to also have taken place on the ninth
day of the month of Av on the Jewish calendar.

19. Many thanks to University of Iowa Hillel Executive Director Gerald L.
Sorokin for sharing this liturgical practice with me.

20. See Mark 15:34; Matt. 27:46.

21. For instance, Pss. 46–48 or Ps. 87.

22. To view the fragments of the Prayer of Nabonidus (4Q242), which
reads a lot like Dan. 4:29–37, visit the IAA's Leon Levy Dead Sea
Scrolls Digital Library, http://www.deadseascrolls.org.il/explore-the
-archive/manuscript/4Q242-1?locale=en_US. To learn more, see Cross,
"Fragments of the Prayer of Nabonidus."

23. Note that the same editor who wrote the last chapter of 2 Kings was
also likely the editor of the book of Jeremiah; he included nearly identi-

cal texts in each account, as the fates of Jeremiah and King Jehoiachin were closely tied together. For an explanation of this parallel, see Schniedewind, *How the Bible Became a Book*, 154. Note also that the Hebrew text of Jeremiah is one-sixth longer than the LXX version.

24. For more on the inviolability of Jerusalem, see Hayes, "The Tradition of Zion's Inviolability."

25. Cyrus Cylinder, lines 14–15. For the full translation, see Irving Finkel, *The Cyrus Cylinder: The King of Persia's Proclamation from Ancient Babylon*.

26. The Babylonian Talmud (Bavli for short) is the larger and better known of the two Jewish Talmuds, the other being the Jerusalem Talmud (Yerushalami for short).

Chapter 5: Megiddo

1. Loud, *Megiddo Ivories*.

2. To view one of the game boards, visit the Palestine collection at the Oriental Institute Museum at the University of Chicago online, https://oi.uchicago.edu/collections/highlights/highlights-collection-palestine.

3. To read about the battles that have taken place at Armageddon, see Cline, *The Battles of Armageddon*.

4. Levin, "Did Pharaoh Sheshonq Attack Jerusalem?"

5. It is worth pointing out, however, that when 2 Chron. 12:2–12 retells this episode, it adds in v. 4: "And he took [or captured] the fortified cities of Judah and came as far as Jerusalem." Thus the Chronicler expands the record of Shoshenq's campaign, perhaps to better reflect the documented reality that his campaign was *not* against Jerusalem, but only up *until* Jerusalem as part of a much larger campaign, and that Jerusalem paid off Shoshenq.

6. My colleague Eric Cline states: "The Megiddo Stele fragment is a small piece of stone that preserves the nomen and prenomen (the first two of three typical names in antiquity) of Shoshenq I. Broken off from a much larger monument, it comes from an unstratified context at Megiddo. Many earlier scholars have argued that its presence at Megiddo indicates that Shoshenq did indeed capture and occupy the city. Therefore, according to these scholars, it provides confirmation that Shoshenq's topographical list inscribed back at Karnak in Egypt is indeed an accurate list of cities that he conquered during the campaign." See Cline, "Review of *The Campaign of Pharaoh Shoshenq I into Palestine*," 131.

Chapter 6: Athens

1. The Elgin Marbles are located in the Duveen Gallery (Room 18) of the British Museum in London. They are comprised of friezes from the Parthenon as well as objects from other buildings on the Acropolis, including the Erechtheion, the Propylaia, and the Temple of Athena Nike.

2. The seat of Persian provincial power in Yehud shifted from Beth'el to Miṣpah (likely modern Tel en-Naṣbeh) and finally to Jerusalem.

3. Cf. Gen. 1:5: "And there was evening and there was morning, the first day." See also Gen. 1:8, 13, 19, 23, 31.

4. Antiochus IV came to power as the Seleucid king in 175 BCE. His first attack on Egypt (in which he marched past Jerusalem) came in 170, and his second attack on Egypt in 167. It was upon his return to Syria after this that he attacked Jerusalem (including the "desolating sacrilege" in the Jerusalem Temple; see Dan. 8:13), and his death occurred in 164. The time element of six years is likely a reference to the period in between two of these events.

5. Diogenes Laertius, *Lives of Eminent Philosophers* 10. This section describes Epicurus, and 10.131–32 describes his Letter to Menoeceus, which states explicitly that his philosophy "is *not* an unbroken succession of drinking-bouts and of revelry, not sexual love, not the enjoyment of the fish and other delicacies of a luxurious table, which produce a pleasant life," but rather, "it is sober reasoning, searching out the grounds of every choice and avoidance, and banishing those beliefs through which the greatest tumults take possession of the soul."

6. We know of Porphyry's *Against the Christians* only from those early (mostly Christian) authors citing it for the purpose of refuting it. You can read the known excerpts at http://www.tertullian.org/fathers/porphyry_against _christians_02_fragments.htm.

7. Qohelet is the Hebrew name of Ecclesiastes. It is derived from the second word of the book, which means "teacher," or more literally "one who convenes or addresses an assembly," as קהלת is derived from the Hebrew root קהל (*qhl*), meaning "to assemble." The word Ecclesiastes is actually the Greek translation of Qohelet, made up of the words ἐκ (*ek*, meaning "out") and καλέω (*kaleō*, meaning "to call, call forth"), similar to the word for "church," ἐκκλησία (*ekklēsía*, meaning "called out").

8. Mishnah *Yadayim* ("Hands") 3:5 reads: "The Song of Songs and Ecclesiastes render the hands impure. Rabbi Yehudah says: The Song of Songs renders the hands impure, but there is a dispute regarding Ecclesiastes. Rabbi Yose says: Ecclesiastes does not render the hands impure, and there is a dispute regarding the Song of Songs. Rabbi Shimon says: Ecclesiastes is among the [relative] leniencies of Beit Shammai and the [relative] strin-

gencies of Beit Hillel. Rabbi Shimon ben Azzai said, 'I have a received tradition from the mouths of seventy-two elders, on the day they inducted Rabbi Elazar ben Azaria into his seat [as head] at the Academy, that the Song of Songs and Ecclesiastes render the hands impure.' Rabbi Akiva said, 'Mercy forbid! No one in Israel ever disputed that the Song of Songs renders the hands impure, since nothing in the entire world is worthy but for that day on which the Song of Songs was given to Israel; for all the Scriptures are holy, but the Song of Songs is the Holy of Holies! And if they did dispute, there was only a dispute regarding Ecclesiastes.' Rabbi Yochanan ben Yehoshua, the son of Rabbi Akiva's father-in-law, said, 'In accordance with words of Ben Azzai, thus did they dispute, and thus did they conclude.'" To "make the hands impure" was a euphemism for "canonical" or "holy." Jews do not touch scrolls of scripture out of respect for their holiness and instead use a pointer called a *yad* ("hand") to move along the text as it is read. Therefore, touching a biblical text is problematic because of its sanctity or holiness, while a noncanonical, common, or "profane" text can be easily touched because it isn't holy.

9. See also Eccl. 2:15–17.

10. Gehenna (Gk. γέεννα) is the hellenization of the Hebrew word for the "Valley of (Ben-)Hinnom" (גיא בן־הנם, *gai ben-hinom*). The Valley of Hinnom runs from the southwest of Jerusalem to the south of the City of David, where it intersects the Kidron Valley. This was where Cana'anites and some Israelites ('Aḥaz in 2 Chron. 28:3; Manasseh in 33:6) sacrificed their children by fire to deities (Jer. 7:31), including Molech (32:35). The place was later considered to be cursed (19:2–6).

11. Matt. 5:22, 29–30; 10:28; 18:9; 23:15, 33; Mark 9:43, 45, 47; Luke 12:5; James 3:6.

12. Matt. 11:23; 16:18; Luke 10:15; 16:23; Acts 2:27, 31; Rev. 1:18; 6:8; 20:13–14.

13. Cf. Gen. 1:20, 21, 24, 30, and numerous other instances. Note that *nefesh* is used of *all* living creatures, not only humans. In Gen. 9:4, *nefesh* is equated with blood, which also gives living creatures life. Thus, *nefesh* simply meant "living" in the early HB. It was only later that it came to be understood as the Hebrew equivalent of the Greek "soul."

14. Gen. 3:19 states clearly that we humans were made from the dust of the earth "and to dust [we] shall return." Eccl. 3:19–20 echoes this understanding of death, and 3:21 ("Who knows whether the human spirit goes upward and the spirit of animals goes downward to the earth?") shows us that various ideas of life after death were being discussed (perhaps by the Greeks). Passages such as Gen. 37:35; Num. 16:30; 1 Kings 2:6; Isa. 14:15; 38:10; and many others mention She'ol

as the place that *all* people go when they die. In fact, Job 14:10–14 offers a descriptive example of how the HB conceives the afterlife: "But mortals die, and are laid low; humans expire, and where are they? As waters fail from a lake, and a river wastes away and dries up, *so mortals lie down and do not rise again;* until the heavens are no more, *they will not awake or be roused out of their sleep.* Oh that you would hide me in Sheol, that you would conceal me until your wrath is past, that you would appoint me a set time, and remember me! If mortals die, will they live again?" Following the prevalent worldview of the time, She'ol was considered to be under the ground, which reflects the burial custom in the ancient Near East of burying the deceased in graves or pits, which is practiced today.

15. For instance, when Saul asked the medium at 'En-Dor to summon the prophet Samuel from the dead in 1 Sam. 28 (note first that *it worked!*, and) note that the text first says that the woman saw a "god" (Heb. *'elohim*) coming up "out of the ground" (v. 13) and that he appeared not as a disembodied spirit, but as "an old man wrapped in a robe" (v. 14). Note that this is not evidence of transcendence, but of resurrection, which is how many early Jews (and Christians) who believed in the afterlife envisioned it—resurrection from the ground of a living being who looks a lot like the previously living being when he or she died, and not a disembodied spirit. See also Dan. 12:2, a very late Hellenistic Jewish text that states, "Many of those who sleep in the dust of the earth shall awake," referencing *resurrection* (of both the righteous and the *wicked!*) and not a disembodied spirit that has been living apart from its host body since the host's death.

16. Some have pointed out that this dualistic notion of a soul that can exist apart from the body (especially after death) may have been introduced into what became Judaism by Zoroastrian religious beliefs while the Jewish exiles were in Babylon. As Zoroastrianism was one of the popular religions of the Persians, who conquered Babylon and funded the reconstruction of the Temple in Jerusalem, this is a viable possibility; Jews may have been more sympathetic to Zoroastrian influence while in Babylon.

17. For instance, Edmonds attributes the maxim to the comic poet Menander in *Thaïs* (*Fragments of Attic Comedy,* 627). In a footnote, Edmonds explains that the saying was "probably quoted by Menander from Euripides; it is the last line of four in a tragic metre in an Anthology of which some fragments are preserved in a papyrus of the 3rd Cent. B.C."

18. Interestingly, Paul's quotation of Euripides in 1 Cor. 15:33 follows a quotation in 15:32, "Let us eat and drink, for tomorrow we die," which sounds like false Epicureanism, but is actually a direct quotation of Isa. 22:13.

19. Socrates of Constantinople, *Ecclesiastical History,* 3.16: "Whence did he get the saying, 'The Cretans are always liars, evil beasts, slow-bellies,' but from a perusal of the *Oracles* of Epimenides, the Cretan Initiator?"

20. See *Callimachus: Hymns and Epigrams, Lycophron and Aratus,* 36–37, lines 6–9. Read the poem at http://www.theoi.com/Text/Callimachus Hymns1.html.

21. Plato, *Apology* 40c–e. About 390 BCE, Plato, cites the words of Socrates right before his death: "For the state of death is one of two things: either it is virtually nothingness, so that the dead has no consciousness of anything, or it is, as people say, a change and migration of the soul from this to another place. And if it is unconsciousness, like a sleep in which the sleeper does not even dream, death would be a wonderful gain. For I think if any one were to pick out that night in which he slept a dreamless sleep and, comparing with it the other nights and days of his life, were to say, after due consideration, how many days and nights in his life had passed more pleasantly than that night,—I believe that not only any private person, but even the great King of Persia himself would find that they were few in comparison with the other days and nights. *So if such is the nature of death, I count it a gain;* for in that case, all time seems to be no longer than one night. But on the other hand, if death is, as it were, a change of habitation from here to some other place, and if what we are told is true, that all the dead are there, what greater blessing could there be, judges?"

22. Plato, *Crito* 49c.

23. Plato, *Republic* 10.12 [613c]. See *Plato in Twelve Volumes.*

24. The Greek in *Politics* 3.8.2 reads: κατὰ δὲ τῶν τοιούτων οὐκ ἔστι νόμος: αὐτοὶ γάρ εἰσι νόμος. See *Aristotle: The Politics,* 240–41 (3.8.2, 1284a lines 13–14). Benjamin Jowett's translation of this same passage reads: "and that for men of preeminent virtue *there is no law—they are themselves a law*" (*Politics of Aristotle,* 93 [3.13]).

25. Gk. πρὸς κέντρα λακτίζειν (*pros kentra laktizein*).

26. Gk. πρὸς κέντρα μὴ λάκτιζε, (*pros kentra mē laktize*). Aeschylus II: *Agamemnon, Libation-Bearers, Eumenides, Fragments,* 144–45, line 1624.

27. Note that Paul claims that Jesus said this *in Hebrew* (Acts 26:14), meaning that it is much more difficult to claim that Paul was simply repeating a popular Greek idiom of the day. If what Paul claims is true, the idiom would have been translated into Hebrew and employed by Jesus, which is less likely than simply repeating a Greek idiom.

28. Tertullian's phrase in Latin is *Seneca saepe noster,* "often one of ours" or "whom we so often find on our side" (*Treatise on the Soul* 20). Tertullian's endorsement of Seneca may have been due to the fact that

so much of what Paul writes here is similar to Seneca's work. Seneca's suicide, which was ordered by the hated Emperor Nero following the Pisonian Conspiracy, a failed assassination plot to kill Nero in which Seneca was believed to have conspired, likely aided in painting him as an early "Christian martyr." Tertullian's comment also likely prompted the composition of the *Letters of Paul and Seneca* in the fourth century CE (which are universally recognized as forged), as Tertullian's positive reference to the esteemed Roman adviser and tutor to the emperor Nero led many to believe Seneca was sympathetic to Christianity. Bart Ehrman says the *Letters of Paul and Seneca* were forged to resolve the question of "why, if Paul was such a brilliant and astute thinker, none of the other great thinkers of his day mentions him" (*Forged*, 91).

29. Seneca, *De Beneficiis (On Benefits)* 7.7.3 (*Seneca: Moral Essays*, 472–73).

30. Lactantius, *Divine Institutes* 6:25.

31. Seneca, *Epistulae Morales ad Lucilium (Moral Letters to Lucilius)* 95.47 (*Seneca: Epistles, Volume III*).

32. Seneca, *Epistulae Morales ad Lucilium* 95.52 (*Seneca: Epistles, Volume III*).

33. Seneca, *Epistulae Morales ad Lucilium* 41.1 (*Seneca: Epistles, Volume I*).

34. Seneca, *Epistulae Morales ad Lucilium* 41.2 (*Seneca: Epistles, Volume I*).

35. Aratus, *Phaenomena* lines 4–7, trans. mine. Cf. *Callimachus: Hymns and Epigrams, Lycophron and Aratus*, 206–7.

36. In this line (Latin *et te quoque dignum finge deo*), Seneca actually quotes Virgil's *Aeneid* (8.364), which was written between 29 and 19 BCE.

37. Seneca, *Epistulae Morales ad Lucilium* 31:11, trans. mine. Cf. *Seneca: Epistles, Volume I*.

Chapter 7: Alexandria

1. To see how papyrus is made, watch this video shot at the Papyrus Museum in Cairo at https://www.youtube.com/watch?v=DCR8n7qS43w.

2. Acts 6:9; 18:24. Alexandria is also mentioned in passing in 3 Macc. 3:1.

3. Khater, "Alexandria Hit by Floods."

4. The Muses were given specific names and responsibilities for different fields of knowledge and arts: Kalliope, epic poetry; Kleio, history; Ourania, astronomy; Thaleia, comedy; Melpomene, tragedy; Polyhymnia, religious hymns; Erato, erotic poetry; Euterpe, lyric poetry; and Terpsichore, choral song and dance. The Muses were always depicted as beautiful young women usually holding the tool or instrument of their trade. (And before you go and Google it, Erato holds a small *kithara*, a lyre that charms young lovers.)

5. Plutarch, *Life of Caesar* 49.6. See especially n. 552 in Plutarch, *Lives,* which references Dio Cassius, who mentions that the library was burned, but argues that Cleopatra rebuilt the library, which went on to serve the people for some time. Dio Cassius notes: "After this many battles occurred between the two forces both by day and by night, and many places were set on fire, with the result that the docks and the storehouses of grain among other buildings were burned, and also the library, whose volumes, it is said, were of the greatest number and excellence" (*Roman History,* 42.38.2).

6. See the comment made by Socrates Scholasticus of Constantinople in *Ecclesiastical History* 5.16, which you can read at http://www.new advent.org/fathers/26015.htm. Others have argued that the library was destroyed during the 641 CE Siege of Alexandria, part of the larger Muslim conquest of Egypt in 642 CE; see Lerner, *Story of Libraries,* 30.

7. Menecles of Barca, *FGrH* 270, F9: "He expelled all intellectuals: philologists, philosophers, professors of geometry, musicians, painters, schoolteachers, physicians and others, with the result that these brought 'education to Greeks and barbarians elsewhere,' as mentioned by an author who may have been one of the king's victims." See Jacoby, "Menecles of Barca."

8. Alexandria is credited with this distinction even though parts of the LXX (especially later parts) may have been written elsewhere.

9. Ameling, "Epigraphy and the Greek Language in Hellenistic Palestine."

10. Metzger, *Bible in Translation,* 15.

11. James Davila argues that the *Letter of Aristeas* had to be "old enough to fool Josephus, but young enough for the writer not to have had accurate knowledge of some important historical matters regarding the reign of Ptolemy II" ("Aristeas to Philocrates").

12. Josephus, *Antiquities* 12.1.1–12.2.2 (12:1–118).

13. Philo of Alexandria, *On the Life of Moses* 2.25–44, esp. v. 34. Philo continues in v. 38: "And yet who is there who does not know that every language, and the Greek language above all others, is rich in a variety of words, and that it is possible to vary a sentence and to paraphrase the same idea, so as to set it forth in a great variety of manners, adapting many different forms of expression to it at different times. But this, they say, did not happen at all in the case of this translation of the law, but that, in every case, exactly corresponding Greek words were employed to translate literally the appropriate Chaldaic words, being adapted with exceeding propriety to the matters which were to be explained." Thus, even Philo argues that the Greek translation of every single one of the "Chaldaic" (Heb.) words of the HB was inspired and thus perfect.

14. *Let. Arist.* 12–27 makes the gracious king look all the more accommodating and receptive to the Jewish faith by coupling the translation of
the HB with a story of how the Greek king emancipated one hundred
thousand Jewish slaves taken captive by his father during a campaign
into Coelesyria and Phoenicia.

15. Charles, ed. and trans., *Apocrypha and Pseudepigrapha,* 121.

16. The *Letter of Aristeas* goes a step farther in the assurance of translational
perfection by invoking a curse upon anyone who might change it: they
"bade them *pronounce a curse in accordance with their custom upon any
one who should make any alteration either by adding anything or changing
in any way whatever any of the words which had been written or making
any omission.* This was a very wise precaution to ensure that the book
might be preserved for all the future time unchanged" (311).

17. Charles, ed. and trans., *Apocrypha and Pseudepigrapha,* 121.

18. For instance, D. M. Turpie studied 275 NT passages that quote the HB
and concluded that the NT, LXX, and HB agree only about 20 percent of
the time. This statistic is telling in itself, as it reveals that many of the
NT quotations of the HB are not exact, but rough paraphrases. The NT's
favoring of the LXX over the HB became apparent when, of the remaining 80 percent of the verses where some disagreement occurred, about
33 percent of the quotations agree with the LXX over the HB, while only
5 percent agree with the HB over the LXX. See Turpie, *Old Testament
in the New,* 267–69. Archer and Chirichigno argue that there are 340
places where the NT cites the LXX, but only 33 places where the NT
cites from the MT of the HB, so 91 percent of the time (*Old Testament
Quotations in the New Testament,* 25–32).

19. The Bar-Kokhba Rebellion (132–135 CE) attempted to re-take Jerusalem
militantly for Jews. Simon Bar-Kokhba issued letters in Hebrew, even
though in one Greek letter (*P. Yadin* 52:11–15) he admits he has no one
on staff who knows how to write in Hebrew, and on his coins, Bar-
Kokhba employed Palaeo-Hebrew script in a propagandistic attempt
to rekindle the memories of an independent Jewish state. For more
evidence of Jewish "re-hebraisation" (a return to traditional ethnic and
cultural practices), including de-hellenization and the reestablishment
of Hebrew as a linguistic indicator of Jewish independence, see Collar,
Religious Networks in the Roman Empire: The Spread of New Ideas, 167
ff. Cf. Tcherikover and Fuks, *Corpus Papyrorum Judaicarum,* 47–93.

20. E.g., Exod. 10:19; 13:18; 15:4, 22; 23:31.

21. See Aristophanes, *Birds,* line 145.

22. Portions of the following originally appeared in my article, "Bible
Secrets Revealed, Episode 4: 'The Real Jesus.'"

23. Cf. Isa. 36–39 and its parallel in 2 Kings 18–20.

24. The definition of *betulah* as "one who has not yet had sex" is evident in the story of the punishment for men caught raping a woman in Deut. 22:28–29, as the woman is described as a "virgin" (בתולה, *betulah*) prior to the rape, but as a "young woman" (נערה, *na'arah*) after the rape. Gen. 24:16 even defines *betulah* specifically as one who has not had sex: "The girl (נער, *na'ar*) was very fair to look upon, a *virgin* (בתולה, *betulah*), *whom no man had known* (ידע, *yada'*)."

25. Gen. 24:43 is the only other time, out of nine total instances, that *'almah* is translated in the LXX using the term *parthenos*.

26. Justin Martyr, *Dialogue with Trypho* 67.

27. It is worth noting that beginning in *Dialogue with Trypho* 71, the "proof" that Justin Martyr offers Trypho that his apology of Jesus's virgin birth is correct lies in his claim that the Septuagint is a perfect translation of the Hebrew text! He claims the differences between the two versions are the result of Jews *removing* portions of the text from the Hebrew version, and *not* because the Septuagint may be flawed in portions of its translation. Of course, Justin Martyr bases his reasoning on the assumption that the story of the Septuagint's perfect translation as told in the Letter of Aristeas (written around 125 BCE) is true. Still, the fact that Justin Martyr is pitting the text of the Septuagint against the Hebrew once again demonstrates that there were acknowledged differences between the two versions, and that many of the Christian claims about Jesus were only made possible by quoting the Septuagint's translation.

28. Cf. Mark 12:20–23; Luke 20:29–32.

29. Dan. 2:4b–7:28 is in Aramaic, but this is not entirely unexpected, as these chapters tell stories of Daniel and his experiences in Aramaic-speaking Babylon and were likely composed at a time when Jews spoke Aramaic as their primary language. Ezra 4:8–6:18 and 7:12–26 are also in Aramaic; these chapters largely preserve the text of several letters sent from Aramaic-speaking Persia, and the narrative in between the letters is simply preserved in Aramaic as well. There is also a single Aramaic place-name in Gen. 31:47. Thus, Jer. 10:11 stands out, as it is an Aramaic verse likely inserted into the middle of Jeremiah's prophecy by a later editor.

30. In fact, the roots of the two words עבד (*avad*) and אבד (*'avad*) are homonyms in Aramaic (and Hebrew for that matter), because the letters that begin both of the words are called "glottal spirant consonants," commonly called "gutterals," which had lost their consonantal sounds by the time the LXX was written. (For those of you nonlinguists, *'aleph* (א) and *'ayin* (ע) are the silent letters in Hebrew and Aramaic that get

mixed up all the time when you first learn Hebrew and Aramaic vo-
cabulary.) And because they were silent and frequently mixed up, the
author of this verse utilized the similarly sounding Aramaic words for
"make, create" (עבד, *'avad*) and "perish, destroy" (אבד, *'avad*) to create a
pun warning against the worship of idols: "The gods who did not *make*
(עבד, *'avad*) the heavens and the earth shall *perish* (אבד, *'avad*) from the
earth and from under the heavens."

31. The 13-inch-high Prism of Esarhaddon, located in the British Museum,
mentions Manasseh of Judah as a loyal vassal of the Assyrian king
Sennacherib's son and successor, Esarhaddon. The Prism of Esarhaddon,
discovered in Nineveh, dates to 673–672 BCE. Col. 5, line 55 of the
hexagonal clay prism mentions "Ba'lu, king of Tyre, Menasi, king of
Judah." Cf. *ANET* 291. Manasseh is listed among twenty-two other
kings who provided tribute in the form of raw materials to Esarhaddon
for his various building projects. Esarhaddon's son, Ashurbanipal, also
names Manasseh as a loyal vassal who actually assisted the Assyrian
king in his war against Egypt.

32. "Outside the number" means it was not among the canonical psalms as
determined at least by the composition of the LXX.

33. See Harrington, *Invitation to the Apocrypha,* 185. For an excellent
commentary on 2 Esdras, see *Early Jewish Writings,* http://www.early
jewishwritings.com/2esdras.html.

Chapter 8: Jerusalem

1. For more information, visit http://www.tweetyourprayers.info/.

2. McCarthy, "Letters to God."

3. Ironically, although Caliph 'Abd al-Malik commissioned the Dome of
the Rock as an Islamic shrine to commemorate the Prophet Muḥammad's
Night Journey (see Qur'an Sura 17) and create an alternate pilgrimage
destination closer to his capital in Damascus, he hired the best architects
of the time to build it, who just happened to be Byzantine Christians.
This is why the Dome of the Rock's architecture and octagonal floor
plan resemble Byzantine churches, and specifically the Byzantine
Chapel of St. Mary between Jerusalem and Bethlehem.

4. Armstrong, *Jerusalem,* 6.

5. For more on Egyptian execration texts, see Ritner, *Mechanics of Ancient
Egyptian Magical Practice,* 136–53.

6. Interestingly, sympathetic magic shows up in the Bible. In Num. 5:11–
31, we find the odd story of how the Israelites determined if a woman
had committed adultery. The solution involved writing down curses,
washing the writing off in water that also contained dust from the

tabernacle floor, and making the woman drink it. The point of writing down the curses is the same as the execration texts above: the power of the curse lies in the written word, the ink of which is then washed into the potion, activating the curse.

7. Rev. 3:5; 13:8; 17:8; 20:12, 15; 21:27.

8. For an excellent discussion on the numinous power of writing, see Schniedewind, *How the Bible Became a Book*, chap. 2.

9. *EA* 287, 290. Note that *EA* 287 and 289 also preserve the name with an *s* sound instead of an *sh* sound, yielding *U-ru-ša-lim*.

10. Later Jewish works from the third and second centuries BCE, like the *Genesis Apocryphon* and the still later targumic tradition, demonstrate the late Second Temple–period tradition of associating Shalem with Jerusalem. The book of Hebrews (chaps. 6–7) also appeals to this association. The study of the Melchizedek tradition and the association of Shalem with Jerusalem in the late Second Temple period is the subject of my forthcoming book, *Melki-Ṣedeq, King of Sodom*.

11. James Hoffmeier, "Exploring David's Strange Antics After Defeating Goliath," Biblical Archaeology Society's *Bible and Archaeology Fest* Lecture, 2009. See also James Hoffmeier, "The Aftermath of David's Triumph over Goliath."

12. The man who would ultimately become the high priest in Jerusalem under Solomon was named Ṣadoq (2 Sam. 8:17, Zadok), whose name is suspiciously close to the names of priests and kings that the biblical tradition says had already lived in Jerusalem prior to the Israelite conquest, namely, Melki-ṣedeq ("My king is Ṣedeq") and 'Adoni-ṣedeq ("My lord is Ṣedeq"). Because Ṣedeq was a well-known Phoenician deity, the presence of these three individuals with the Ṣedeq theophoric element in their names may suggest that there was a cult (and temple) of Ṣedeq in Jerusalem prior to the arrival of the Israelites.

13. Translation taken from Barkay et al., "Amulets from Ketef Hinnom."

14. Translation taken from Barkay et al., "Amulets from Ketef Hinnom."

15. Smoak, *Priestly Blessing in Inscription and Scripture,* 80–83.

16. Prov. 3:1–14 and 6:20–22 offer evidence that amulets were worn, instructing children to "tie [them] around your neck" the commandments and the teachings of their fathers and mothers.

17. Cf. Matt. 21:1–11, Luke 19:29–40; John 12:12–18.

18. Note how Matt. 21:2 actually has the disciples retrieve *two* animals instead of just the one—a donkey *and* a colt—and has Jesus ride them *both* (like a trick rodeo rider), rather than just the single animal as depicted in Mark 11:2, 7 and Luke 19:31, 35. This is due to Matthew's misunder-

standing of the Hebrew poetic parallelism in Zech. 9:9, which states that Jesus is "riding on a donkey, on a colt, the foal of a donkey." While Mark and Luke rightly understand this as a parallel poetic description of the *same* animal, Matthew mistakenly sees it as *two separate* animals and tells his story with Jesus riding both animals. It's the equivalent of my wife, Roslyn, writing me a love poem saying, "I love my husband, I love my broad-shouldered, handsome man," and a friend asking, "I know your wife loves *you,* but who is that *other* handsome man your wife *also* loves?"

19. Luke states that as a child Jesus visited Jerusalem on the eighth day after his birth, as was the custom for newborn Jewish males (2:22), and at age twelve the lost prepubescent Jesus was discovered by his parents sitting among the teachers in the Temple (2:41–50).

20. Eusebius of Caesarea, *Life of Constantine* 3:25–41.

21. Cf. Mark. 15:26; Matt. 27:37; Luke 28:38; John 19:19. Note that John 19:20 states that the inscription "was written in Hebrew, in Latin, and in Greek." The Latin INRI is actually an acronym standing for *Iesus Nazarenus, Rex Iudaeorum,* meaning "Jesus the Nazarene, King of the Jews."

22. Socrates of Constantinople, *Ecclesiastical History* 1.17.

23. Twain, *Innocents Abroad,* chap. 35. Read it online at https://www.guten berg.org/files/3176/3176-h/3176-h.htm.

Chapter 9: Qumran

1. For an excellent summary of the discovery of the DSS, see Davies, Brooke, and Callaway, *Complete World of the Dead Sea Scrolls.* See also the Leon Levy Dead Sea Scrolls Digital Library page on the discovery of the scrolls at http://www.deadseascrolls.org.il/learn-about-the-scrolls /discovery-and-publication?locale=en_US.

2. Of course, the UN vote was immediately followed by the 1947–48 Civil War in Mandatory Palestine, which, following the end of the British Mandate in Palestine on May 15, 1948, immediately led to the full-scale 1948 Arab-Israeli War, which the Israelis refer to as their "War of Independence" and Palestinians refer to as *al-Nakba,* or "The Catastrophe."

3. Remember, the caves around Qumran where the scrolls were discovered were considered part of the Kingdom of Transjordan, which had captured the West Bank during the 1948 Arab-Israeli War. And because the Director of the Department of Antiquities of Jordan headed the excavations at Qumran, Mar Samuel feared potential interference from the Jordanian government.

4. See Robert Cargill, "The Fortress at Qumran: A History of Interpretation."

5. See page 35 of New York District Attorney, The People of the State of New York v. Raphael Golb, Indictment No. 2721/2009, "Affirmation in Response to the Defendant's Motions to Dismiss, Motion to Suppress Evidence Recovered via Search Warrant, and Request for an Advisory Opinion, Exhibit C: Summary of, and Excerpts of, Certain Email Communications," Jan. 19, 2010.

6. New York District Attorney, The People of the State of New York v. Raphael Golb, Indictment No. 2721/2009, 35.

7. See Leland, "Online Battle Over Sacred Scrolls."

8. See Steve Kolowich, "Harassment of Dead Sea Scroll Scholars Leads to Arrest of Professor's Son," and "The Fall of an Academic Cyberbully.

9. In one e-mail exchange between Raphael Golb (posing as alias "Robert Dworkin") and his brother, Joel Golb, concerning me, Joel Golb wrote, "Clearly, for all who read this, one of *the purposes of Dworkin's devastating letter will be, precisely, to destroy the career prospects* of a really nice guy." See page 17, §78 of New York District Attorney, The People of the State of New York v. Raphael Golb, Indictment No. 2721/2009, "Affirmation in Response to the Defendant's Motions to Dismiss, Motion to Suppress Evidence Recovered via Search Warrant, and Request for an Advisory Opinion, Exhibit C: Summary of, and Excerpts of, Certain Email Communications," Jan. 19, 2010.

10. The Israel Antiquities Authority has recently added interactive digital high-resolution scans of several of the major DSS, which are available for free on your browser at the IAA website, http://www.deadseascrolls .org.il/. Pnina Shor and Shai Halevi have done magnificent work overseeing the photography of the scrolls and making them available to the public for study.

Chapter 10: Bethlehem and Nazareth

1. Justin Martyr, "Dialogue of Justin," 233–34.

2. Isa. 33:16 in the LXX reads: οὖτος οἰκήσει ἐν ὑψηλῷ σπηλαίῳ πέτρας ἰσχυρᾶς (*houtos oikēsei en hupsēlō spēlaiō petras ischuras*), which in English reads: "he shall dwell in a *high cave of a strong rock*."

3. Origen of Alexandria, *Contra Celsum* 1:51 (Origen, "Contra Celsus," 395–669 [418–19]).

4. Pummer, *Early Christian Authors on Samaritans and Samaritanism,* 431.

5. Hamilton, *Church of the Nativity, Bethlehem.*

6. Bethlehem is also called Efrat, which means "fertile" or "fruitful" (cf. Gen. 35:16; 48:7; Ruth 4:11). W. F. Albright suggests that the name Bethlehem originates from the Cana'anite version of the fertility deities

Laḫmu and Laḫamu, whose names always appeared together and who were worshipped together. Thus one can see why Laḫmu and Laḫamu might be worshipped in a place called *Bit-Laḫmi* in ancient Cana'an. As Israel and Judah became monotheistic worshippers of YHWH, the etymology of the name was likely altered to *Bet Leḫem,* thus ridding the name of any connection to a foreign god. For more on the name of Bethleḫem, see Cole, "Bethlehem," and Cazelles, "Bethlehem."

7. Levirate marriage laws (Deut. 25:5–6) allow for the protection of child-less widows by requiring the brother (or relative) of the dead husband to marry the widow to provide a child for her and a legacy for her dead husband. The offspring is legally considered the child of the dead hus-band, not of the "redeemer."

8. Wright, "Establishing Hospitality in the Old Testament," 177. Cf. Matthews, "Hospitality and Hostility."

9. John 7:42 does mention Bethleḫem, but it does so in the context of *ques-tioning* Jesus's association with Bethleḫem, highlighting the problem that Jesus was from Nazareth when Scripture said the Messiah must come from Bethleḫem.

10. This practice of conflating a series of citations from multiple books of the HB is actually quite common in Second Temple Jewish texts, as well as in the Jewish Talmud. One scroll among the DSS, 4QFlorilegium (4Q174), also referred to as the "Midrash on the Last Days," is a series of quotations from the HB strung together around a central theme—in this case, the Last Days. This particular scroll strings together citations from 2 Sam. 7, Psa. 1–2, Exod. 15, Ezek. 37, and Isa. 8 and 65 present-ing them as a prophetic preview of what the eschatological Last Days will be like. Another scroll, 4QTestimonia (4Q175) or the "Messianic Anthology," strings together passages that appear to describe a messi-anic figure that will appear in the Last Days. The texts include passages from Deut. 5:28–29 and 18:18–19 (two texts referring to the prophet-figure who is like Moses); Num. 24:15–17 (a portion of prophecy of Bil'am about the Messiah-figure, who is similar to David); Deut. 33:8–11 (a blessing of the Levites, and of the Priest-Messiah who will be a teacher like Levi); and Josh. 6:26, which is then expounded by means of a quotation from the non-canonical Psalms of Joshua (4Q379). Thus, we have evidence that the merging of quotations from the HB isn't a mistake, or an anomaly, but was actually a widely practiced technique in the Second Temple and Rabbinic periods.

11. This episode of infanticide only appears in Matthew's Gospel. Not only does it *not* appear in Luke's account, but it also is never mentioned in any of Josephus's writings. This has caused several scholars, including Geza Vermes (*Nativity,* 22) and E. P. Sanders (*Historical Figure of Jesus,*

85), to suggest that Matthew embellished the story with Herod's infanticide for the dual purpose of once again citing a prophecy (in this case, Jer. 31:15) that casts events in Jesus's life as the fulfillment of prophecy, therefore adding support to Matthew's claim that Jesus is the promised Messiah of David, and to provide a motive for Jesus and his family to go to Egypt (so that he could cite yet another prophecy in support of Jesus's messiahship, in this case, Hos. 11:1) and ultimately to relocate to Nazareth, in order that he might be raised as "Jesus of Nazareth."

12. Josephus, *Antiquities* 17.13.5 (17:354); 18.1.1 (18:1–2).

13. Lewis, *Life in Egypt Under Roman Rule,* 156. The census edict of Gaius Vibius Maximus of 104 CE from Alexandria is written on papyrus and cataloged as P.London 904 in the British Museum. See also Hunt and Edgar, *Select Papyri.*

14. Josephus, *Antiquities* 17.13.5 (17:354); 18.1.1 (18:1–2).

15. Bernegger, "Affirmation of Herod's Death."

16. Some scholars conclude that Luke simply made an error in regard to the timing of the census, citing the census of Quirinius instead of a census of either Gaius Sentius Saturninus or Publius Quinctilius Varus, both of whom actually ruled during the reign of Herod the Great. See Fitzmyer, *Gospel According to Luke I–IX,* 401. A more likely candidate for governor of Syria overseeing a census at the time of Jesus's birth comes from the early Carthaginian Christian author Tertullian (155–240), who stated that Jesus was born during the time when Gaius Sentius Saturninus (*not* Quirinius) was the *Legatus Augusti pro praetore* (or imperial governor) of the Roman province of Syria from 9 to 7 BCE. Publius Quinctilius Varus, who was governor from 6 to 4 BCE is another candidate for governor of Syria during Jesus's birth. Josephus states that Varus crucified two thousand Jewish rebels following a messianic revolt in Judea following the death of Herod the Great in 4 BCE (*Antiquities* 17.10.10 [17:295]). Quirinius could not have held a census during the reign of Herod the Great.

17. The traditional translation, "in the inn," is problematic. It suggests that Mary and Joseph were forced to stay in a barn because there was no room in the local hotel in Bethlehem. The Greek word *kataluma* actually describes a guest room within a house, which was apparently occupied, forcing Mary and Joseph to stay on the home's lower level with the animals, explaining the manger. See Carlson, "The Accommodations of Joseph and Mary in Bethlehem."

18. See Lev. 12:1–5 for the rules concerning purification after childbirth. The requirement is 7 days plus 33 days for purification after the birth of male children. (Note that the purification period is twice that for a

female child.) For more on the discrepancies between Matthew and Luke's accounts of Jesus's birth, see Brown, *Birth of the Messiah,* 46.

19. If you *really* want to have fun, read the *Infancy Gospel of Thomas,* which recounts some disturbing tales of Jesus's childhood.

Chapter 11: Rome

1. See Pliny, *Natural History* 3.66.

2. Woodpeckers are sacred to the god of war because their tenacity and powerful beaks are capable of toppling mighty oaks. Regarding the woodpecker, see Plutarch, *Roman Questions* 21; Plutarch, *Life of Romulus* 4.2; Ovid, *Fasti* 3.37. Regarding the wolf, see Livy, *History of Rome* 10.27.9.

3. Livy, *History of Rome* 1.4.1–2.

4. Livy, *History of Rome* 1.7.2.

5. Livy, *History of Rome* 1.13.

6. The celebration of the Feast of the Most Holy Saints Peter and Paul takes place in Rome annually on June 29. Cf. Eusebius, *Ecclesiastical History* 3.2.

7. See Dan. 9:27; 11:31; 12:11; 1 Macc. 1:54; 6:7.

8. See Mark 13:14; Matt. 24:15–16; Luke 21:20–21.

9. Josephus, *Jewish War* 1.14.4 (1:282–85).

10. For instance, when he took the throne in Jerusalem, he did not defile the Temple as Antiochus IV and Pompey had done prior to him. In fact, when Herod announced that he would be refurbishing and doubling the size of the Jerusalem Temple and building the massive retaining walls and platform around it known today as the Temple Mount, he had members of the tribe of Levi, the priestly tribe, trained as carpenters and masons so that only those religiously eligible individuals would operate in and around the Temple, and so that no one could accuse Herod of profaning the Temple. Herod also allowed the Jewish religious establishment to select its own High Priest (subject to his preliminary approval, of course). Herod offered generous tax relief and distributed grain during a time of famine in 25 BCE. He avoided erecting pagan temples and statues in heavily populated Jewish areas in and around Jerusalem, although he built them freely in less Jewish-populated areas, including three Augusteums (or Temples to Augustus) in the northern parts of his kingdom. Josephus, *Jewish War* 1.21.2 (1:403) mentions the Augusteum in Samaria. *Jewish War* 1.21.3 (1:404) describes the Augusteum in the region of the Panion (Caesarea Philippi). *Jewish War* 1.21.7 (1:414) mentions the Augusteum and a Colossus of Caesar at Caesarea Maritima. And when he minted

coins, he avoided putting his portrait on the coins in order to comply with the command not to make graven images (cf. Lev. 19:4; 26:1; Exod. 20:4; Deut. 5:8).

11. View the Pilate Stone at http://www.english.imjnet.org.il/popup?c0= 13142.

12. Byrne, *Romans*.

13. In the first three chapters alone, for example, Rom. 1:17 cites Hab. 2:4; Rom. 2:24 cites Isa. 52:5; Rom. 3:4 cites Ps. 51:4 (51:6 HB); and Rom. 3:10–12 cites Ps. 14:2–3. Of the fifty-seven citations of or allusions to the HB, the majority come from Isaiah, Genesis, and Psalms.

14. Note that Paul says in Romans that he is raising funds for the "poor in Jerusalem" (15:26) and hopes to stop in Rome when he goes to Spain, asking that they assist him on his journey there (15:24).

15. Barber, "Loose Canons (Part 1)"; "Loose Canons (Part 2)"; "Loose Canons (Part 3)."

16. Scholars believed that Yavne (Jamnia) was chosen as the place for the council, because the Jewish Babylonian Talmud (*Gittin* 56a–b) relates that Rabbi Yohanan ben Zakk'ai had relocated to the city of Yavne just prior to the destruction of the Jerusalem Temple in 70 CE and had received permission from Rome to establish a school of Jewish religious law (*halakha*).

17. *Ḥagigah* 13a; *Yebamoth* 63b; cf. *Erubin* 54a.

18. *Baba Kamma* 92b.

19. Joshua, Judges, 1–2 Samuel, and 1–2 Kings are considered books of the prophets, because, although they are written as histories more closely related to the Torah, they mention the names and works of prophets like Deborah (Judg. 4–5), Samuel (1–2 Sam.) Nathan (2 Sam. 7–1 Kings 1), Elijah (1–2 Kings), Elisha (1–2 Kings), and others and are thus counted among the prophetic books.

20. Bart Ehrman has written an excellent introduction to the world of the Apocrypha, including summaries of many of the books that did not make it into the canon; see Ehrman, *Lost Scriptures*. For a look at the phenomenon of writing books in the names of the apostles and others close to Jesus, including letters written in the name of Paul, see Ehrman, *Forged*.

21. For the text of the Muratorian Fragment, see http://www.homepage .villanova.edu/christopher.haas/muratorian_fragment.htm.

22. Scholars debate whether Irenaeus referenced the books of Hebrews and James.

23. Eusebius, *Ecclesiastical History* 3.25; 6.25. You can read *Ecclesiastical History* 6.25 at http://www.newadvent.org/fathers/250106.htm.

24. The "twenty-two books of the Hebrews" is the ancient Jewish way of counting the thirty-nine books of the Christian OT. Modern Jews count twenty-four books. The earliest mention of a fixed number of books of the HB comes from Josephus, who says that there are *twenty-two* books of the Hebrews: "It follows, I say, that we do not possess myriads of inconsistent books conflicting with each other. Our books, those which are justly accredited, are but *two and twenty,* and contain the record of all time" (*Against Apion* 1.8 [1:38]). The discrepancy between twenty-four and twenty-two likely comes counting Ruth as part of Judges and Lamentations as part of Jeremiah in an artificial attempt to force the number of Hebrew books to match the number of letters in the Hebrew alphabet (see *The Philocalia of Origen* 3; Jerome, *Preface to the Books of Samuel and Kings*).

25. Origen, *Letter to Africanus* 9.

26. Origen also quotes Sir. 21:18 as Scripture in *Against Celsus* 7.12.

27. The argument is that if the earliest copies of the NT do not possess these clauses and verses, then these disputed portions of the text must have been added at a later date, *after* the biblical books had initially been written. Examples of disputed texts that are in our Bibles today but are *not* present in Sinaiticus include the long ending of Mark's Gospel (16:9–16), the story of the woman caught in the act of adultery (John 8:3–11), the ascension of Jesus in Luke 24:51, the designation of Jesus Christ as the Son of God in Mark 1:1, and many more. Read Codex Sinaiticus for yourself online at http://codexsinaiticus.org.

28. Eusebius, *The Life of the Blessed Emperor Constantine (Vita Constantini)* 4:36.

29. Athanasius, *Apologia ad Constantium* 4.

30. See Brakke, "Canon Formation and Social Conflict in Fourth Century Egypt: Athanasius of Alexandria's Thirty-Ninth Festal Letter." There is a debate among scholars whether Athanasius's canonical list was the basis for the official canon, or whether it was simply coincidence that his was the first to list what would eventually become the twenty-seven canonical New Testament books. Note also that Athanasius rejected Esther in a fashion similar to that of the Qumran sectarians, who also apparently did not preserve a copy of Esther, as it is the only canonical book of the Hebrew Bible not discovered at Qumran. You can read this portion of Athanasius's 39th Festal Letter here: http://www.ccel.org/ccel/schaff/npnf204.xxv.iii.iii.xxv.html.

31. Jerome, *Letter to Augustine* 75.5 (19).

32. Jerome, *Preface to Proverbs, Ecclesiastes, and the Song of Songs*. A portion of the preface reads: "As, then, the Church reads Judith, Tobit, and the books of Maccabees, but does not admit them among the canonical Scriptures, so let it read these two volumes [Sirach and the Wisdom of Solomon] for the edification of the people, not to give authority to doctrines of the Church." The text is available online in *Nicene and Post-Nicene Fathers,* Second Series, vol. 6, at http://www.tertullian.org /fathers2/NPNF2-06/Npnf2-06-21.htm#P7993_2595461.

33. Barber, "Loose Canons (Part 2)."

34. Jerome, *Preface to Judith*.

35. Jerome, *Letter to Eustochium* 21.

36. Perhaps what is most fascinating about this list is that most scholars consider it to be inauthentic, that is, it was added at a much later date by some editor wishing to make a list of authorized books of the Bible *appear* to be earlier that it actually was. Scholars believe this list to be inauthentic because several authors summarizing this same synod's canons shortly after this time do *not* list Canon 60, instead ending their lists at Canon 59. The lists of Dionysius Exiguus, John of Antioch, and Bishop Martin of Braga do not include Canon 60. See "Council of Laodicea," in Schaff and Wace, trans. and eds., *Nicene and Post-Nicene Fathers,* Second Series, vol. 14, 159. Although the later authors could have omitted the Canon 60 because it left out the book of Revelation or because other known canon lists were in use—note that both reasons support the argument that by the late fourth century there still was no definitive list of canonical books—it is far more likely that it did not exist at the time of the Synod of Laodicea and was added at a later time.

37. See "The Canonical Epistle of St. Gregory, Bishop of Nyssa, to St. Letoïus, Bishop of Melitene," in Schaff and Wace, trans. and eds., *Nicene and Post-Nicene Fathers,* Second Series, vol. 14, 612.

38. The Code of Canons of the African Church, or "African Code," is the name of the summary of the earlier church councils, as Carthage is in northern Africa (present-day Tunis, Tunisia). See "The Code of Canons of the African Church A.D. 419," in Schaff and Wace, trans. and eds., *Nicene and Post-Nicene Fathers,* Second Series, vol. 14, 437–510.

39. Translation in Westcott, *General Survey of the History of the Canon,* 436.

ACKNOWLEDGMENTS

No book writes itself, and no author completes a work without the help of many others. I offer my thanks to my University of Iowa colleagues in the Departments of Classics and Religious Studies, especially my department chairs, Diana Cates and John Finamore, and to the late Carin Green, who hired and mentored me in my first years at Iowa. I miss you, Carin! Thank you also to my colleagues Paul Dilley, Sarah Bond, Jordan Smith, and Craig Gibson, whose feedback, advice, and humor were much appreciated. Thank you to Jon Winet and the Digital Studio for your support, and I am forever grateful to my Tel 'Azeqah colleagues, Oded Lipschits and Yuval Gadot, at Tel Aviv University, and Manfred Öeming, at the University of Heidelberg, for the research and travel opportunities they have provided for my Iowa students and me.

I wrote this book while at the Obermann Institute for Advanced Studies in Iowa City while on a Spring 2015 Fellow-in-Residence fellowship. I am grateful to Obermann Director Teresa Mangum, to Chaden Djalali, Raúl Curto, and Joe Kearney at the University of Iowa College of Liberal Arts and Sciences, to Lynette Marshall at the University of Iowa Foundation, Dan Reed, Ann Ricketts, and to Provost Barry Butler for being supporters of my research at Iowa.

I could not have written this book without the help of my graduate assistant, Cale Staley, whose almost daily presence in my office provided a sounding board (and the coffee) necessary to develop many of the ideas in this book. Thank you to my UCLA *Doktorvater* Bill Schniedewind and my colleagues Jeremy Smoak, Matthew Suriano, Peter Lanfer, Roger Nam, Kyle Keimer, Eric Cline, and Mark Goodacre for reading drafts of this book and providing helpful suggestions.

This book would not exist without my literary agent at Foundry, Roger Freet, who championed the idea for this book early on, and my editor, Katy Hamilton, her assistant, Anna Paustenbach, and Lisa Zuniga, whose keen eyes and endless patience make my writing seem palatable. Thank you to Richie Kern for his advocacy on my behalf. And many thanks to everyone at HarperOne who made this process possible and pleasurable, especially to Claudia Boutote, Melinda Mullin, Adia Colar, Kim Dayman, and Ann Edwards. I offer special thanks to my colleague and friend Candida Moss, who was instrumental in the early development of this book. Special thanks also go to Amalyah Keshet and the Israel Museum, John F. Wilson, Christopher A. Rollston, and Stewart M. Perkins for assistance with photos and charts in this book.

I also want to offer a special word of thanks to Rabbi Jeff Portman and the Agudas Achim Congregation in Iowa City for inviting me regularly to speak and try out ideas for this book. Your feedback and encouragement meant the world to me. I also want to thank Rev. Dr. Sam Massey and the First Presbyterian Church in Iowa City for repeatedly inviting me to speak at the Finn Memorial Lecture series promoting Jewish-Christian interfaith dialogue. If only every congregation could be as wonderful as First Pres and Agudas Achim in Iowa City!

Thank you Mom and Dad, for raising me with an inquisitive mind and adventurous heart. And perhaps most important, I am thankful to my partner, Roslyn, who has made this process possible with her encouragement, love, and tender touches on stressful nights and for managing our home and our litter of children. And to Tali, Mac, Quincy, Rory Kate, and Judah, this book is why Daddy had to go to the office every day over the summer of 2015. I love you and cannot wait to watch you grow and explore the world around you.

BIBLIOGRAPHY

Albright, William F. *Yahweh and the Gods of Canaan: A Historical Analysis of Two Contrasting Faiths.* Winona Lake, IN: Eisenbrauns, 2001.

———. "The Name of Yahweh." *Journal of Biblical Literature* 43 (1924): 370–78.

Alster, B. "Tammuz." In *Dictionary of Deities and Demons in the Bible,* 2nd ed., edited by Karel van der Toorn, Bob Becking, and Pieter W. van der Horst, 828–34. Grand Rapids, MI: Eerdmans, 1999.

Ameling, Walter. "Epigraphy and the Greek Language in Hellenistic Palestine." *Scripta Classica Israelica* 34 (2015): 1–18.

Archer, Gleason L., and G. C. Chirichigno. *Old Testament Quotations in the New Testament: A Complete Survey.* Chicago: Moody, 1983.

Armstrong, Karen. *Jerusalem: One City, Three Faiths.* New York: Ballantine, 2005.

Bagnall, Roger S. "Alexandria: Library of Dreams." *Proceedings of the American Philosophical Society* 146/4 (December 2002): 348–62.

Barber, Michael. "Loose Canons: The Development of the Old Testament (Part 1)." *The Sacred Page,* March 4, 2006. http://www.thesacredpage.com/2006/03/loose-canons-development-of-old.html.

———. "Loose Canons: The Development of the Old Testament (Part 2)." *The Sacred Page,* March 6, 2006. http://www.thesacredpage.com/2006/03/loose-canons-development-of-old_06.html.

———. "Loose Canons: The Development of the Old Testament (Part 3)." *The Sacred Page,* March 9, 2006. http://www.thesacredpage.com/2006/03/loose-canons-development-of-old_09.html.

Barkay, Gabriel, et al. "The Amulets from Ketef Hinnom: A New Edition and Evaluation." *Bulletin of the American Schools of Oriental Research* 334 (May 2004): 41–70.

Bartoloni, Piero. "Commerce and Industry." In *The Phoenicians,* edited by Sabatino Moscati, 92–100. London and New York: Tauris, 2001.

Baumgarten, Albert I. *The Phoenician History of Philo of Byblos: A Commentary.* Leiden: Brill, 1981.

Bernegger, P. M. "Affirmation of Herod's Death in 4 B.C." *Journal of Theological Studies* 34/2 (1983): 526–31.

Brakke, David. "Canon Formation and Social Conflict in Fourth Century Egypt: Athanasius of Alexandria's Thirty-Ninth Festal Letter." *Harvard Theological Review* 87 (1994): 395–419.

Brown, Raymond. *The Birth of the Messiah: A Commentary on the Infancy Narratives in the Gospels of Matthew and Luke.* Anchor Yale Bible Reference Library. New Haven, CT: Yale Univ. Press, 1999.

Byrne, Brendan. *Romans.* Sacra Pagina 6. Collegeville, MN: Liturgical, 1996.

Cargill, Robert R. "Bible Secrets Revealed, Episode 4: 'The Real Jesus.'" *Bible History Daily,* January 3, 2014. http://www.biblical archaeology.org/daily/biblical-topics/bible-secrets-revealed-episode -4-"the-real-jesus"/.

———. "Why Christians Should Adopt the BCE/CE Dating System." *Bible and Interpretation,* September 2009. http://www.bible interp.com/opeds/why_3530.shtml.

———. "The Fortress at Qumran: A History of Interpretation." *Bible and Interpretation*, May 2009. http://www.bibleinterp.com /articles/qumfort.shtml.

Carlson, Stephen C. "The Accommodations of Joseph and Mary in Bethlehem: Κατάλυμα in Luke 2.7." *New Testament Studies* 56 (2010): 326–42.

Cazelles, Henri. "Bethlehem." *Anchor Bible Dictionary.* Vol. 1, edited by David Noel Freedman, 712–15. New York: Doubleday, 1992.

Charles, R. H., ed. and trans. *Apocrypha and Pseudepigrapha of the Old Testament in English.* Oxford: Clarendon, 1913.

Cline, Eric H. *1177 B.C.: The Year Civilization Collapsed.* Princeton, NJ: Princeton Univ. Press, 2014.

———. "Review of *The Campaign of Pharaoh Shoshenq I into Palestine,* by Kevin A. Wilson." *Journal of Near Eastern Studies* 70/1 (April 2011): 129–32.

———. *The Battles of Armageddon: Megiddo and the Jezreel Valley from the Bronze Age to the Nuclear Age.* Ann Arbor: Univ. of Michigan Press, 2002.

Cole, R. Dennis. "Bethlehem." In *Eerdmans Dictionary of the Bible,* edited by David Noel Freedman, 172–73. Grand Rapids, MI: Eerdmans, 2000.

Collar, Anna. *Religious Networks in the Roman Empire: The Spread of New Ideas.* New York: Cambridge Univ. Press, 2013.

Cook, Ed. "Hair of the Ugaritic Dog." *Ralph the Sacred River,* October 7, 2005. http://ralphriver.blogspot.com/2005/10/hair-of-ugaritic-dog.html.

Cross, Frank Moore. "Fragments of the Prayer of Nabonidus." *Israel Exploration Journal* 34/4 (1984): 260–64.

Crowell, Bradley L. "The Development of Dagan: A Sketch." *Journal of Ancient Near Eastern Religions* 1 (2001): 32–83.

Curtis, Adrian. *Ugarit (Ras Shamra).* Cambridge: Lutterworth, 1985.

Davies, Graham, ed. *Ancient Hebrew Inscriptions: Corpus and Concordance.* Vol. 1. Cambridge: Cambridge Univ. Press, 1991.

———. *Ancient Hebrew Inscriptions: Corpus and Concordance.* Vol. 2. Cambridge: Cambridge Univ. Press, 2004.

Davies, Philip R., George J. Brooke, and Phillip R. Callaway. *The Complete World of the Dead Sea Scrolls.* London: Thames & Hudson, 2011.

Davila, James. "Aristeas to Philocrates." University of St. Andrews Divinity School lecture, February 11, 1999. https://www.st-andrews .ac.uk/divinity/rt/otp/abstracts/aristeas/.

Day, John. *Yahweh and the Gods and Goddesses of Canaan*. Journal for the Society of the Old Testament Supplement Series 265. Sheffield: Sheffield Academic, 2002.

Dever, William G. *Did God Have a Wife? Archaeology and Folk Religion in Ancient Israel*. Grand Rapids, MI: Eerdmans, 2008.

Dietrich, Manfried, Oswald Loretz, and Joaquín Sanmartín, eds. *Cuneiform Alphabetic Texts from Ugarit, Ras Ibn Hani, and Other Places*. 3rd ed. Alter Orient und Altes Testament 360/1. Winona Lake, IN: Eisenbrauns, 2013.

Driver, D. R. "The Original Form of the Name of 'Yahweh.'" *Zeitschrift für die Alttestamentliche Wissenschaft* 46 (1928): 7–25.

Edmonds, John Maxwell. *The Fragments of Attic Comedy*. Vol. 3B. Leiden: Brill, 1961.

Ehrman, Bart D. *Forged: Writing in the Name of God—Why the Bible's Authors Are Not Who We Think They Are*. San Francisco: HarperOne, 2011.

———. *Lost Scriptures: Books That Did Not Make It into the New Testament*. Oxford: Oxford Univ. Press, 2003.

Finkel, Irving, and Michael Seymour. *Babylon: City of Wonders*. London: British Museum Press, 2008.

Fitzmyer, Joseph. *The Gospel According to Luke I–IX: Introduction, Translation, and Notes*. Anchor Bible 28. New York: Doubleday, 1982.

Fontenrose, Joseph. "Dagon and El." *Oriens* 10/2 (December 1957): 277–79.

Frye, Richard N. "Review of G. R. Driver, *Aramaic Documents of the Fifth Century B.C.*" *Harvard Journal of Asiatic Studies* 18/3–4 (1955): 456–61.

Gadd, C. J. "Inscribed Prisms of Sargon II from Nimrud." *Iraq* 16/2 (Autumn 1954): 173–201.

Glassner, Jean-Jacques. *Mesopotamian Chronicles*. Writings from the Ancient World 19. Atlanta: Society of Biblical Literature, 2004.

Golb, Norman. *Who Wrote the Dead Sea Scrolls?: The Search for the Secret of Qumran*. New York: Scribner, 1995.

Grayson, A. K. *Assyrian and Babylonian Chronicles*. Texts from Cuneiform Sources 5. Locust Valley, NY: Augustin, 1975.

Hallo, William W., and K. Lawson Younger, Jr., eds. *The Context of Scripture*. Vol. 1, *Canonical Compositions from the Biblical World*. Leiden: Brill, 2003.

———. *The Context of Scripture*. Vol. 2, *Monumental Inscriptions from the Biblical World*. Leiden: Brill, 2003.

Hamilton, R. W. *The Church of the Nativity, Bethlehem*. 2nd ed. Jerusalem: Department of Antiquities and Museums, 1968.

Hardy, Ernest George, ed. and trans. *Roman Laws and Charters*. Oxford: Clarendon, 1912.

Harper, Robert Francis. *The Code of Hammurabi King of Babylon About 2250 BC*. Chicago: Univ. of Chicago Press, 1904.

Harrington, Daniel J. *Invitation to the Apocrypha*. Grand Rapids, MI: Eerdmans, 1999.

Haupt, P. "Der Name Jahwe." *Orientalistische Literaturzeitung* 12 (1909): 211–14.

Hayes, John H. "The Tradition of Zion's Inviolability." *Journal of Biblical Literature* 82 (1963): 419–26.

Healey, J. F. "Dagon." In *Dictionary of Deities and Demons in the Bible,* 2nd ed., edited by Karel van der Toorn, Bob Becking, and Pieter W. van der Horst, 216–19. Grand Rapids, MI: Eerdmans, 1999.

Herdner, Andrée. *Corpus des tablettes en cunéiformes alphabétiques découvertes à Ras Shamra-Ugarit de 1929 à 1939.* 2 vols. Paris: Imprimerie nationale et librairie orientaliste Paul Geuthner, 1963.

Hoffmeier, James. "The Aftermath of David's Triumph over Goliath." *Archaeology in the Biblical World* 1 (1991): 18–23.

Hunt, A. S., and C. C. Edgar. *Select Papyri, Volume II: Public Documents*. Loeb Classical Library 282. Cambridge, MA: Harvard Univ. Press, 1934.

Jacoby, Felix. "Menecles of Barca (270)." *Die Fragmente der griechischen Historiker*. Vol. 3a. Brill: Leiden, 1940.

Jenkins, Ferrell. "Nabopolassar, Father of Nebuchadnezzar, Destroyed Nineveh." *Ferrell's Travel Blog,* February 1, 2012. https://ferrell jenkins.wordpress.com/2012/02/01/nabopolassar-father-of-nebuchadnezzar-destroyed-nineveh/.

Jowett, Benjamin. *The Politics of Aristotle*. Oxford: Clarendon, 1885.

Katzenstein, H. Jacob. "Tyre in the Early Persian Period (539–486 B.C.E.)." *Biblical Archaeologist* 42/1 (1979): 23–34.

Kenyon, Kathleen M. *Digging up Jericho: The Results of the Jericho Excavations, 1952–1956.* New York: Praeger, 1957.

Khater, Menan. "Alexandria Hit by Floods." *Daily News Egypt*, October 25, 2015. http://www.dailynewsegypt.com/2015/10/25/prime-minister-heads-to-alexandria-to-assess-damages-from-flooding/.

Kolowich, Steve. "Harassment of Dead Sea Scroll Scholars Leads to Arrest of Professor's Son." *Chronicle of Higher Education,* March 6, 2009. http://chronicle.com/daily/2009/03/13090n.htm.

———. "The Fall of an Academic Cyberbully." *Chronicle of Higher Education,* March 20, 2009. http://chronicle.com/article/The-Fall-of-an-Academic/30977.

Leland, John. "Online Battle Over Sacred Scrolls, Real-World Consequences." *New York Times,* February 16, 2013. http://www.nytimes.com/2013/02/17/nyregion/online-battle-over-ancient-scrolls-spawns-real-world-consequences.html?_r=0.

Lerner, Fred. *The Story of Libraries*. London: Continuum, 2001.

Levin, Yigal. "Did Pharaoh Sheshonq Attack Jerusalem?" *Biblical Archaeology Review* 38/4 (2012): 42–52, 66–67.

Lewis, Naphtali. *Life in Egypt Under Roman Rule*. Oxford: Clarendon, 1983.

Lewis, Theodore J. "El's Divine Feast." In *Ugaritic Narrative Poetry*, edited by Simon B. Parker, 193–96. Society of Biblical Literature Writings from the Ancient World 9. Atlanta: Scholars, 1997.

Lightfoot, Neil R. *How We Got the Bible*. 3rd ed. Grand Rapids, MI: Baker, 2003.

Ling-Israel, Pinna. "The Sennacherib Prism in the Israel Museum, Jerusalem." In *Bar-Ilan: Studies in Assyriology Dedicated to Pinḥas Artzi*, edited by J. Klein and A. Skaist, 213–47. Ramat-Gan: Bar-Ilan Univ. Press, 1990.

Lipiński, Edward. "Hiram of Tyre and Solomon." In *The Books of Kings: Sources, Composition, Historiography and Reception*, edited by André Lemaire and Baruch Halpern, 251–72. Supplements to Vetus Testamentum 129. Leiden: Brill, 2010.

Loud, Gordon. *The Megiddo Ivories*. Oriental Institute Publications 52. Chicago: Univ. of Chicago Press, 1939.

Luckenbill, Daniel David. *Ancient Records of Assyria and Babylonia*. Vol. 2, *Historical Records of Assyria from Sargon to the End*. Chicago: Univ. of Chicago Press, 1927.

Margalit, Baruch. "The Legend of Keret." In *Handbook of Ugaritic Studies*, edited by Wilfred G. E. Watson and Nicolas Wyatt, 203–33. Leiden: Brill, 1999.

Matthews, Victor H. "Hospitality and Hostility in Genesis 19 and Judges 19." *Biblical Theology Bulletin* 22/1 (1992): 3–11.

McCarter, P. Kyle. "Kuntillet 'Ajrud (2.47)." In *The Context of Scripture*. Vol. 2, *Monumental Inscriptions from the Biblical World*, edited by William W. Hallo and K. Lawson Younger, Jr., 171. Leiden: Brill, 2003.

———. "Khirbet el-Qom (2.52)." In *The Context of Scripture*. Vol. 2, *Monumental Inscriptions from the Biblical World*, edited by William W. Hallo and K. Lawson Younger, Jr., 179. Leiden: Brill, 2003.

———. " 'Yaw, Son of 'Omri': A Philological Note on Israelite Chronology." *Bulletin of the American Schools of Oriental Research* 216 (December 1974): 5–7.

McCarthy, Rory. "Letters to God: Jerusalem's Faithful Delivery of Messages from the World." *Guardian,* December 20, 2009. http://www.theguardian.com/world/2009/dec/20/israel-jerusalem -letters-to-god.

McDonald, Lee M., and James A. Sanders, eds. *The Canon Debate.* Peabody, MA: Hendrickson, 2002.

Mettinger, T. N. D. "Yahweh Zebaoth." In *Dictionary of Deities and Demons in the Bible,* 2nd ed., edited by Karel van der Toorn, Bob Becking, and Pieter W. van der Horst, 920–24. Grand Rapids, MI: Eerdmans, 1999.

Metzger, Bruce. *The Bible in Translation.* Grand Rapids, MI: Baker Academic, 2001.

Metzger, Bruce M., and Bart D. Ehrman. *The Text of the New Testament: Its Transmission, Corruption, and Restoration.* 4th ed. Oxford: Oxford Univ. Press, 2005.

Moberly, R. W. L. *The Old Testament of the Old Testament: Patriarchal Narratives and Mosaic Yahwism.* Eugene, OR: Wipf & Stock, 2001.

Mondriaan, M. E. "Anat-Yahu and the Jews at Elephantine." *Journal for Semitics* 22/2 (2013): 537–52.

Moran, William L. *The Amarna Letters.* Baltimore and London: Johns Hopkins Univ. Press, 1992.

Moscati, Sabatino, ed. *The Phoenicians.* London and New York: Tauris, 2001.

Mulder, M. J. "Baal-Berith." In *Dictionary of Deities and Demons in the Bible,* 2nd ed., edited by Karel van der Toorn, Bob Becking, and Pieter W. van der Horst, 141–44. Grand Rapids, MI: Eerdmans, 1999.

Naveh, Joseph. *Early History of the Alphabet: An Introduction to West Semitic Epigraphy and Palaeography.* 2nd ed. Jerusalem: Magnes Press, 1987.

O'Brien, Julia M. "Nineveh." *Bible Odyssey.* http://www.bible odyssey.org/en/places/main-articles/nineveh.aspx.

O'Connor, Daniel J. "The Keret Legend and the Prologue-Epilogue of Job." *Irish Theological Quarterly* 55/1 (1989): 1–6.

O'Conor, John Francis Xavier. *Cuneiform Text of a Recently Discovered Cylinder of Nebuchadnezzar King of Babylon*. Baltimore: John Murphy, 1885.

Pardee, Dennis. "The Kirta Epic (1.102)." In *The Context of Scripture*. Vol. 1, *Canonical Compositions from the Biblical World*, edited by William W. Hallo and K. Lawson Younger, Jr., 333–43. Leiden: Brill, 2003.

———. "The 'Aqhatu Legend (1.103)." In *The Context of Scripture*. Vol. 1, *Canonical Compositions from the Biblical World*, edited by William W. Hallo and K. Lawson Younger, Jr., 343–56. Leiden: Brill, 2003.

———. "The Ba'lu Myth (1.86)." In *The Context of Scripture*. Vol. 1, *Canonical Compositions from the Biblical World*, edited by William W. Hallo and K. Lawson Younger, Jr., 241–74. Leiden: Brill, 2003.

Pettinato, G., and H. Waetzoldt. "Dagan in Ebla und Mesopotamien nach den Texten aus dem 3. Jahrtausend." *Orientalia* 54 (1985): 234–56.

Porten, Bezalel. *The Elephantine Papyri in English*. Rev. ed. Atlanta: Society of Biblical Literature, 2011.

Pritchard, James B., ed. *Ancient Near Eastern Texts Relating to the Old Testament*. 2nd ed. Princeton, NJ: Princeton Univ. Press, 1955.

Pummer, Reinhard. *Early Christian Authors on Samaritans and Samaritanism*. Texts and Studies in Ancient Judaism 92. Tübingen: Mohr Siebeck, 2002.

Renz, Johannes, and Wolfgang Röllig. *Handbuch der althebräischen Epigraphik*. 3 vols. Darmstadt: Wissenschaftliche Buchgesellschaft, 1995.

Ritner, Robert Kriech. *The Mechanics of Ancient Egyptian Magical Practice*. 4th ed. Studies in Ancient Oriental Civilization 54. Chicago: Oriental Institute, 2008.

Rollston, Christopher A. "Writing and Literacy in the World of Ancient Israel: Epigraphic Evidence from the Iron Age." *Archaeology and Biblical Studies* 11. Atlanta, Society of Biblical Literature, 2010.

Rosenthal, Franz. *A Grammar of Biblical Aramaic*. Wiesbaden: Otto Harrassowitz, 1961.

Rush, George, Joanna Molloy, Jo Piazza, and Chris Rovzar. "Nicole Calls In A Scripture Doctor." *New York Daily News*, April 21, 2005. http://www.nydailynews.com/archives/gossip/nicole-calls-scripture -doctor-article-1.610796.

Sanders, E. P. *The Historical Figure of Jesus*. London: Penguin, 1993.

Schaff, Philip, and Henry Wace, eds. *Nicene and Post-Nicene Fathers*. Second Series. New York: Scribner, 1900.

Schniedewind, William M. *A Social History of Hebrew: Its Origins Through the Rabbinic Period*. New Haven, CT: Yale Univ. Press, 2013.

———. *How the Bible Became a Book*. Cambridge: Cambridge Univ. Press, 2004.

Sigrist, M., R. Zadok, and C. B. F. Walker, eds. *Catalogue of the Babylonian Tablets in the British Museum*. Vol. 3. London: British Museum Press, 2006.

Smelik, Klaas A. D. "The Inscription of King Mesha (2.23)." In *The Context of Scripture*. Vol. 2, *Monumental Inscriptions from the Biblical World,* edited by William W. Hallo and K. Lawson Younger, Jr., 137–38. Leiden: Brill, 2003.

Smith, Mark S. *The Early History of God*. 2nd ed. Grand Rapids, MI: Eerdmans, 2002.

———. *The Ugaritic Baal Cycle*. Leiden: Brill, 1994.

Smith-Spark, Linda. "Syria: ISIS Destroys Ancient Muslim Shrines in Palmyra." *CNN.com,* June 24, 2015. http://www.cnn .com/2015/06/24/middleeast/syria-isis-palmyra-shrines/.

Smoak, Jeremy D. *The Priestly Blessing in Inscription and Scripture: The Early History of Numbers 6:24–26*. Oxford: Oxford Univ. Press, 2015.

Tcherikover, Victor A., and Alexander Fuks, eds. *Corpus Papyrorum Judaicarum*. Vol. 1. Cambridge: Harvard Univ. Press, 1957.

Turpie, D. M. *The Old Testament in the New*. London: Williams & Norgate, 1868.

Twain, Mark, *Innocents Abroad*. Hartford, CT: American Publishing, 1869.

Tzaferis, Vassilios. "Crucifixion: The Archaeological Evidence." *Biblical Archaeology Review* 11/1 (January/February 1985): 44–53.

———. "Jewish Tombs at and near Giv'at ha-Mivtar, Jerusalem." *Israel Exploration Journal* 20/1–2 (1970): 18–32.

Van der Toorn, K. "Anat-Yahu, Some Other Deities, and the Jews of Elephantine." *Numen* 39 (1992): 80–101.

Vermaseren, Maarten J. "The Miraculous Birth of Mithras." In *Studia Archaeologica*, edited by László Gerevich, 93–109. Leiden: Brill, 1951.

Vermes, Geza. *The Nativity: History and Legend*. London, Penguin, 2006.

Westcott, Brooke Foss. *A General Survey of the History of the Canon of the New Testament*. 4th ed. London: Macmillan, 1875.

Whiston, William, trans. *The Works of Josephus: Complete and Unabridged*. New updated ed. Peabody, MA: Hendrickson 1980.

Wiener, Noah. "Hanging Gardens of Babylon . . . in Assyrian Nineveh." *Bible History Daily*, May 13, 2015. http://www.biblical archaeology.org/daily/ancient-cultures/ancient-near-eastern-world /hanging-gardens-of-babylon-in-assyrian-nineveh/.

Wilson, Robert Dick. "Aramaisms in the Old Testament." *Princeton Theological Review* 23/2 (1925): 234–66.

Wright, David P. *Inventing God's Law: How the Covenant Code of the Bible Used and Revised the Laws of Hammurabi*. Oxford: Oxford Univ. Press, 2009.

Wright, R. A. "Establishing Hospitality in the Old Testament: Testing the Tool of Linguistic Pragmatics." Ph.D. dissertation, Yale Univ., 1989.

Yon, Marguerite. *The City of Ugarit at Tell Ras Shamra*. Winona Lake, IN: Eisenbrauns, 2006.

Younger, K. Lawson, Jr. "Assyrian Involvement in the Southern Levant at the End of the Eighth Century B.C.E." In *Jerusalem in Bible and Archaeology: The First Temple Period,* edited by Andrew G. Vaughn and Ann E. Killebrew, 235–63. Society of Biblical Literature Symposium Series 18. Atlanta: Society of Biblical Literature, 2003.

———. "Nimrud Prisms D & E (2.118D)." In *The Context of Scripture.* Vol. 2, *Monumental Inscriptions from the Biblical World,* edited by William W. Hallo and K. Lawson Younger, Jr., 295–96. Leiden: Brill, 2003.

Classical Works Cited

Aeschylus II: Agamemnon, Libation-Bearers, Eumenides, Fragments. Translated by Herbert Weir Smyth. Loeb Classical Library (LCL) 146. Cambridge, MA: Harvard Univ. Press, 1926.

Aristophanes. *Birds: The Complete Greek Drama.* Vol. 2. Translated by Eugene O'Neill, Jr. New York: Random House, 1938.

Aristotle: The Politics. Translated by H. Rackham. LCL 264. London: William Heinemann, 1932.

Athanasius of Alexandria. "Apologia ad Constantium." In *Nicene and Post-Nicene Fathers,* Second Series, vol. 4. Translated by M. Atkinson and Archibald Robertson and edited by Philip Schaff and Henry Wace. Buffalo, NY: Christian Literature, 1892.

Callimachus: Hymns and Epigrams, Lycophron and Aratus. Translated by A. W. Mair and G. R. Mair. LCL 129. London: William Heinemann, 1921.

Dio Cassius: Roman History: Volume IV, Books 41–45. Translated by Earnest Cary. LCL 66. Cambridge, MA: Harvard Univ. Press, 1916.

Diogenes Laertius: Lives of Eminent Philosophers, Books 6–10. Vol. 2. Translated by R. D. Hicks. LCL 185. Cambridge, MA: Harvard Univ. Press, 1925.

Eusebius of Caesarea. "The Life of the Blessed Emperor Constantine." In *Nicene and Post-Nicene Fathers,* Second Series, vol. 1.

Translated by Ernest Cushing Richardson and edited by Philip Schaff and Henry Wace. Buffalo, NY: Christian Literature, 1890.

———. "Ecclesiastical History." In *Nicene and Post-Nicene Fathers,* Second Series, vol. 1. Translated by Arthur Cushman McGiffert and edited by Philip Schaff and Henry Wace. Buffalo, NY: Christian Literature, 1890.

Herodotus: The Persian Wars, Volume 1, Books 1–2. Translated by A. D. Godley. LCL 117. Cambridge, MA: Harvard Univ. Press, 1920.

Herodotus: The Persian Wars, Volume 3, Books 5–7. Translated by A. D. Godley. LCL 119. Cambridge, MA: Harvard Univ. Press, 1922.

Homer: Odyssey, Volume 1, Books 1–12. Translated by A. T. Murray. LCL 104. Cambridge, MA: Harvard Univ. Press, 1919.

Homer: Odyssey, Volume 2, Books 13–24. Translated by A. T. Murray. LCL 105. Cambridge, MA: Harvard Univ. Press, 1919.

Jerome. "Letters." In *Nicene and Post-Nicene Fathers,* First Series, vol. 1. Translated by J. G. Cunningham and edited by Philip Schaff. Buffalo, NY: Christian Literature, 1887.

———. "Prefaces." In *Nicene and Post-Nicene Fathers,* Second Series, vol. 6. Translated by W. H. Fremantle, G. Lewis and W. G. Martley and edited by Philip Schaff and Henry Wace. Buffalo, NY: Christian Literature, 1893.

Josephus: Jewish Antiquities, Books 12–13. Vol. 5. Translated by Ralph Marcus. LCL 365. Cambridge, MA: Harvard Univ. Press, 1943.

Josephus: Jewish Antiquities, Books 16–17. Vol. 7. Translated by Ralph Marcus and Allen Wikgren. LCL 410. Cambridge, MA: Harvard Univ. Press, 1963.

Josephus: Jewish Antiquities, Books 18–19. Vol. 8. Translated by Louis H. Feldman. LCL 433. Cambridge, MA: Harvard Univ. Press, 1965.

Josephus: The Jewish War, Books 1–2. Vol. 1. Translated by H. St. J. Thackeray. LCL 203. Cambridge, MA: Harvard Univ. Press, 1927.

Josephus: The Life, Against Apion. Translated by H. St. J. Thackeray. LCL 186. Cambridge, MA: Harvard Univ. Press, 1926.

Justin Martyr. "Dialogue of Justin, Philosopher and Martyr, with Trypho, a Jew." In *Ante-Nicene Fathers,* vol. 1. Translated by Marcus Dods and George Reith and edited by Alexander Roberts, James Donaldson, and A. Cleveland Coxe. Buffalo, NY: Christian Literature, 1885.

Lactantius. "The Divine Institutes." In *Ante-Nicene Fathers,* vol. 7. Translated by William Fletcher and edited by Alexander Roberts, James Donaldson, and A. Cleveland Coxe. Buffalo, NY: Christian Literature, 1886.

Livy: History of Rome, Volume I: Books I and II. Translated by B. O. Foster. LCL 114. Cambridge, MA: Harvard Univ. Press, 1919.

Livy: History of Rome, Volume IV: Books VIII–X. Translated by B. O. Foster. LCL 191. Cambridge, MA: Harvard Univ. Press, 1926.

Origen of Alexandria. "Contra Celsus." In *Ante-Nicene Fathers,* vol. 4. Translated by Frederick Crombie and edited by Alexander Roberts, James Donaldson, and A. Cleveland Coxe. Buffalo, NY: Christian Literature, 1885.

————. "Letter to Africanus." In *Ante-Nicene Fathers,* vol. 4. Edited by Alexander Roberts, James Donaldson, and A. Cleveland Coxe. Buffalo, NY: Christian Literature, 1885.

————. *Philocalia*. Translated by George Lewis. Edinburgh: Clark, 1911.

Ovid: Fasti. Translated by James G. Frazer and revised by G. P. Goold. LCL 253. Cambridge, MA: Harvard Univ. Press, 1931.

Philo: Volume VI: On Abraham. On Joseph. On Moses. Translated by F. H. Colson. LCL 289. Cambridge, MA: Harvard Univ. Press, 1935.

Plato: Euthyphro. Apology. Crito. Phaedo. Phaedrus. Vol. 1. Translated by Harold North Fowler. LCL 36. Cambridge, MA: Harvard Univ. Press, 1914.

Plato in Twelve Volumes. Vols. 5–6. Translated by Paul Shorey. Cambridge, MA: Harvard Univ. Press, 1969.

Plato: Republic, Books 1–5. Vol. 1. Edited and translated by Chris Emlyn-Jones and William Preddy. LCL 237. Cambridge, MA: Harvard Univ. Press, 2013.

Plato: Republic, Books 6–10. Vol. 2. Edited and translated by Chris Emlyn-Jones and William Preddy. LCL 276. Cambridge, MA: Harvard Univ. Press, 2013.

Pliny: Natural History, Books 3–7. Vol. 2. Translated by H. Rackham. LCL 352. Cambridge, MA: Harvard Univ. Press, 1942.

Plutarch. *Lives*. Translated by Aubrey Stewart and George Long. Vol. 3. London: George Bell, 1892.

Plutarch: Lives, Theseus and Romulus. Lycurgus and Numa. Solon and Publicola. Vol. 1. Translated by Bernadotte Perrin. LCL 46. Cambridge, MA: Harvard Univ. Press, 1914.

Plutarch: Moralia, Volume IV. Translated by Frank Cole Babbitt. LCL 305. Cambridge, MA: Harvard Univ. Press, 1936.

Porphyry's Against the Christians: The Literary Remains. Edited and translated by R. Joseph Hoffman. Amherst, NY: Prometheus, 1994.

Seneca. *Physical Science in the Time of Nero, Being a Translation of the Quaestiones Naturales of Seneca*. Translated by John Clarke. London: Macmillan, 1910.

Seneca: Epistles, Volume I, Epistles 1–65. Translated by Richard Mott Gummere. LCL 75. Cambridge, MA: Harvard Univ. Press, 1917.

Seneca: Epistles, Volume III, Epistles 93–124. Translated by Richard Mott Gummere. LCL 77. Cambridge, MA: Harvard Univ. Press, 1925.

Seneca: Moral Essays, Volume III, De Beneficiis. Translated by J. W. Basore. LCL 310. Cambridge, MA: Harvard Univ. Press, 1935.

Socrates of Constantinople. "Ecclesiastical History." In *Nicene and Post-Nicene Fathers,* Second Series, vol. 2. Translated by A. C. Zenos and edited by Philip Schaff and Henry Wace. Buffalo, NY: Christian Literature, 1890.

Strabo: Geography, Volume II: Books 3–5. Translated by Horace Leonard Jones. LCL 50. Cambridge: Harvard Univ. Press, 1923.

Strabo: Geography, Volume VII: Books 15–16. Translated by Horace Leonard Jones. LCL 241. Cambridge: Harvard Univ. Press, 1930.

Tactius: Annals, Books 13–16. Translated by John E. Jackson. LCL 322. Cambridge, MA: Harvard Univ. Press. 1937.

Tertullian. "Treatise on the Soul." In *Ante-Nicene Fathers,* vol. 3. Translated by Peter Holmes and edited by Alexander Roberts, James Donaldson, and A. Cleveland Coxe. Buffalo, NY: Christian Literature, 1885.

Virgil. *Aeneid.* Translated by Theodore C. Williams. Boston: Houghton Mifflin, 1910.

SCRIPTURE INDEX

SUBJECT INDEX

(The transliteration of the letters 'aleph, 'ayin, as well as supra- and sub-linear diacritical marks (ā ḥ ḫ ṣ ś š ṭ û) are ignored for purposes of English alphabetization.)

Aaronic blessing, 182
'Abd al-Malik, 167–68
'Abednego, 157–158
'Abinadab, 106
'Abino'am, 104
abomination of desolation ("desolating sacrilege"), 242
Abraham ('Abraham), 46, 95, 174
Abram ('Abram), 50–51, 175
Acca Larentia, 238
Achaemenid, 20, 25, 96, 117, 180
Acropolis: of Athens, 112–14, 129–31; Museum (Athens), 112; of Ugarit, 32–33, 37;
acrostic, 87–88
Actium, Battle of, 241
Acts of Andrew, 256
Acts of John, 256
Acts of Paul, 256
Adad-nirari II, 54
Adam ('Adam), 130
Adapa, 56
Adasi, 54
'Adoni-bezeq (Adoni-bezek), 176
'Adoni-ṣedeq (Adoni-zedek), 175
Aegean Sea, 18, 113
Aegisthus, 128
Aelia Capitolina, 190
Aeneas, 238
Aeneid, 238
Aeschylus, 114, 128
Against Celsus, 220
Against Heresies, 254

Agamemnon (play), 128
Agamemnon (king), 128
Agrippa II (Herod), 128
Ahab ('Aḥ'ab) son of 'Omri, 37
'Aḥaz, 148–49
Aḥaziah ('Aḥazyahu), 107
'Aḥiqam, 84
'Ain Dāra, 179
Akkad(ian): kingdom, 33, 55, 83; language, 20; 75–79, 159
Al-Aqṣā Mosque, 169, 171
Alamo, 108
Alawite, 31
Alba Longa, 238
Alexander, bishop of Constantinople, 258
Alexander the Great, 10, 25, 92, 111, 115–17, 133, 136, 138, 166
Alexandria: archbishop of, 258; bishop of, 193; city, 116, 135–39, 141, 153, 161–62, 164, 264; Clement of, 255; Library of, 10, 127, 136–39, 143, 164; Lighthouse of, 136; Musaeum of, 138; Origen of, 220; Philo of, 126, 143, 145; Siege of, 138, 243
All Along the Watchtower, 140
Allegory of the Cave, 121
Allenby, Edmund Henry Hynman, 108
alphabet, 9, 10, 13, 17–21, 28, 41, 87, 263

CREDITS

Map on page viii courtesy Google Earth, Data SIO, NOAA, U.S. Navy, NGA, GEBCO, and Image Landsat.

Photographs on insert pages xvi, xvii (bottom), xviii, xix, xx, xxi (top), xxii, xxiii, xxiv, xxv, xxvi, xxvii (top), xxviii, xxx, xxxi, and interior pages 14, 73, 79, 101, 103, 112, 131, 135, 167, 169, 170, 188, 191, 199, 202, 204, 205, 217, 229, and 236 by Robert R. Cargill. Used with permission.

Photograph on insert page xvii (top) by Benjamin Sitzmann. Used with permission.

Photograph on insert page xxi (bottom) by Roslyn Cargill. Used with permission.

Photograph on insert page xxvii (bottom) by Yuval Peleg (ז״ל). Used with permission.

Chart on page 20 created by Robert R. Cargill. Used with permission.

Images on insert page xxix and interior pages 37, 38, 48, 49, 63, 102, 182, 237, and 246 copyright © The Israel Museum, Jerusalem. Used with permission.

Photograph on page 137 by Stewart M. Perkins. Used with permission.

Photograph on pages 171, 197, and 198 by John Fothergill. Used with permission.

Photograph on page 244 of obverse and reverse of Herodian coin from the John F. Wilson collection by Robert R. Cargill, courtesy John F. Wilson. Used with permission.